CHANGING BEHAVIOR IN ORGANIZATIONS

Changing Behavior in Organizations

Minimizing Resistance to Change

ARNOLD S. JUDSON

First published 1966 by John Wiley & Sons Ltd.

All rights reserved

This edition Copyright © Arnold S. Judson, 1991

This edition first published 1991

Basil Blackwell, Inc.
3 Cambridge Center
Cambridge, Massachusetts 02142, USA

Basil Blackwell Ltd
108 Cowley Road, Oxford, OX4 1JF, UK

All rights reserved. Except for the quotation of short passages for the purposes of criticism and review, no part of this publication may be reproduced, stored in a retrieval system, or transmitted, in any form or by any means, electronic, mechanical, photocopying, recording or otherwise, without the prior permission of the publisher.

Except in the United States of America, this book is sold subject to the condition that it shall not, by way of trade or otherwise, be lent, re-sold, hired out, or otherwise circulated without the publisher's prior consent in any form of binding or cover other than that in which it is published and without a similar condition including this condition being imposed on the subsequent purchaser.

Library of Congress Cataloging in Publication Data

Judson, Arnold S.
    Changing behavior in organizations: how to approach and manage change/Arnold S. Judson.
      Rev. ed. of: A manager's guide to making changes. 1966.
      Includes bibliographical references and index.
      ISBN 0-631-17803-1:
      I. Judson, Arnold S. Manager's guide to making changes.
II. Title.
HD58.8.J83 1991
658.4′063—dc20
90-47802 CIP

British Library Cataloguing in Publication Data
A CIP catalogue record for this book is available from the British Library.

Typeset in 10½ on 12pt Times
by APS Ltd, Salisbury, Wilts
Printed in Great Britain by
T.J. Press (Padstow) Ltd, Padstow, Cornwall.

Contents

	Acknowledgements	vi
	Introduction	1
1	Defining the Change and Its Causes	5
2	How People are Affected by Change	15
3	How Personal Attitude to a Change is Formed	23
4	How People React to Change	47
5	Predicting the Extent of Resistance	55
6	Minimizing Resistance to Change: Concepts	77
7	Minimizing Resistance to Change: Methods	99
8	Process Skills	139
9	Differences in the Perception of Change	149
10	A Systematic Approach to Making Change	165
11	Implications for Managerial Competence	191
	Conclusion	205
	Notes	207
	Index	213

Acknowledgments

This book represents the accumulated learning from my more than forty years' involvement in improving organizational effectiveness and productivity. I want to cite the more important influences that contributed to this learning.

First and foremost was my association with Douglas McGregor and the other faculty involved in the innovative graduate program in organizational behavior that he established at the Massachusetts Institute of Technology in 1947. Another strong influence in that program was Joseph Scanlon.

For help in the areas of individual psychology and development, I want to thank Drs Jacob and Louis Brenner in addition to my wife, June, who has been an unflagging source of insight, as well as support.

For helping me in the development and production of my manuscript, I want to thank Stacy Curtis. Also, thanks to Ralph Moxcey for his jacket design.

Introduction

In 1789 Ben Franklin wrote to a friend, "But in this world nothing is certain but death and taxes." He neglected to mention a third certainty: change. Changes have been, are, and will continue to be an ever present feature of our lives. The process of life itself is continuous change.

Business organizations, too, are continuously changing. Any organization operates within a dynamic social-political-economic environment. Changes in its external environment require that appropriate changes be made within the organization. Its objectives, strategies, policies, organization structures, personnel and methods of operation must change so that it can become or remain financially sound and socially responsible. Thus, any organization can be viewed as having needs that require fulfillment, needs for changes aimed at maintaining economic and social viability and vitality.

Each of us who works in an organization also has needs requiring fulfillment. Although our needs may be manifold and complex, we need above all to maintain our integrity and sense of security. The satisfaction of this need requires in large part that our environment remain relatively familiar and consistent; in short, unchanging.

Thus, there is a fundamental conflict between any organization's need for change and our personal need for maintaining a sense of security. This conflict becomes apparent whenever changes are introduced within an organization. If the organization's objectives are to be met, management must find ways of resolving such conflict. Their effectiveness in doing so has a direct bearing on how well the organization manages to improve or even to sustain its market and financial performance in its competitive environment. For this reason, effectiveness in making changes can be viewed as a prime criterion in assessing a manager's performance. Carrying out changes successfully is a key requirement of managers and supervisors at every organizational level.

Pressures for change originate both within and outside organizations. Management may initiate innovations, or may react to economic, social, technological and political forces entirely external to the organization. Whether management are pursuing their own desires for improvement, or whether they are responding to external pressures,

Introduction

how they act to change the status quo will determine the enterprise's long-term ability to survive.

Three independent variables determine the extent to which any management achieve the full potential benefits available from a change:

1 Skill in identifying and analyzing problems demanding solutions, and determining the objectives of any required changes.
2 Skill in formulating strategies, tactics and methods to accomplish these objectives and solve these problems.
3 Skill in developing and implementing processes to gain acceptance and support for both the objectives and the means for their achievement from the people affected by and involved in the change.

In order for management to introduce and implement any change smoothly, and to achieve fully the objectives of that change, they must be skillful in all three areas. When management are deficient in any one of these areas, the actual benefits realized from a change are less than the full potential. Management's analysis of a problem might be brilliant. Their identification of the objectives that should be achieved might be correct. Their approach to the attainment of these objectives might be imaginative and clever. Yet, the expected results will not be realized if the managers are not also skillful in dealing with any resistance to the change from those involved.

But the skills involved in the first and second areas are very different from those in the third. Any manager, in relative isolation, can identify and analyze both problems and objectives, and devise methods for their solution and achievement. To do these things well requires a keen, logical and imaginative mind working with sufficient reliable data. When a manager performs these tasks, the outcome depends primarily on these personal abilities.

However, a manager, no matter how brilliant, cannot alone achieve acceptance of and support for a change from those affected or otherwise involved. Such an outcome requires interaction among and inputs from many managers, supervisors and employees. Here, the manager cannot control the situation or solely determine the outcome. Rather, the manager must be able to influence the thoughts and attitudes of those involved in a change in order to secure their buy-in and active cooperation. When this effort is unsuccessful, any change, no matter how well conceived, will fail.

How can managers improve their skills in introducing and implementing changes? A manager's ability to identify and analyze prob-

Introduction

lems depends largely on intellectual power and the quality of available information. This skill can be developed in several ways: formal academic training; personal experience of trial and error; informed and constructive criticism from his seniors, peers and subordinates; and knowledge of the effects of decisions.

In the training of management, considerable attention has been devoted to developing those skills involved in the invention of solutions to problems. An early example stemmed from the Gilbreths' techniques of work study and work simplification.[1] "Brainstorming," synectics[2] and the work of Kepner and Tregoe[3] exemplified attempts to free the mind and stimulate creative thinking through the application of systematic procedures to identify and analyze problems and to formulate innovative solutions.

When I wrote the initial version of this book in 1965,[4] comparatively few efforts had been made to develop methods for getting people to be more cooperative and supportive with respect to the changes in which they are directly involved, Since 1965, organizational behavior has developed as a separate discipline and is currently a required first-year course in virtually every graduate program in business administration and management. A primary focus of this new discipline is the management of change. Many larger corporations have established the separate function of organizational development, with a charter to facilitate changes within the organization.

Both research and practice in organizational behavior and organizational development over the past two and a half decades now lend solid support to the ideas and approaches set forth in this book – a revised, expanded and updated version of my original work. A systematic, planned approach to the implementation of changes and the management of any associated resistance is clearly necessary and practicable. Any manager can and must develop some facility in coping with resistance to and in gaining people's acceptance of changes.

In this book, I present some concepts, principles and guidelines intended to help managers at every organizational level improve the way in which they introduce and implement changes in business situations. Any capable manager should be able to apply these concepts.

The question of whether or not a change should be made, and how such a decision should be reached, is outside the scope of this book. This subject is treated extensively in many books on management, decision-making, strategic analysis and planning, and the like. In this book, I assume that the decision to make a change has already been reached. I also assume that the objectives of the change are in the best

Introduction

long-term interests of the organization. This book focuses on how the change can be made so that its full benefits are actually realized.

It is not my intent that the ideas presented here help managers manipulate their employees into accepting changes that are neither in their nor in the organization's best long-term interests. On the contrary, it is my hope that by applying these concepts management can become aware of any poorly conceived or miscalculated decisions in time to retract or alter them. I doubt that any management could, by using the approaches suggested here, get their employees to accept a change that would ultimately prove harmful to them.

The particular approaches discussed in the following pages should not be regarded as formulas that can be applied with certain success in any business situation. Each change as well as each organization has its own unique characteristics. Often, these present special problems. To solve these, managers will need to adapt and modify the approaches described here. Nevertheless, it is my hope that the fundamental principles underlying these approaches will prove to be broadly applicable in helping management improve their present ability to make changes successfully.

1

Defining the Change and Its Causes

There is nothing in this world constant, but inconstancy.

Jonathan Swift

Consider the following examples of changes:

1. The desks in an office are rearranged to accommodate three new clerks and their equipment.
2. An improvement is made in the quality of rubber thread used to manufacture golf balls. The number of thread breaks occurring in the winding operation is reduced.
3. As a result of studies made by industrial engineers, coating machine operatives in the consumer packaging division of a large paper company are told that each of them will no longer be operating a single paper-coating machine as had been the custom. Instead, each operative will be required to operate two coating machines simultaneously. Redundant operatives will be moved to different jobs.
4. The private secretaries to middle-level managers in the sales department at head office are notified that because they are frequently underutilized by their bosses who travel frequently, they will be moved into a secretarial pool, reporting to a newly hired female manager.
5. An announcement is made to the employees of the Ion Electronics Company Ltd that within six months the firm's manufacturing facilities will be moving to a new plant. This will be located in Stevenage New Town, 20 miles from their present location in London.
6. As part of a strategy to improve service quality and customer satisfaction, the senior management of an insurance company decide to change the compensation system for all employees.

Rather than consisting of fixed salaries based on job evaluation with individual merit increases determined by annual performance reviews, the new pay system will be performance-based. This means standard fixed rates for each job with potentially substantial bonuses determined every four months, based on departmental performance.

7   The directors of Halox Photographic Products Inc. decide to pursue a strategy of diversification. In addition to continuing their business of manufacturing and marketing cameras and film for amateur and professional use, they plan to enter a niche in the office duplicating equipment market. Immediately, they begin planning for the design, development, manufacture and sale of these new products.

What common threads link these seven examples? How can these actual situations help to clarify our understanding of change in a business environment? And, how can these illustrations illuminate the basic reasons for change? Clearly, in all seven cases, some aspect of the status quo either is about to change or is in the process of changing.

All seven changes were instituted by management. They acted in each instance because there was a need to change the existing situation. In some cases, this need was a manager's perception that operating efficiency needed improvement. In other cases, decisions to act were responses to external pressures. These might have been initiated by senior management, or by economic, social and political forces in the business environment. Wherever the source of pressures to change, management acted because they wanted certain improvements or benefits.

Some of these benefits will be immediate. Others will result in time. In several of the cases, only a segment of the company's operations is affected. In others, the entire organization will be involved. In each of these seven examples, the scope of change varies widely. Nevertheless, we can develop some principles that can be used both to explain what is happening in each change and to improve the way in which it is carried out.

In all seven cases, others in addition to management are vitally involved. Some of these people are affected directly by the changing circumstances. They must alter their established patterns of behavior. Others are required to contribute their efforts toward realizing the changes, but will not be affected directly. In every case, the extent of benefits or improvements resulting from each change depends on the behavior both of those affected and of the managers and supervisors who are implementing the change. In the next four chapters, I discuss the ways in which people are affected by change and how they react.

Means or Ends?

To carry out a change successfully, any manager must first understand fully what is about to happen. Four questions must be answered:

- What is to be accomplished?
- Why?
- How is this to be accomplished?
- What will be changed as a consequence?

Answering these questions about a particular change enables a manager to distinguish means from ends. Why is this distinction vital to the successful introduction and implementation of any change?

In most situations, ends or objectives are what really count. Objectives can be both near- and long-term. These are often quite different. Several different means are usually available for achieving any given objective. Assuming that all options are equally moral and ethical, the choice should depend primarily on which can best achieve long-term objectives.

To enhance success in implementing any change, it is desirable that managers be flexible in selecting or modifying the means for achieving desired objectives. Such flexibility is best achieved when there is a clear separation in thinking between objectives and the methods for their accomplishment. When this distinction is blurred, a manager can confuse means with ends. A method can itself become the prime objective. When this occurs, a manager can become so commited to one particular method that both flexibility and objectivity are lost.

But the success of change depends heavily on flexibility and objectivity. They are important at the outset because they enhance the probability of selecting the best means for achieving the desired ends. They continue to be important throughout the change until the objectives are achieved. Although one method might initially seem attractive and appropriate, it might require subsequent modification as unforeseen developments occur. Modification of the original method might also become desirable when others involved contribute worthwhile suggestions. These can occur at any time during a change.

Defining the Change and Its Causes

Because adopting suggestions can enhance the effectiveness of changes and their outcomes, managers must remain sufficiently flexible to incorporate new ideas throughout the change process. To do so is in the best interests of both the manager and the organization.

In my experience, managers often have a hard time maintaining objectivity and flexibility about the means for achieving particular ends. Typically, day-to-day business and organizational pressures foster a focus on immediate and near-term issues. This makes it difficult to sustain a clear separation in one's thinking between immediate means and long-term ends. All too often, means become ends. Furthermore, many managers become obsessive about control. A kind of management *machismo* stiffens one's resolve "to do it my way" and to resist any suggestion to swerve from a set course. When a particular method for carrying out a change is originated by the manager accountable for the outcome, the personal investment in that method tends to create a state of mind that is anything but objective, open and flexible. I discuss this issue in greater detail in chapter 9.

When a manager accountable for carrying out a change is resistant to modifying the approach, the probability for successful outcomes will be reduced. Such a manager will find it difficut to react appropriately to unexpected developments in the situation. S/he will be resistant to constructive criticism and suggestions. A manager who from the outset can clearly distinguish what is to be accomplished from how it is to be achieved, will tend to be more open to subsequent alterations in the way the change is approached. Successful results will be far more likely.

We can now analyze the seven changes at the beginning of this chapter, in order to distinguish clearly methods from objectives. This analysis can also clarify how the specification of objective can influence the method employed.

1 Rearranging the desks was the method chosen to accomplish an immediate objective: providing for sufficient space to accommodate three new clerks, together with their desks, chairs and files. The long-term objective was to increase office capacity to support increased business. In this case, immediate and long-term objectives are quite different. If the immediate objective were the sole consideration, then rearranging the desks was the inevitable method for its accomplishment. If, however, the long-term objective were the primary consideration, several alternative methods might have been contemplated: (a) introducing more automation into the office without increasing the number of clerks; (b) streamlining clerical procedures without increasing the number of clerks;

Defining the Change and Its Causes

or (c) acquiring more space for expanding the office. Methods (a) and (b) might have been more desirable in the long term. Yet, they were not considered because management focused only on the immediate objective.

2   Improving the quality of rubber thread was the method chosen to accomplish the immediate objective of reducing the number of thread breaks occurring in the golf ball winding operation. The long-term objectives were to reduce manufacturing costs and to improve the quality of product. In this case, both immediate and long-term objectives are consistent. Nevertheless, alternative methods might have been considered: (a) redesigning the winding equipment; (b) redesigning the method for maintaining a constant thread tension during the winding operation; or (c) redesigning the product to eliminate the use of rubber thread.

3   Doubling the number of coating machines to be operated by a single operative was the method chosen to accomplish the immediate objective of improving employees' utilization. The long-term objective was to reduce operating costs so as to maintain or improve the profit margin. Immediate and long-term objectives are different but consistent. Yet there are alternative methods of approach, such as incorporating other functions (e.g. inspection, maintenance and record-keeping activities) into the operative's job. This approach could reduce the number of service personnel required.

4   Creating a secretarial pool was the method selected to achieve the near-term objective of better utilizing the formerly private secretaries. Perhaps a longer-term objective was to improve secretarial productivity and reduce costs (although this is by no means clear). Near- and longer-term objectives are different but consistent. At least one alternative approach to achieving both ends would be to work out a scheme whereby two or more sales managers would share a single secretary. This solution would be far less disruptive for both secretaries and managers, and would result in more substantial cost reductions than was achieved by creating the secretarial pool.

5   Moving manufacturing operations to a new plant located in a nearby suburb was the method chosen to accomplish two near-term objectives: (a) modernizing the manufacturing process; and (b) providing additional capacity for expected business growth. These objectives are consistent with two longer-term objectives – increasing share of market and improving profitability. Because all these objectives are broad, there is wide scope for alternative

methods for their accomplishment. Other locations closer to the present plant might have been selected for the new factory. The existing plant might have been rebuilt and modernized. Or it might have been closed altogether, and manufacturing operations could have been either subcontracted or reinsituted elsewhere in the UK or in another country.

6 Instituting performance-based compensation was the means chosen to achieve a near-term objective of improving employees' motivation. The longer-term strategic objectives, entirely consistent with the near-term one, were the improvement of service quality and customer satisfaction, and organizational productivity. Several other options would also address these objectives. Alternative approaches to compensation might be considered such as gainsharing, profit sharing or a company stock bonus plan. Other approaches to improving motivation would be a comprehensive, organization-wide quality improvement program, or some form of an employee involvement strategy.

7 A diversification strategy was the approach selected to accomplish three long-term strategic objectives: (a) increasing revenues; (b) increasing profitability and ensuring the firm's financial stability; and (c) reducing wide seasonal fluctuations in both revenues and operations. As in the previous two cases, many alternative approaches might have been employed to accomplish these objectives.

The Nature of Change and Its Causes

Here are some generalizations about the nature of change and its causes. In the context of this book, we can define change as any alteration to the status quo in an organization initiated by management, that impacts either or both the work and the work environment of an individual. The purpose of any change is to achieve certain objectives or outcomes. These may be both immediate and long-term. How effectively the change is managed and implemented will determine the extent to which the intended objectives or outcomes are actually realized.

For any change to be successful, it is essential first to identify the objectives for which that change is a means of accomplishment. Commitment to a set of objectives depends on understanding their

Defining the Change and Its Causes

underlying rationale: why are these objectives necessary and important, and how were they determined? Immediate objectives must be distinguished from long-term ones. Any inconsistencies must be recognized. Generally, long-term objectives permit considerable variety in the choice of options for their accomplishment. To maximize the probability for success, managers must have the widest possible choice in the method of change. When managers focus only on immediate objectives, they risk having a very narrow range of options from which to choose. Thus, in determining the method of change, managers are more likely to be successful when they focus primarily on long-term objectives.

There are no more than about eight types of long-term objectives most likely to create the need for changes within business organizations:

- Improving market offerings (products and services) in terms of quality, uniformity, reliability, visual appeal, ease of use, functionality.
- Reducing total costs by improving operating effectiveness and efficiency, better utilization of human resources, plant and equipment, materials, energy and capital.
- Improving the delivery of products and services to customers in terms of time-to-market for new and modified market offerings, consistency and reliability, and responsiveness to unexpected customer demands.
- Changing productive capacity to meet the needs of business growth or decline, changes in market geography, changes in location of facilities, and changes in sourcing.
- Improving organizational effectiveness in terms of structural improvement, better employee motivation and teamwork, less friction and less diversion of human energies toward nonproductive activities, improved policies, systems, procedures and processes, and better opportunities for employees to realize to the full their potential capabilities.
- Improving the ability of the organization to innovate and learn from its experience in order to anticipate or respond to market opportunities, demands and changes, changes in technology equipment, materials and methods, and changes in its economic, political and social environment.
- Improving the company's public image and reputation through better relations with customers, suppliers, shareholders and the general public, and through more socially responsible behavior.

Defining the Change and Its Causes

- Changing the business(es) by redefinding the product or service concept, changing markets and customers served, changing the mix of market offerings (goods versus services), changing the portfolio mix (diversification, acquisition, merger, divestiture).

Here are some of the more common types of changes that are typically employed to accomplish these long-term objectives.

Changes in operations

Ways in which work is performed and flows.

Location of work.

Layouts of work areas.

Processes.

Materials.

Plant and facilities.

Machinery, tools and equipment.

Sourcing.

Subcontracting.

Safety and housekeeping practices.

Operating procedures and methods.

Systems (planning, budgeting, control, communications, rewards, information).

Changes in market offerings

Design of products and services.

Materials and components.

Quality specifications and standards.

Breadth of products/services offered.

Defining the Change and Its Causes

Changes in organization

Structure of organization and allocation of responsibilities (functional, strategic business unit, matrix).

Levels of management and supervision.

Extent of delegation; management style.

Size and nature of work groups.

Supervision of work groups.

Placement of individuals in jobs.

Geographical dispersion/concentration.

Policies, procedures and processes.

Systems (planning, budgeting, control, communications, rewards, information).

Employee/management relationships.

Vehicles for interfunctional interaction.

Vehicles for employee involvement.

Unions and industrial relations.

Cultural norms and beliefs.

Changes in the working environment

Working conditions.

Systems of measurement and control.

Standards of performance.

Policies and procedures.

Safety and housekeeping.

Summary

At the outset of introducing and implementing a change, the accountable managers should first answer several questions before taking any action:

Defining the Change and Its Causes

- What are we trying to accomplish in the long-term, and why?
- Why is it necessary to make any change at all, and what will be the value of doing so?
- What optional methods should be considered for accomplishing the long-term objectives? Why have we selected the particular option to be implemented?
- What precisely will be changed as a consequence of the particular method selected?

Clarifying these points at the outset will provide the manager with the widest possible choice of methods in accomplishing the intended objectives. Also, it will enable personal flexibility in the way the changing situation is managed. The manager will be able, when necessary, to modify the initial approach and to incorporate any worthwhile ideas contributed by others. Consequently, there will be a greater probability that the change will be implemented successfully.

2

How People are Affected by Change

*All changes are irksome to the human mind,
especially those which are attended with
great dangers and uncertain effects.*

John Adams

Every change has some impact on people. They are the operatives, clerks and other workers who must alter their working behavior so that the objectives of the change can be achieved. They are the other employees who might later be affected by the outcome. They are also the supervisors at lower levels in the management hierarchy. They are the managers accountable for carrying out the change. They are the staff specialists who are invited to contribute their expert knowledge. And they are the union stewards and officials when the workers involved are unionized. The people most affected are all those directly involved in carrying out management's intentions. But in order to realize the full benefits of the change, everyone mentioned above must to some extent alter both their attitudes and behavior.

Maximum benefits from a change can be achieved only when any resistance to it by those affected is minimized. In order to minimize resistance and maximize acceptance and support, managers must first understand the nature of resistant behavior, of resistant attitudes and feelings, and of the complex, dynamic relationships that exists between these and the several factors that influence them. These factors derive from three sources: each individual affected by the change; the organizational setting, culture, environment and context; and the nature of the change itself.

In the following three chapters, I discuss the factors derived from these three sources that influence both attitudes and behavior. I then discuss the relationship between resistant attitudes and resistant behavior. Based on this analysis, I suggest a method by which any individual or group of managers might anticipate in their planning how those affected might react to an intended change.

Before attempting any analysis of attitudes and behavior, however, consider first the objective effects that changes have on the people involved. Understanding in some detail just how a change impacts those affected, enables us to establish a frame of reference for considering resistant attitudes and behavior. In this chapter, I examine three distinct ways in which people are affected by changes. One of these is operational: whatever alterations in behavior are required. Another effect is psychological: whatever changes occur to the way in which each individual relates to and regards his or her work. The third effect is social: whatever alterations are made to established relationships among those affected and between them and the organization.

Operational Effects

Most changes require those doing the work to alter the way in which they perform the physical routines involved. The following examples illustrate some typical operational effects of changes on people's behavior:

- Mary is told that several of her movements in assembling electronic amplifiers are no longer necessary if she rearranges the sequence of assembly operations. Mary must learn to perform a different sequence of operations along with different arm-hand-finger movements.
- A new automatic machine is introduced to replace the skilled manual process of sewing buttonholes in men's clothing. Skilled buttonhole sewers must now either become machine operatives or move to different jobs, requiring different skills.
- To improve the quality of its services, a bank offering mortgages to prospective home buyers decides to maintain contact with the mortgage applicant during the lengthy mortgage approval process. Relevant bank managers must now telephone customers weekly to provide them with a progress report on the processing of their application.
- A centralized stockroom in a large machine shop is decentralized into several small stockrooms located at various points in the

plant. Each of the smaller stockrooms may not carry all the tools and parts required by craftsmen. Some craftsmen will have to spend more time than before to get tools and parts, while others will spend less.
- There is a reduction of 12 percent in the tensile strength of paper that is receiving several chemical coatings. Coating machine operatives must either adjust to more frequent paper breaks, or learn new operating techniques.
- All company employees are notified that they must wear safety glasses at all times while in particular sections of the laboratories. Employees must learn to don their safety glasses whenever they enter these areas.
- First-line clerical supervisors in a large insurance company are now provided with weekly computerized print-outs listing detailed information about each clerk's attendance and performance. Each supervisor is directed to meet weekly with the clerks reporting to her, to review this information and discuss ways to improve.

In each instance, the operational effects of the change caused the people impacted to alter the way in which they performed their work.

Most of these alterations in behavior were, in fact, the immediate purpose of the change. Successful implementation usually depends on such alterations. But changes in behavior do not simply occur automatically at management's request or direction. Desired alterations depend entirely on active cooperation of those directly involved. The extent and nature of cooperation depend in part on personal attitudes. The formation of these attitudes is profoundly influenced by the psychological and social effects of the change.

Psychological Effects

Almost every change has a psychological as well as an operational impact on the people involved. Any change tends to alter how each person impacted relates to and feels about what he or she is doing. When a change is first announced, everyone affected begins to wonder how the change will impact accustomed ways of working. Questions arise, because any change creates uncertainty at first. Often, such uncertainty is related to each individual's ability to cope with required operational changes. Concerns about ability to cope are triggered both by individual personality characteristics, and by the nature of the change itself. In chapter 3, I discuss how the variety of one's questions and the intensity of one's feelings relate to personality and experience. But, characteristics of the change itself also tend to stimulate certain types of questions. These are quite predictable. Consider two examples.

A new and extremely complicated automated machine is introduced to perform a sequence of several operations. These were previously done on several more simple machines. Brian, an operative on the old equipment, is selected to run the new machine. This change will probably stimulate several questions for Brian. These questions will probably arise regardless of the particulars of his personality and experience. For example, Brian will probably wonder how well he will be able to master the new technology and skills required, and how well he will meet the new job standards. Also, it is likely that he will wonder whether or not he will be compensated fairly for what he considers will be his new, added responsibilities.

Stephen manages a branch office located in a provincial city. He is promoted to a position in the company's head office in London. He has never before lived there. Without any knowledge of Stephen's personality or background, we can predict that this change will probably cause him to have several questions. He will probably wonder how well he will adjust to a new environment with greater and different pressures. He might also wonder about the effects of this move on his personal finances, on his wife and two children, and on his relationship to them.

Thus, because changes generate psychological effects we can anticipate that certain questions are likely to occur to each individual affected. These questions usually center on personal concerns about learning, competence, performance, fair treatment, status and personal worth, all arising from changes in the work and its environment.

Social Effects

Changes also tend to generate social effects. These effects are alterations that take place in a person's established relationship with others in his or her work group, and with management, union officials and the organization as a whole. Almost any change in the work and work environment will tend to alter established relationships among those doing the job and between them and other employees of the organization, including managers and supervisors. Often, the basic framework for these relationships (the need for interactions and their frequency) is established by the technology and organization of the work, along with its physical environment.[5] For example, the pattern of interactions among a group working on an assembly line differs from that of teams of individuals all performing the identical operation. Other aspects of the working environment that affect the pattern of interactions are the physical location of the operations, the level of skills involved, the means by which the work flows from one point to another and the pay system.

In addition to the basic framework for relationships set by the technology and organization of the work and its environment, the nature of these relationships is determined in large part by the individual personal needs of the people involved. All of us tend to adjust the character of our social relationships to fit certain needs arising out of our individual personalities. Anyone who has worked on a job for an appreciable length of time will have tried to satisfy some personal needs by establishing rapport with others in the working environment. When the procedures and systems of work are changed, these often comfortable and satisfying relationships are disrupted or altered.

As with psychological effects, a change's social effects cause those involved to wonder at the outset what alterations will be taking place in their existing relationships. They will also wonder what their future relationships will be like. When we understand these existing relationships and the intended change, we can then predict the likelihood that certain questions will arise.

Let us return to the prior two cases of Brian and Stephen and consider the social effects involved. Brian, in his new job as a machine operative, will be relatively isolated in a new location, separated from his present workmates. Although we know nothing about Brian personally, it is likely that such a change will raise certain questions in his mind. He will probably wonder what it will feel like to be cut off from opportunities to chat with fellow workers. Also, he will probably be concerned that in the future he will be less well informed about what is going on around him in the organization. He will likely wonder how his performance on the new job will affect the regard that his supervisor, his workmates and his union have for him. He might also have some concern about the effects of this change on his future in the organization.

As a consequence of his impending move from the provinces to London, Stephen, the promoted branch manager, will undoubtedly have some questions about his new social situation. He will probably wonder how well he will compete with many other peer-level managers in a highly politicized environment, one very different from his familiar situation where he was the most senior executive in a small office. He will probably wonder about his response to the loss of status as an important member of the provincial community. Also, he will be concerned about the kind of person to whom he will now be reporting, and the effect of this move on his future career with the company.

A third example might help to clarify further the nature of these social effects. A group of widely separated, noisy machines are used to wind rubber thread onto cores for the manufacture of golf balls. Operatives depend on Arthur, their supplier of materials, for communicating with each other and for maintaining contact with what is going on around them in the organization. Because the rubber thread broke frequently, fresh spools were ofen required. Also, the spools of defective thread had to be removed. Arthur performed both these tasks, and his contacts with each operative were frequent. When a different company was contracted to supply thread, its quality improved greatly and the number of breaks diminished sharply. As a consequence, Arthur had fewer contacts with the operatives. The entire social situation altered. As a result, rather than receiving a wholehearted welcome from the operatives, the improvement in quality was regarded with mixed feelings.

The social effects of a change can have critical consequences on the way in which it is regarded, particularly when there is a possiblility of alterations in personal status. This is especially the case in any organizational change, whether it be structural or personal.

Importance of Psychological and Social Effects

Since the early 1900s, considerable attention and effort have been devoted to improving methods for dealing with the behavioral effects of changes. Many techniques have been developed and applied to make it easier for people to alter their routines for performing work: engineering design, time and motion study, work simplification, industrial engineering and industrial training techniques.

Although increasing attention and effort have been devoted in recent industrial research to developing ways of dealing with the psychological and social effects of changes, the results of this work have only recently begun to influence managers in business organizations. The level of sophistication achieved in this area is far from that in engineering design, industrial engineering and the training of skills.

Yet, for a change to be introduced and implemented successfully, *all three* effects must be considered and dealt with systematically. Often, the success of a change depends primarily on how it is perceived by everyone involved. All too often the originators and managers making a change assume that everyone will view the change as they do: namely, focusing only on the positive benefits expected and being concerned only with the operational impact. Unfortunately, this assumption is both naive and wrong. There is often a strong likelihood that the potentially adverse psychological and social effects will outweigh any perceived benefits, and generate resistance. Without acceptance and support, even changes that are brilliantly conceived and that are obvious improvements are likely to yield disappointing results. Consider the following examples.

The engineering department of a North American company manufacturing hypodermic syringes developed a high-speed automatic machine that was capable of increasing the rate of manufacture of the syringe body from 400 to 1,500 bodies per hour. There was a history of mistrust and hostility between the management and labor of this firm. When the new machine was unveiled, union representatives stated that they did not believe the machine could increase the production rate to more than 700 bodies per hour. Because this figure was less than half the amount predicted by the engineers, management protested vigorously. Nevertheless, after the machine was installed, the production rate gradually rose to about 700 and then levelled off.

In the United Kingdom, the large tank trucks used to deliver petroleum products were initially limited by law to a maximum speed of 20 m.p.h. With modified legislation, this maximum speed was subsequently raised to 30 m.p.h. The industry-wide agreement between the Transport and General Workers' Union and the association of petroleum companies was amended in the late 1950s to provide a bonus payment of sixpence per hour "for achieving the full improvement in running times from 30 m.p.h. operation." Most drivers were infuriated with what they regarded as a paltry pay settlement. As a consequence, the average driving speeds at many operating points were actually reduced rather than increased.

Summary

Any change has three kinds of effects on the people involved. The operational effects are whatever alterations they must make to the way in which they do their work. The psychological effects are whatever alterations are made to the way in which individuals relate to and regard their work. The social effects are the changes that occur to the established relationships among those involved and between them and the organization. All three effects tend to stimulate questions in the minds of the people involved. When enough is known about the nature of both the existing situation and the intended change, it is possible to anticipate the kinds of questions that will probably arise.

For a change to be realized successfully, management must act systematically to address all its effects – operational, psychological and social – in order to minimize resistance to and maximize support for the change. Specific constructive action requires that managers understand as much as possible about how these effects shape people's attitudes toward the change. In chapter 3, I discuss the relationship between these effects and attitudes.

3

How Personal Attitude to a Change is Formed

No passion so effectively robs the mind of all its powers of acting and reasoning as fear.

Edmund Burke

Change is not only an intellectual process but a psychological one as well.

Peter Drucker

Any change's operational, psychological and social effects tend to stimulate those involved to have certain predictable kinds of questions. Many of these questions evoke feelings and attitudes that are particular to each person, deriving both from individual personality and background of experience, and from a variety of factors in the situation. These questions, feelings and attitudes can have a profound effect on the way that each individual regards the change. Attitudes toward the change, however, are only one of several factors that determine behavior. How each person actually behaves when involved in the change is determined by the interaction of these attitudes with other forces generated by the work group and by the organization as a whole.

Any management's ability to achieve maximum benefits from a change depends, in part, on how effectively they create and maintain a climate that minimizes resistant behavior and encourages acceptance and support. In addition, they must also be able to anticipate many of the specific questions and problems that are likely to arise as a consequence of that change. Management can create a supportive climate and address these problems when they understand the

How Personal Attitude to a Change is Formed

dynamics of the relationship between attitudes and behavior, both with individuals and with groups.

The relationship between attitudes and behavior is far from direct. That is, someone who feels apprehensive and resistant toward a change may not necessarily resist it in a way that directly reflects his or her attitude. Actual behavior might appear quite unrelated to the person's actual feelings. But these feelings may nevertheless influence behavior in other, more subtle, ways. I discuss this relationship in chapters 4 and 5.

But first, consider how attitudes are formed. We can predict the generic questions stimulated by a particular change in the minds of the people affected (see chapter 2). But, is it possible to predict how each individual will regard the change? What will be his or her specific questions? What feelings and attitudes will be evoked by these questions? What fears and expectations will be triggered? How intense will these feelings and attitudes be? And what will be the relationship between these feelings and attitudes and the way the person actually behaves?

Our understanding of human motivation and of organizational behavior has developed substantially since World War II. Nevertheless, we have not yet reached the level of sophistication where we can make accurate predictions with certainty. We can, however, accumulate sufficient information about the nature of any particular change, about the individuals involved and about the organizational environment and context in which they are operating, so that many of their probable specific reactions can be forecast and anticipated. Such predictions cannot be entirely accurate. Nor can they be all-inclusive. Nevertheless, despite their limitations, such forecasts can be extremely useful in planning the introduction and implementation of that change. This and the next two chapters are concerned with how such predictions can be developed.

When confronted with a change that is to effect us, our attitude toward it is influenced by eight complex factors. Two derive from our own individual personality. Four arise primarily from more objective characteristics of the change itself, its organizational environment and its broader context. The two factors stem from conflicts that are generated by the change and how it is introduced. These are conflicts between our personal interests and those of the organization. All eight factors interact in complicated ways to determine our individual feelings and attitudes.

Fundamental Feelings about Change

One factor that influences our attitudes toward any change is both individual and deeply personal. It is a rather vague, predisposed, fundamental feeling about changes of any kind. This feeling is likely to be deeply ingrained in our mind. We are likely to be unaware of its existence, and unable to describe it. Yet it often influences profoundly our attitude toward any change.

What is the source of this deeply ingrained feeling? To understand this, we must recall how our unique personality developed. From the moment of birth, each of us had to deal with an unrelenting series of changes, the earliest ones being especially profound. At birth, the relatively cold, unpredictable and hostile world outside was substituted for the certain, warm comfort of the womb. Such a change could not fail to have evoked unpleasant and distasteful feelings. Next, many of us experienced another profound change, that of being weaned from mother's nipple to that of a bottle. Again, this substitution of an impersonal object for one that was warm, reassuring and comfortable must have been unpleasant.

Further profound changes occurred during our early years. Learning to deposit body wastes in toilets required us for the first time to exercise self-discipline and control over our bodily functions. This response to perhaps the first major demand made of us meant giving up the freedom we previously enjoyed. Then, if we were the first child in the family, the sudden appearance of an infant brother or sister must have been unsettling, because we then had to share the previously exclusive attention of our parents. Later, our initial introduction to school may well have generated mixed feelings of both anxiety and pleasure.

These profound changes are experiences that all of us have in common. Furthermore, these changes were, in most instances, imposed on us without the benefit of discussion or consultation, and therefore without our understanding. In no case could we really have understood what was happening to us, or why. All of these changes involved our giving up pleasures that yielded almost instantaneous gratifications. Although other pleasures were substituted in their place (e.g. parental approval and affection), the gratifications from these new pleasures were not necessarily as immediately satisfying. We had to learn to accept the increased time interval between our action and the pleasure and gratification that followed.

It is very difficult for an infant or young child to forgo immediate gratifications for others that might come later on. For example, it is

How Personal Attitude to a Change is Formed

unlikely that any very young child could be persuaded to give up sucking a lolly for a promised bag of lollies to be provided 30 minutes later. The natural reaction of any child to such changes (particularly the profound changes of childhood) is to resist them. Initially, at least, these changes are unpleasant. It should not be suprising, then, that each of us tends to develop in our early years some suspicion and distrust of change. Unpleasant memories of these significant childhood changes, and of the associated feelings of suspicion and distrust, tend to persist in adulthood.

Although everyone has undergone these early experiences, the resultant effect on any adult's fundamantal attitude toward change varies widely. This variation is caused both by the manner in which parents handled early changes and by the individual's inherited physical and mental characteristics.

From the very outset of life itself, how effectively the *process* of change is managed (by parents and other family members) has a profound impact. There is an enormous difference between the demands made on a child by parents who are patient, flexible and understanding, and those made by parents who are demanding, rigid and unreasonable. Parents with the former characteristics can help their child to realize that there can be certain compensations for the loss of pleasures that yield immediate gratifications. If the rewards offered for making a change are sufficiently great (e.g. approval and love), then the child may begin to regard future changes in a more attractive light. Any unpleasantness in a child's initial experience of these changes will be offset. Later on, the adult might regard changes with less suspicion and distrust, facing the unknown with some degree of self-confidence. Any questions arising about a particular change would tend to be less subjective and more objective, based more on the realities of the situation than on self-centered generalized apprehensions and fears.

By contrast, a child whose parents were constantly making unreasonable demands, unyielding, and forcing conformance might have developed very different fundamental feelings about change. To this child, every major change was probably an agonizing experience. The adult would tend to regard almost every change with suspicion and fear. Facing an unknown future, the inevitable consequence of any change, this adult would confront the change subjectively, conjuring up a wide variety of questions about how the change might affect him or her. These questions would probably be based more on personal fears and imaginings than on the realities of what is about to take place.

How valid is this comparison between changes experienced as adults and those experienced as children? All changes involve giving up the familiar for the unfamiliar, the certain for the uncertain. In any present situation, both the sources and nature of gratification are known. Confronted with a change, anyone faces a future in which both the sources of gratification and the gratifications themselves are either unknown or uncertain. No one in such circumstances can know with assurance what is really going to happen to him or her. Thus, individual perceptions of the impending change and its impact become especially important in shaping each person's attitudes toward the change.

An adult's childhood experiences with changes leaves a legacy in the form of a residue of faint but persistent memories. These memories of the past can exert a pervasive influence on current attitudes when changes are confronted in the present. For many, the prospect of an unknown or uncertain future stimulates anxiety in the form of doubts and fears. A measure of courage and self-assurance is required to enter into any new situation. Few people can approach changes with comfort and confidence. The intensity of anxiety generated by a prospective change will vary widely among those affected.

Feelings of Insecurity

Very closely related to our fundamental, predisposed feelings about change is another individual and deeply personal factor that influences our attitudes whenever we confront a changing situation. This factor is our basic feeling of security, which is primarily a function of our individual personality, and to a lesser extent a reflection of our financial circumstances. Clearly, anyone with independent means is less likely to fear changes on the job than the person entirely dependent on wages or salary.

The extent to which we feel secure is primarily a result of our cumulative experiences from birth. As in the case of our fundamental feelings about change, we would find it difficult to recognize or articulate any feelings of insecurity. These, too, are deeply ingrained and have a profound influence on many aspects of our behavior.

These feelings are particularly important because they can cause a person to have fears without objective justification. Such a person would tend to be apprehensive about any event perceived as threatening with potentially adverse effects. This person would probably find many more reasons for objecting to a particular change than someone who felt more secure.

How secure or insecure we may feel affects other aspects of our behavior. These feelings are closely related to self-confidence. They are also related to the extent of our resourcefulness and intiative. They determine in part how flexible and adaptable we are.

Relevance of Fundamental Feelings about Changes and Security

Of what value to managers is an understanding of these deeply ingrained feelings about changes and security? These feelings are beyond the reach of any manager's ability to influence them. We might even question whether or not they can be altered to any appreciable extent.

Nevertheless, it is important that managers appreciate the existence of these feelings. Managers must recognize that most people have some suspicion and discomfort when facing any change. They must also accept that it is their task to minimize these feelings (it is these same feelings that probably account for the glib references to the "fact" that "it is human nature to resist change"). Furthermore, a manager who understands the nature of these feelings will appreciate that in any group of people about to be affected by a change, there will be a wide range of personal responses. Each individual will have his or her own special questions, fears and expectations. These will vary widely from person to person in both variety and intensity.

Therefore, it is misleading and risky for any manager to implement a change assuming that everyone involved will regard it in the same way. A more sound, useful view is that despite any apparent similarities in behavior, underlying attitudes will vary. These will range widely - from opposition that is unreasoning and intense, to some kind of acceptance, however uncomfortable and resigned it may be, to active support.

A manager who knows his or her people should be able to predict who will probably have feelings of opposition and who will tend to be more accepting and supportive. Sometimes, the manager can predict whether or not these feelings of opposition are likely to be intense. Clearly, then, an intimate and detailed knowledge of each individual involved in the change is helpful in anticipating personal behavior.

Cultural Beliefs and Norms

Those cultural beliefs and norms of behavior that are characteristic of the societies in which we operate also influence our attitudes toward changes. All of us operate simultaneously in several different societies, each with its own culture: the work group; the deparment or division of the organization; the organization as a whole; the community; the region; the nation; etc. Each of these societies has identifiable cultural beliefs and behavioral norms.

The existence and significance of cultural beliefs and behavioral norms have long been familiar to anthropologists. In their study of primitive societies they were able to identify in each particular culture certain implicit ideas that were universally accepted and unquestioned. Typically, these ideas were concerned with the value of both objectives and practices. Because of these ideas, certain practices or norms were institutionalized as rituals and then perpetuated by myths. They became an essential element in the lives of the members of the primitive societies. Consider this example of a primitive society's cultural belief and consequent behavioral norm:

> EXAMPLE
>
> In the Betsileo and Tanala societies on the island of Madagascar, there existed the cultural belief that a child born on an "unlucky" day would ulimately destroy its family. As a consequence of this belief, children born in a particular month were killed either by being drowned or by having cattle walk over them. Children born on other "unlucky" days at other times of the year were thrown on the village rubbish heap for a period, or were washed in a jug of dirty dishwater. These practices were supposed to avert evil destiny.[6]

In our contemporary societies certain cultural beliefs and norms of behavior also exist. although these may appear to have somewhat of a more rational basis than the one cited above.

Research on the relationship between personality and culture has led to the conclusion that people tend to create culture and society to fulfill their own needs.[7] The creation of a culture with its associated beliefs and behavioral norms provides us with a means for ensuring an outlet for the expression of our needs and tendencies towards particular forms of action. In any organization, the cultural beliefs and behavioral norms that take root are the consequence of that organization's history, its experience with past leadership, successes and failures. These beliefs and norms serve to maintain equilibrium and continuity among the organization's employees.

Once established, any culture tends to influence the attitudes and behavior of its members (especially the more recent entrants) to conform to accepted beliefs and norms. After considerable time in a culture, this cultural and group pressure may cause a member to develop new needs. These are a rationalization of his or her more deeply ingrained, fundamental needs which would otherwise be in conflict with the cultural (or organizational) conditions and demands.[8] It is for this reason that some question how relevant it is to be concerned about fundamental personal needs in the study of behavior in organizations, particularly during periods of change.

In any organization (as well as in its subdivisions) there are cultural beliefs concerned with the value of or necessity for perpetuating certain practices. As in primitive societies, these beliefs are accepted implicitly. They are rarely, if ever, questioned. They determine what behavior is regarded as acceptable, and what is viewed as unacceptable. They influence people's choices in making decisions and in taking action.

Consider some examples of cultural beliefs and behavioral norms that have existed (many are still prevalent) both in British and in some American business organizations. Despite the general acceptability of the positive values that have been attached to these practices, each can in fact be challenged.

Belief Skilled craftsmen must have "mates" or "helpers" to assist them.
Norm Where collective bargaining agreements exist, provisions are explicitly included requiring and defining the job category of "mate".

Belief Systematic, regular overtime in large amounts is an essential and unavoidable element of work schedules.
Norm "Acceptable" standards of performance are set that ensure the "necessity" of regularly scheduled overtime.

Belief Skilled workers must not perform any work that they consider to be outside the boundaries of their craft.
Norm Job descriptions and work rules carefully specify who should do what work. Any deviation gives rise to grievances and disputes.

Belief Long service with a single organization is intrinsically desirable.
Norm Long service is rewarded and recognized by prizes, ritual celebrations, and preferential treatment in career advancement.

How Personal Attitude to a Change is Formed

Belief The length of an employee's service with an organization should be the determinant of his "rights" to tenure, of the extent of his benefits and of his "rights" to advancement.

Norm Long-service employees are never sacked; the length of holidays and magnitude of other benefits are related to length of service; when several employees are being considered for advancement, the longest-service employee is selected.

Belief The extent of "perks" should be proportional to the status of the job.

Norm Size and location of a manager's office, along with the nature of its furnishings, is a function of hierarchical level.

Prevailing cultural beliefs and behavioral norms become an important factor when they influence people's attitude toward any change. This occurs when the real or imagined effects of the change are in direct conflict with the established cultural belief or norm. For example, in a large British petroleum refinery a change is proposed that would result in the elimination of craftsmen's "mates" Both craftsmen and mates react immediately by dismissing this proposal as nonsense. They believe implicitly that the craftsman-mate system is both useful and necessary. They cannot conceive that this system would be eliminated.

As another example, for many years the construction and maintainance division (CMD) of a large American electric utility established a reputation in both the company and its industry for outstanding performance in constructing nuclear power plants. The resultant culture in this division was more consistent with that of a successful engineering construction company than with that of a service function in an electric utility. When the company's top management stopped the construction of any further nuclear plants, CMD was assigned the role of providing maintenance services to existing nuclear, fossil fuel, and hydro power plants. CMD's cultural characteristics of pride, autonomy, and massive-project orientation made it very difficult for it to change to a service-oriented function working on small and medium-sized projects.

Any manager must be aware of the existence and the potential power of established cultural beliefs and behavioral norms in both the entire organization and its subdivisions. The more prevalent beliefs and norms should be identified. With this knowledge, it is possible to recognize when a specific change is in conflict with one or more of these beliefs and norms. Such conflicts can then be lessened by addressing them directly. Before it is possible to carry out a change that is in conflict with cultural beliefs, it is necessary first that the beliefs themselves be changed. This often requires extensive discussion and re-education.

Trust

Another factor that influences an individual's attitudes toward a change stems from the nature of his or her relationships in the organization and its subgroups. The more important relationships are those with the immediate supervisor, manager, colleagues or fellow workers, the organization as a whole and the union. The key element in all these relationships is trust and loyalty.

When there is considerable trust in supervision and management, the individual will probably have faith that whatever the change his or her welfare will be looked after. If, on the other hand, there is little trust, s/he will find it difficult to believe any promises. Thus anyone's willingness to change depends in part on how much s/he trusts management.

Similarly, the extent of trust in the union or fellow workers to help protect individual interests may also influence attitudes toward a change. When an employee is confident that personal interests will be protected, s/he might be more favorably inclined to "go along with it," especially on an experimental basis. Lack of confidence in the power of either the union or workmates might cause one to feel opposed to the change. Such an attitude might stem from a belief that one's future security depends primarily on one's own ability to protect personal interests.

Feelings of trust and loyalty between two individuals are first formed by the way they interact and "hit it off." But these feelings become firmly established only after a series of incidents "prove" that the supervisor, manager or fellow worker really is to be trusted. The opportunity to experience such incidents is affected by the frequency of interactions permitted by both the technology of the operation and the organizational circumstances. Established cultural beliefs also influence the development of feelings of trust. But only through direct observation and personal experience can one develop a deep conviction that one's trust is justified.

Loyalty and trust for the more abstract "company," "management" or "union" are also developed through a series of direct personal experiences. However, because these are less frequent and often more impersonal and symbolic, cultural beliefs may be a more important influence. It is unlikely, for example, that anyone either could or would have the desire to test and disprove a prevailing cultural belief about the insincerity or general untrustworthiness of management.

There is some evidence that a supervisor is trusted more when it is believed that s/he has a significant amount of influence with his or her supervisors.[9] When supervisors who were found to have above-average influence or power with their own superior followed procedures considered generally to be good supervisory behavior, their subordinates reacted favorably. On the other hand, when supervisors with below-average influence upwards practiced the same desirable supervisory procedures, they failed to obtain a favorable reaction from their subordinates; often the reaction was adverse. From these findings, Pelz termed upwards influence a "conditioning variable" affecting the results of supervisory behavior.

At the outset of instituting a change, no manager can alter the patterns of trust that have already become established with employees and between them and the union and the organization as a whole. It takes a long time to achieve such alterations. Nevertheless, managers must recognize both the significance and the nature of the patterns of trust that already exist. These are "givens" at the time of any change.

A manager must recognize that when there is little trust, problems of carrying out the change will be far more difficult than they would be if there were considerable trust. When there is little trust, the manager must greatly increase efforts to gain acceptance. A little-trust situation can be somewhat offset by providing explicit and firm facts and guarantees, and by gradually introducing the change as a series of experimental trials.

Historical Events

Our attitudes toward any change are also influenced by the objective historical events that have preceded it. The significant ones are those perceived as relevant to the change, occurring within the organization, in the locality, and possibly in the nation.

Relevant historical events within an organization are:

- Its past policies, practices and customs.
- Actions of its past and present managements.
- The extent to which these managements have proved themselves trustworthy.

How Personal Attitude to a Change is Formed

- How past changes have been carried out.
- The after-effects of past changes.

Important historical factors of the region or nation are:

- Patterns of unemployment.
- Forces that influence the mobility of labor.
- The extent of government involvement or control with respect to businesses and their employees.

History influences attitudes toward change. People often regard past events as precedents for what is likely to occur in the future. These events are often cited as "evidence" of management's true attitudes. Assumptions are often made that because events followed a particular course in the past, these will be repeated in the future.

As with the issue of trust, managers can do nothing about history. Past events cannot be undone. Nor can they be ignored. Managers must be aware of their existence. Furthermore, they should be able to identify those events of special relevance to the change at hand. With such knowledge, they can act to offset the influence of any historical events which might affect attitudes negatively. Likewise, they might also be able to exploit advantageously any past happenings that might impact attitudes positively.

Threats Inherent in the Change

Any change is potentially threatening to those affected because there is the real possibility that they will suffer some kind of a loss. The seriousness of any perceived potential loss depends on how basic are the human needs that are impacted. The more basic the need affected by the changes, the more threatening will be the perception of that change by those involved.

The concept that there is hierachy of human needs was first postulated by A. H. Maslow.[10] He assumes that everyone has basic needs which can be classified into five hierachical levels:

1 Physiological needs: Food, shelter, sex, rest, exercise, basic protection from the elements.
2 Safety needs: protection against bodily harm from nature; protection against the threat of physical or psychological danger or deprivation.

3   Love needs: association, affection and acceptance.
4   Esteem needs: (a) personal need for achievement, confidence, independence, freedom, and feelings of adequacy and self-respect; and (b) personal need for recognition and appreciation from others.
5   Self-actualization needs: to fulfill one's full potentialities, to become what one is capable of being.

Maslow postulates that the lower-numbered needs are more basic than those with higher numbers. People seek to satisfy the more basic needs which relate essentially to survival, before directing their behavior toward satisfying the higher-numbered needs. Once a more fundamental need is satisfied, it ceases to drive motivation. Thus, once physical and safety needs are met, other higher-order needs become more important in motivating behavior.

But even though a person's more basic needs may be satisfied, they continue to exist. When a person feels that basic needs are threatened in some way by a change, his or her feelings about that change will be strongly negative. The more basic the need that is threatened, the more strongly negative will be the attitude.

Thus, the intensity of person's resistant feelings toward a particular change will be affected by which hierarchical need level is threatened. The more basic the level, the more resistant will be one's feelings. These feelings are likely to amplify the emotions stimulated by the other factors as well. Reconsider two of the examples discussed in chapter 1.

The coating machine operatives facing the requirement that each must now operate two machines, regarded this change as extremely threatening. This change impacted two of their most basic needs: *physiological*, because their very jobs and source of income were threatened by redundancy; and *safety*, because anxiety was stimulated about possibly increased personal hazards associated with the operation of two machines, when the operative's attention will be divided. As a consequence, they developed very resistant feelings which promoted extremely negative responses to every effort made by management to "sell" the change.

The private secretaries facing the move into a secretarial pool felt their needs for *love* and *esteem* threatened. They perceived a loss both of a close association with their former bosses and of personal status. These threatened needs stimulated negative and resistant feelings about the change. But the intensity of the attitudes toward the change was somewhat lower than the intensity of resistant feelings felt by the machine operatives in the former example, because physiological and safety needs are more basic than love and esteem needs.

Apprehensions and expectations

Our attitudes toward a change are influenced by the specific apprehensions and hopeful expectations arising from any conflict or harmony between our personal needs and those of the organization. I have already discussed the fundamental needs that are a function of our personalities and the more superficial needs that stem from the established beliefs and norms of the organizational cultures in which we operate.

Organizations, too, have needs. Any organization's most compelling need is to survive in a state of homeostatic equilibrium with its environment.[11] Most changes introduced by management are aimed at meeting this need (see chapter 1). These changes often bring into sharp focus conflicts between the immediate and long-term needs of the organization and those of the people involved. Sometimes, these needs will be more in harmony than in conflict.

When changes are introduced, those involved become acutely aware of any conflicts or harmony between their interests and those of the organization. When there is harmony, the individual tends to feel reassured and has hopeful expectations. When there is conflict, s/he may become apprehensive and fearful, with specific concerns about the future.

The characteristics of each situation and the individuals involved are unique. The specific questions that might be stimulated in each person's mind by a particular change can be described only in terms of probabilities. The following questions are intended to illustrate the range of possibilities. No single individual will have all these questions about any change. Nor should this list be considered as a complete complication of all the questions that could occur for any change. Yet any manager about to carry out a change should be prepared to encounter and cope with questions such as these.

The individual in relation to the work

- How effective will I be in the new situation?
- What new things will I have to learn? Can I learn them? How difficult will it be for me? How much time will I have to learn these things?
- What are the new standards I shall have to meet? Will I be able to meet them?

How Personal Attitude to a Change is Formed

- Will there be anything in the new situation that I shall find unpleasant or distasteful?
- Will the new situation involve increased responsibility for me? Will more work be required of me? Will I receive increased recognition? Will I be compensated fairly?
- How will the new situation compare with my existing one in terms of job interest? Variety? Challenge? Satisfactions? Rewards?
- Are they asking me to do something unprecedented? Can it be done?

The individual in relation to others

Fellow members of the work group

- How will the new situation affect my present interactions with my workmates? Will there be more or less contact? Will the people be the same, or will I have to work with a new group or with some new people?
- What will the change mean in terms of how others will regard me? What will they think? What will be my status in their eyes?
- Will I be able to continue associating with my mates or colleagues as now? Will I be left out of things?
- How will others feel about my cooperating with this change? Will they think I am being a "company man"? Will I be setting any precedents that might hurt others later on? How will all this affect my future relationships?
- Will others lose their jobs as a consequence of this change?
- Will I continue to be as well informed about what is going on in the group (or organization) as I am now? How will I be able to keep up-to-date on what is happening?
- In this change, am I being singled out or picked on? Will others regard this as discrimination or favoritism?

Supervision

- Will this change mean that I shall be working for a new boss? How will s/he compare with my present one? Will there be different

expectations, and if so, what? What will s/he consider to be especially important? How will we hit it off?
- In the new situation, will I be seeing as much of my boss as before? Can my future performance be judged fairly? How will I feel about being left to myself more often?
- In the new situation, will I be seeing my boss more often than before? Will s/he be looking over my shoulder constantly? How will I feel about that?
- Why was I chosen to try out the change?

Subordinates

- What will my subordinates think of me as a consequence of this change? Will they alter their regard for me? Will they see this as an increase or a decrease in my status?
- What kind of new subordinates will I have working for me? How will they compare with my present group? Will we be able to develop as good a rapport? What influence will they have on how effective a job I can do?

Outside contacts: customers, vendors, suppliers

- How will those outside the company regard me after this change? Will I be able to get their cooperation to the same extent as now? Will they bypass me and work with others in the company because of this change?
- Will my success in this new territory be as good as the success I've had to date? How difficult will it be to establish new contacts?
- Will my outside contacts regard this change as an increase or a decrease in my status in the company? How will my position in my community be affected?

The individual in relation to the organization
- How will my long-term future with the company be affected by this change? How will my chances for advancement be affected? How have others fared in this or similar circumstances?

- How will my future security with the company be affected by this change? Will I be more vulnerable to redundancy? In case of redundancy, what alternative positions might be open to me?
- How important does the company regard this new situation? To what extent will they be watching me? How much is at stake on how good a job I make of it?
- Does the company have as much faith in me as before? How will my new responsibilities and freedom to act compare with before?
- How does this situation compare with what I might have been able to secure elsewhere? Would I be able to do better with another company?

Many such questions will arise out of a genuine conflict of interest. Some, however, may not be realistically based. These would be products of an apprehensive imagination. For the manager, such a distinction is irrelevant. What is important is that these questions exist and are real for the individual to whom they have occurred. So long as these are treated as genuine problems, they must be addressed seriously and constructively.

The Manner of Change

The way in which a change is introduced and implemented also influences the attitudes of those involved. The effects of how a change is brought about may be quite independent of the effects generated by the change itself. The former depend on how those involved regard the methods management use to achieve desired changes in employees' behavior. When negative attitudes are generated, they typically are directed against the change itself, not the manner of its realization.

Whenever management institute a change, the number of orders given to subordinates increases substantially. Such an increase in the extent of direction can be, in itself, a cause of opposing the change. Many people resent taking any orders. Others adjust themselves to a degree of control by management, but may become upset when this degree of control is increased. Furthermore, some people, once they have become expert in their jobs, require very little supervision. They often regard this state of affairs with satisfaction and pride. When changes are instituted, these people are subjected to unaccustomed pressures and orders, not only from their immediate supervisors but also from staff specialists and more senior managers. In such circumstances, these people tend to lose their feelings of autonomy and self-sufficiency. Their dependence on management is emphasized, and their resentment of the change can be heightened.

There are many other aspects of how the way in which a change is instituted can influence people's attitudes toward it. One of these is the extent to which the orders for the change appear to be arbitrary and unilateral. When people feel they must alter their behavior without any apparent reason, they are likely to be more stubborn in their opposition. Moreover, the feeling that a change is being imposed in a dictatorial manner can also result in hostile attitudes. When people feel that a change is being rammed through, they will tend to feel little responsibility for its success.

There will be additional problems if a change is presented as irreversible and irrevocable. When those affected believe that they are being made to travel down a one-way road and to cross a bridge that will then be burned behind them, their suspicions and fears about the change will inevitably rise.

Insufficient information about the change and its probable effects and implications can cause those involved to become apprehensive. When someone's mind is filled with unanswered questions about a change and its possible impact, that person is likely to invent the answers. These will be products of that individual's own imagination, hopes and fears. Nevertheless, s/he will come to believe that these invented answers are factual. Typically, such self-developed "facts" can cause one's suspicions and fears of the change to be intensified.

When the people affected are not considered as individuals and are instead treated as an undifferentiated group, category or class, they can resent the apparent lack of concern for and recognition of their individual needs. This resentment can find a ready outlet in negative and resistant feelings toward the change. There is considerable research evidence to support this need for individual treatment:

> Consistently, in study after study, the data show that treating people as "human beings" rather than as "cogs in a machine" is a variable highly related to the attitudes and motivation of the subordinates at every level of the organization. The extent to which the superior conveys to the subordinate a feeling of confidence in him and an interest in his on-the-job and off-the-job problems exercises a major influence upon the attitudes and performance goals of the subordinate.[12]

The timing of a change can also be a source of difficulty. Most of us require time to adjust to new situations. Time is necessary for us to adjust our thinking to the new conditions. When sufficient time is not allowed for such adjustments, those involved in a change could become bewildered or apprehensive, and develop feelings of opposition.

There is a common root to most of these reasons why the way a change is managed might adversely affect people's attitudes. This root is the effect of the manner of change on two fundamental needs common to everyone: namely, a sense of both importance and personal worth. There is considerable evidence to support the concept that subordinates in any organizational situation react favorably to experiences which they feel support and contribute to this sense of importance and personal worth, and that they react unfavorably to experiences that threaten to decrease or minimize their sense of importance and personal worth.[13] When a change is introduced in a way that serves to increase the amount of direction and control on those affected in an apparently arbitrary and unilateral way with little or no explanation and involvement, and when the change is apparently being imposed irrevocably with no seeming concern for their needs, the people who must carry out the change can scarcely escape the feeling that their sense of importance and personal worth is being threatened and reduced. It should be no surprise, then, if they respond with hostile and resistant feelings.

Therefore, the way in which a change is introduced and implemented can be in itself a major source of difficulty. In chapters 6 and 7, I discuss in greater detail the significance of this problem, together with some possible solutions.

Attitude Determinants and Resistant Feelings

Eight factors have been described that interact to determine how anyone might feel about a change. A person's fundamental, predisposed feelings about any change and feelings of personal security are both functions of his or her own background of experience and personality. Existing cultural beliefs and behavioral norms, patterns of trust, the threats inherent in the change, and the historical context are all functions of the change itself, the organizational situation and its environment. One's reactions to the specifics of the change itself and its manner of introduction and implementation are the product of whatever conflicts and harmony are generated between that person's interests and those of the organization. How then, do these eight factors interact and combine to form the individual's overall feeling toward the change?

The interrelationship among these factors cannot be described precisely. Nevertheless, we can postulate a model based on mathematical concepts to help clarify these interrelationships. It is important to recognize that any such model will be inexact. Yet, it can suggest how these eight factors might interact and combine.

Six factors will tend to vary directly with feelings of resistance. That is, anyone's resistant feelings will be more intense when any of the following is greater: (a) the extent to which fundamental, predisposed feelings about any change are apprehensive and fearful; (b) the extent of conflict between prevailing cultural beliefs and norms and what is to be changed; (c) the number of specific unanswered apprehensions that arise stimulated by how s/he might be affected by the change; (d) the number and importance of past historical events that might cause anxiety about the change; (e) the extent to which the change threatens basic needs; and (f) the extent to which feelings of self-importance and self-worth are threatened and reduced by how the change is being introduced and implemented.

Some of the other influencing factors will tend to vary inversely with feelings of resistance. That is, anyone's resistant feelings will be less intense when any of the following is greater; (a) the extent to which s/he feels personally secure; (b) the extent of trust in management, the union and the work group; (c) the number and importance of any historical events that might cause positive feelings about the change; (d) the number of specific, confirmed hopeful expectations about the impact of the change; and (e) the extent to which the manner of instituting the change contributes to an increase in feelings of self-importance and self-worth.

We know that some of these factors tend to exert an influence on the intensity and significance of some of the others. For instance, anyone's predisposed feelings about changes in general will probably pervade all thoughts and feelings about any particular change. Likewise, when a change threatens very basic needs, the strong negative feelings aroused will impact all other factors associated with the change. The more anyone fears and is apprehensive about changes of any kind, the more s/he will tend to feel intensely fearful and suspicious toward, and to have a greater number of questions about, a particular change. Every available bit of data would probably be interpreted in the most pessimistic and negative terms possible.

Likewise, anyone's sense of personal security and feelings of trust will tend to pervade: (a) interpretations of past events that are

How Personal Attitude to a Change is Formed

prejudicial in favor of the change; (b) hopeful expectations of any benefits that might stem from the change; and (c) general satisfaction with the manner in which the change is being carried out. When an individual's sense of security and trust are considerable, s/he will tend to place an optimistic interpretation on the significance of events, both past and present, as well as on the magnitude of any expected benefits. An individual's early experiences and basic personality determine both predisposed apprehensiveness about any change and a sense of personal security. By adulthood, these tend to be relatively fixed or given.

We can see all these direct and inverse relationships together in our model shown in figure 1. When we examine this way of expressing these relationships, we can see that:

- Each element of the model relates to attitudes and feelings. Therefore, the entire model expresses the intensity of a single individual's overall resistant attitude or feeling about a prospective change.
- Resistant feelings are intense when the factors appearing in the numerator of the expression are great and the factors appearing in the denominator are small.
- Resistant feelings are reduced by strong feelings of personal security and trust even though the factors in the numerator might be of substantial magnitude.
- The intensity of threat posed by a particular change depends on which level of need in Maslow's hierarchy of needs is impacted. The more fundamental the need, the greater the intensity of threat. This threat amplifies resistant feelings because it pervades all other factors in the numerator of the model.
- The factors that most influence resistant feelings are one's predisposed feelings about any change, general sense of security and feelings of trust, and the intensity of threat posed by the change itself. When a person is generally apprehensive and the change threatens fundamental needs, the influence of all the other factors in the numerator is increased. When s/he is more confident, this tends to reduce the influence of all these factors. Similarly, if the person feels personally secure and/or has a high degree of trust, these increase the influence of all the other factors in the denominator, therefore reducing resistant feelings.
- Several factors are beyond management's ability to control. Management cannot influence anyone's predisposed feelings about change, or general sense of personal security. Furthermore, because trust develops from past experience, management can do

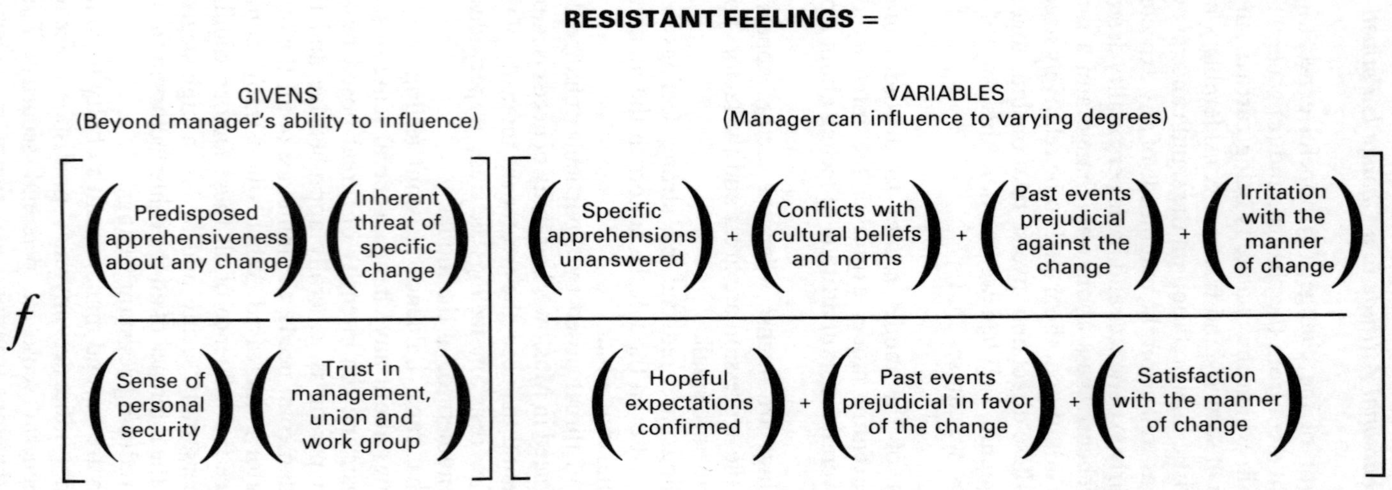

RESISTANT FEELINGS =

GIVENS
(Beyond manager's ability to influence)

- Predisposed apprehensiveness about any change
- Inherent threat of specific change
- Sense of personal security
- Trust in management, union and work group

VARIABLES
(Manager can influence to varying degrees)

- Specific apprehensions unanswered + Conflicts with cultural beliefs and norms + Past events prejudicial against the change + Irritation with the manner of change
- Hopeful expectations confirmed + Past events prejudicial in favor of the change + Satisfaction with the manner of change

f

Figure 1 A model showing relationships between resistant feelings and those factors which influence attitudes toward a specific change

How Personal Attitude to a Change is Formed

little, at the point of instituting a change, to alter already established feelings of trust. Also, there is little that management can do about the influence of historical events to the change.
- When instituting any particular change, management can fully control the influence of only two factors. One of these is the extent to which conflicts between people's interests and those of the organization are rationalized, and how many and how effectively questions about their unknown futures are answered. This applies even to changes that threaten fundamental personal needs. Management can also control the manner in which the change is introduced and implemented.
- Management have limited control over the influence of two other factors. One is apparent conflicts with prevailing cultural beliefs and norms. The other is the way in which apparently relevant historical events are interpreted.
- Many changes can be implemented successfully without much concern for the human implications when the people involved have strong feelings of personal security, and/or trust in their management and union. However, if this change later proves to have adverse effects on those involved, their subsequent feelings of trust about future changes will be lessened.
- Implementation of a change can fail even when management demonstrate active concern for those affected. Failure can occur when those involved are: (a) exceptionally apprehensive about changes in general; (b) personally insecure; (c) untrusting; and/or (d) threatened at a very fundamantal need level.

If we could collect sufficient and accurate data about each of the givens and variables in our model, we could then estimate the intensity of an individual's resistant feelings. Such a possibility, however, is remote. Not only would the collection of accurate data be very difficult, but also these factors would be extremely difficult to measure and quantify.

Although our model cannot be regarded as a precise instrument, it is useful for depicting how the eight factors that influence attitudes impact one another and result in an overall feeling about a particular change. The model has little value, however, in helping us to predict how people will actually behave. In chapters 4 and 5, I discuss how behavior is influenced by other factors in addition to the eight already described. Understanding these relationships can help management reduce or minimize resistant behavior.

Attitudes toward any change are based primarily on a person's assumptions and inferences when imagining what it will be like to work in the new situation after the change is made. However, no one can know beforehand with any certainty what this new situation will be like. Furthermore, no one can know about changes in status in these altered circumstances. People make such assumptions and inferences either to reassure themselves and enhance their feelings of personal security, or to justify their worst fears.

Whether or not these assumptions and inferences are in fact correct is irrelevant. To the extent that the individual believes them to be correct, s/he will act upon them. S/he will continue to act upon these assumptions until subsequent experience disproves their validity.

Summary

Anyone's attitudes toward a change are the consequence of eight factors that interrelate and interact in complicated ways:

- Fundamental, predisposed feelings about changes of any kind.
- Feelings of personal insecurity.
- Any prevailing cultural beliefs and behavioral norms that might be in conflict with change.
- The extent of trust in management, the union and the work group.
- Historical events relevant to the change.
- The intensity of threat inherent in the change.
- Specific apprehensions and expectations about the particular change.
- The manner in which the change is introduced and implemented.

Because the characteristics of each situation and each individual involved are unique, no formulas can be applied to predict how a particular change will be regarded by those affected. Nevertheless, a manager must understand the nature and source of the factors that shape personal attitudes before s/he can anticipate with any success their probable attitudes toward a specific change. Identifying such probabilities is a necessary preliminary step for any manager in planning for the introduction and implementation of that change.

4

How People React to Change

But men may construe things after their own fashion, Clean from the purpose of the things themselves.

William Shakespeare

If the changes that we fear be thus irresistible, what remains but to acquiesce with silence, as in the other insurmountable distresses of humanity? It remains that we retard what we cannot repel, that we palliate what we cannot cure.

Samuel Johnson

Our concern to this point has been primarily with attitudes: how changes tend to generate predictable questions in people's minds, and what factors interact to form their attitudes toward a particular change. But attitudes do not necessarily correlate directly with actual behavior. Before examining this relationship, we must first understand the variety of behavior that can occur: what are the various ways in which people can act when confronted with changes? In chapter 5, I discuss the relationship between attitudes and behavior, and to what extent and how it might be possible to forecast reactions to a particular change, so as to minimize any resistance.

Spectrum of Possible Behavior

Individual and group behavior can vary widely across a broad spectrum of possibilities. At one extreme is active resistance; at the other is enthusiastic support for the change (see figure 2). Previously I noted that anyone's assessment of future status is influenced by fears, desires, suspicions and beliefs. To ensure that one's apprehensions will not "come true," the most immediate and obvious action that s/he can take is to protect and defend present (and known) status. S/he does this by resisting the change.

This resistance may take many forms. The particular form depends on the individual's personality, on the nature of the change itself, on attitudes toward it and on forces deriving from the group and from the organization and its environmental context. Whatever the form of resistance, all types of opposition are a kind of aggressive or hostile behavior.

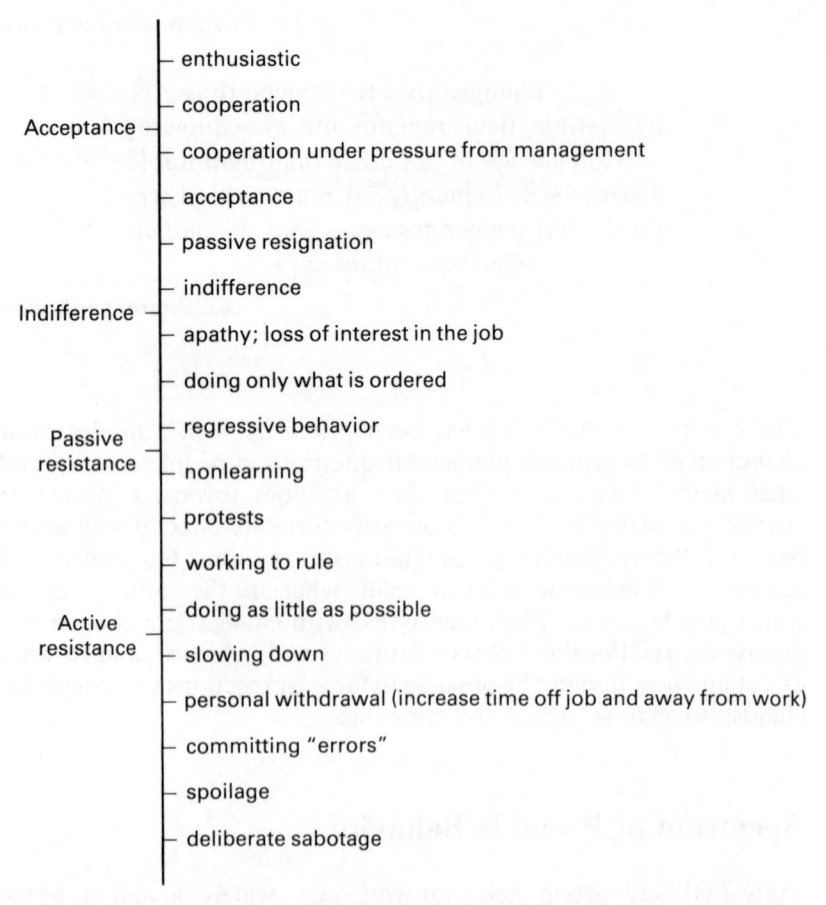

Acceptance
- enthusiastic
- cooperation
- cooperation under pressure from management

Indifference
- acceptance
- passive resignation
- indifference
- apathy; loss of interest in the job

Passive resistance
- doing only what is ordered
- regressive behavior
- nonlearning

Active resistance
- protests
- working to rule
- doing as little as possible
- slowing down
- personal withdrawal (increase time off job and away from work)
- committing "errors"
- spoilage
- deliberate sabotage

Figure 2 The spectrum of possible behavior toward a change

Frustration and Aggression

The relationship among aggressive behavior, hostile feelings and frustration is a well-established psychological concept.[14] Any of us can become frustrated when external forces conflict with and act to deny our personal desires and needs. When one believes that the future consequences of a change will conflict with present desires and needs, s/he will develop feelings of frustration. This frustration, in turn, arouses hostile feelings. Often, these feelings are directed towards the source of the frustration. Sometimes however, they are deflected elsewhere. In some instances, a person might even turn hostile feelings inward, against him or herself.

Anyone involved in a changing situation can become frustrated. In their most extreme form, hostile feelings can find release in aggressive behavior towards some aspect of the change. This behavior can take the form of deliberate sabotage. The following case is an illustration of how a drill press operative successfully resisted the establishment of tighter time-standards on his job:[15]

DIALOG

"Ray knew his drills," said Starkey. "He'd burn up a drill every four or five pieces when they were timing him, and say the speed was too high for the tough stuff he was running. Tough stuff, my ass! They'd lower the speed and feed to where he wasn't burning up the drills, then afterwards he'd speed up and cut through that tough stuff like cheese."

"What I want to know," said Tennessee, "is how in hell could Ward burn up the drills like that? You can't just burn up a drill when you feel like it."

"It's in the way you grind the drill," said Starkey. "Ray used to grind his own drills, and he'd touch them up before they timed him. The wrong kind of a grind will burn up a drill at a lower speed than the drill can take if it's ground right for the job."

"Oh," said Tennessee.

Increasing the amount of spoilage in the work, slowing down the pace of working and committing unintentional "errors" are all overt evidence of aggressive behavior directed toward changes. A more subtle means of sabotaging a change might be the practice of following orders in the most literal fashion, or working to rule. For example, a new machine was introduced into a manufacturing operation. It was intensely opposed by all the operatives on the shop floor. An engineer was supervising the trial runs and a maintenance fitter from the shop was assigned to assist him. When carrying out orders to make certain specific adjustments on the machine, the fitter noticed that several vital bolts had worked themselves loose. He did nothing about the matter because he had not been so instructed. During the next trial run, the machine became so badly damaged that it was withdrawn from the shop for extensive redesign.

Sometimes a person will resist a change by withdrawing entirely from the situation. Absence from work might increase. Or s/he might actively seek a change of job. In extreme cases, s/he might even leave the organization.

Resistance to changes can take passive as well as active forms. Regression to less mature levels of behavior is one possible outlet for feelings of frustration and hostility. We are familiar with the three-year-old child who resumes thumb-sucking when a new baby arrives in the family. Similarly, a manager, faced with a difficult and complicated change, might find it difficult to make any decisions at all. Or a clerk might develop problems in learning new office procedures. In some cases of frustration, a person might give up trying altogether and become indifferent, apathetic, passive or resigned.

There are other outlets for feelings of frustration. A person might direct hostile feelings toward others who are not directly involved in the change. S/he might become a disruptive influence in the work group by picking on members who are more weak and defenseless. Or s/he might direct aggressive behavior towards members of racial or religious minority groups. Another possible way of behaving might be to become fixated on some useless activity, just as Lady Macbeth became absorbed with washing her hands repeatedly. Thus, to avoid facing a difficult change, a frustrated manager might focus on a low-priority task such as reorganizing the files.

Another possible consequence of frustration caused by a change is that the person affected might direct hostile feelings inward, against him or herself. The result might be a psychosomatic exacerbation of illnesses such as high blood pressure, ulcers, heart conditions and asthma.

> Once we observed a group of working supervisors who had been strongly pressured to increase production under difficult circumstances with no backing from management. There were nine men regularly assigned to the day shift. One had a nervous breakdown, another had a fatal heart attack that was generally attributed to overwork and fatigue. Of the remaining seven, five had serious illnesses and in most cases no

organic cause could be determined. All this happened during a period of twelve months. Meanwhile, the men on the night shift, where pressure was much less, had an almost perfect health record.[16]

Finally, a person might turn away altogether from the source of frustration by sublimating hostile feelings. S/he might lose all interest in work and become passionately involved in gardening, local politics or some other personal activity.

These latter forms of resistant behavior are less immediately damaging to the success of a change than sabotage. Nevertheless, they can diminish significantly the extent of that success.

Organized Resistance

So far, the discussion has centered on individual behavior. When a group of people are affected by a change, the intense reactions of some members might have an inflammatory effect on others. This can happen even when members have only mild feelings of frustration. Yet, the majority could be stimulated by a few hotheads who voice loudly their personal fears and dire predictions. When these are infectious, the group often unites and resists the change in an organized way. Those less inclined towards aggressive behavior will nevertheless rally around the leadership provided by the more actively hostile members.

Another reason for any organized resistance to a change is that each individual's need for self-protection, so likely to be stimulated by a change, can find fulfillment in group action. Banding together in a group to resist the change offers people who share this need for self-protection an effective means for ensuring their future security. Collective action is often more successful than separate personal resistance.

Organized group resistance is a familiar phenomenon. One example is the limitation of output by group agreement so that any attempts to increase work standards can be defeated. Another instance is group action to cover up mistakes made by members as they implement new work procedures or quality standards. A group might also act to withhold vital information from management so that they can be kept in ignorance of what is really happening in a changing situation.

Organized resistance by a group occurs when there is conflict between the goals and interests of the group and those of the organization as a whole. These conflicts can occur at any one or more of three levels: (1) the immediate work group; (2) the department or function of which the work group is a part; and (3) the "dominant coalition." The dominant coalition is determined as "the objectives and strategies [for the organization], their personal characteristics, and the internal relationship of that minimum group of cooperating employees who oversee the organization as a whole and control its basic policy making."[17]

The dynamics of group influence on individual behavior is much the same at all three levels. I have already noted in chapter 3 that the need for belonging is one of everybody's most basic needs. Especially when the work itself is not providing much meaning or satisfaction to the individual, social needs tend to rise in importance. When the shared expectations of group members are in conflict with organizational goals, the social controls of the group can be a powerful countervailing force to management's controls to achieve organizational goals.[18] This conflict is often thrown into sharp relief at times when management are instituting changes.

Whether the individual identifies him or herself primarily with the immediate work group, the department or function, or the dominant coalition, the group itself may become a powerful source of resistance to a change. Once formed, any group develops needs for self-preservation and perpetuation. The more cohesive the group, the more powerful these needs, In time, groups meet these needs in part by developing their own subcultures within the organizational culture. Each group may establish their own beliefs and norms of behavior. When a change threatens to violate these beliefs and norms, the group may generate organized resistance to the change.[19]

Sometimes, the union will provide leadership for organized resistance to a change. It will do so if it believes that the interests of its members will genuinely be threatened or damaged by the change. The union might also act, however, if it believes that the change, or the manner of its introduction or implementation, will in some way damage the union's future status or security. It should be remembered that, although any union is formed originally as a self-protective device for its members, once formed it becomes an organizational entity. As such, it exhibits behavior that reflects the need to maintain a typical homeostatic equilibrium with its environment.

Every union has its own institutional requirements that must be fulfilled if it is to continue its existence by retaining the loyalty of its members. One of these requirements is recognition by the company of the union's power and status. If management are careful to recognize this fact by discussing their plans in advance with the union, the union might then be more willing to cooperate in the introduction of the change. If, on the other hand, management ignore or bypass the union, it will inevitably oppose both management and the change so that its status will be preserved.

Unions are particularly concerned with maintenance of membership. This is a fundamental security issue. Consequently, changes of special interest to unions are those that threaten to reduce the number of members or that impinge on or threaten those employees' rights normally associated with length of service with the company. Unions should be involved in discussion of such matters early in the introduction of the change. If this is not done, there will tend to be organized resistance to the change, led by the union.

Acceptance of Changes

Just as there is a variety of behavior in which people can resist changes, so are there also several different ways in which they can be accepting. The most positive form of acceptance is enthusiastic cooperation. Although rare, this can occur when an individual's own desires and needs, as well as those of the groups of which s/he is a member, are fulfilled by expectations about the effects of the change. Even when there are a few minor conflicts between one's desires and needs and that person's estimates of the effects of a change, s/he will still tend to accept that change because less effort is required to accept than to resist.

Group cooperation with a change can be regarded as a kind of defensive action taken by the group.[20] Because the change may be perceived as a threat to the group's stability and continued integrity, members may decide that to cooperate with the change is the lesser of two evils. They might believe that to engage in a joint venture is the best method for preserving the group's stability and integrity. They might also believe that failure to cooperate may exclude the group from any potential benefits to be derived, or may even diminish their present "payoffs" from the organization.

Indifference to Changes

Indifference to a change may be a more common defense against it than is commonly realized.[21] Indifferent behavior is manifested in two ways. Sometimes the individual (or group) appears to be ignoring the problems entirely. In effect, the person is saying, "This is really not *my* problem. I shan't be affected significantly." Alternatively, the individual (or group) may appear to be actively avoiding the pertinent issues by introducing and focusing on subjects that are irrelevant to the problems at hand.

Indifferent behavior can be a subtle form of resistance. The consequences of such behavior may affect adversely the successful implementation of a change. Indifference might result in a slowness or difficulty in comprehending the nature of the change and the requirements of the new conditions. Learning new skills, procedures, etc. would be slowed. Because of lack of interest, any unanticipated problems arising from the change might not become apparent soon enough for ready solution. There would be few suggestions from those involved that might contribute to the success of the change. All these effects would require management to exert more effort and devote more time than might otherwise be necessary for carrying out the change.

Summary

In introducing and implementing changes, the problems of resistance by both individuals and groups are of paramount concern. When resistance exists, it is not so much the change itself that is opposed. Rather, the primary causes for resistance are both the imagined and the real effects of the change on those involved, together with the manner in which the change is being brought about. In reality, the change itself is often only the symbol of what is being opposed.

The key problem in making any change is how to minimize resistance by those involved, in whatever form it occurs. These forms can vary widely, ranging from active outright resistance, through more subtle passive forms including indifference, to acceptance. The manager must be able to anticipate resistance and estimate its intensity. More important, furthermore, s/he must also anticipate many of its specific causes and reasons. Any manager who does this will then be able to plan and implement countermeasures that should at the very least minimize resistance and at best transform it into some form of acceptance.

5

Predicting the Extent of Resistance

Change will meet resistance unless it clearly and visibly strengthens Man's psychological security; and man being mortal, frail and limited, his security is always precarious.

Peter Druker

In order to develop appropriate plans for minimizing any resistance, managers must first be able to anticipate how those about to be affected by a change might react. Furthermore, to implement such plans effectively, managers must understand which situational factors they can influence most. Also, they must understand where and how to direct their efforts so that most of the conflicts between organizational groups and personal needs can be resolved with a minimum of compromise to desired objectives.

To be able to do all this, managers need to know how people form attitudes toward a change, how they might behave, and what the relationship is between resistant feelings, attitudes and resistant behavior. Moreover, managers must appreciate organizational and group influences, and their relevance to personal feelings, attitudes and behavior. Once a manager understands the interrelated and interactive dynamics among all these factors, it is then possible to know where efforts can be applied most effectively with the greatest leverage.

I have already discussed feelings, attitudes and behavior separately. In this chapter, I focus on the relationship among these. I also examine further the influence of organizational and group influences on behavior. Then, I suggest where managers can direct their efforts to influence reactions to a change, and propose an approach whereby reactions to a specific change can be estimated so that effective plans can be developed for its institution.

A Case of Personal Reactions to a Simple Change

So that the complex relationship between feelings, attitudes and behavior toward a change can be seen in sharper focus, imagine yourself about to be affected by a simple change. How might you feel? How might you actually behave?

Imagine that you are about to participate in two-day seminar in a city about 150 miles distant from your home. You have come hoping to learn about the application of strategic management to your business.

Suppose that, prior to your arrival at this seminar, you had received information including a schedule of events. The seminar is scheduled from 9:00 a.m. to 4:30 p.m. on a Thursday and Friday. Each day, there is to be one 15 minute break in the morning and another in the afternoon, and a 90 minute period for lunch. Accordingly, you have arranged to return to your home by a train departing at 5:15 p.m. on Friday.

Now suppose that, during his introductory remarks, the seminar lecturer announces that it will be neccessary to alter the schedule. Because there is more material than can be completed within the scheduled time, the length of the seminar must be extended by two hours. Therefore, you are told that the seminar will end each day at 5:30 p.m. instead of 4:30 as previously announced.

If you were in such a situation, how might you feel immediately after such an announcement? There are several possibilities:

1 Damn! I must now catch a later train on Friday. I shall not be able to return home until nearly midnight. I must ring my wife and tell her to cancel our plans for Friday evening.
2 Impossible! I have an engagement I simply cannot cancel on Friday evening. I must leave the seminar before its completion.
3 Good! This is a fine reason for spending the evening here on Friday. I shall ring X, whom I have not seen for some time. Perhaps we can get together Friday evening.
4 Good! This seminar may prove even more interesting and valuable than I had anticipated. We certainly seem to be getting value for money.

5 So what? I do not have to be back at any particular time. I shall book a later train.
6 Hold on! What kind of seminar is this going to be if the lecturer can't even plan his own schedule properly? I wonder how qualified he is to be handling this subject? I shall certainly listen more critically.
7 Hold on! This is an arbitary and dictatorial way to make such an announcement. Why couldn't he have consulted us? Perhaps we could work out some compromise in which we might shorten our luncheons and breaks so that we could finish at the originally scheduled time after all.

Any of these feelings and attitudes might occur to you. The particular one would depend on your own personality and the extent to which this change either conflicted with or fulfilled your needs and plans at the time. Attitudes 1 or 2 might occur if there were conflict. Attitudes 3 and 4 might occur of the effects of the change to some extent fulfilled your need and plans. You might feel the indifference of response 5 if there were neither conflict nor fulfillment. Attitudes 6 and 7 would result from irritation with the lecturer's manner of introducing the change.

If any of these feelings and attitudes occured to you, how might you actually behave? Just as there are a variety of possible attitudes, so would there also be a variety of possible ways to react. If your attitude were similar to 2, you would be likely to walk out of the seminar before its completion. Attitudes 1, 2, 6 and 7 all involve feelings of frustration and hostility. Your hostile feelings would probably be directed toward the lecturer, the source of your frustration. However, the situation is such that you would be inhibited in resisting the change directly. In a group of strangers this would be considered unmannerly and impolite. Consequently, you might resist indirectly by becoming inattentive, argumentative during discussions, skeptical about the content of the seminar or a disruptive influence in the group. On the other hand, you might take the initiative and suggest that a compromise in the schedule be considered so that the seminar might end at the originally scheduled time on Friday.

Generalizations from the Case

What generalizations can be made from this simple example that would be relevant to any change in a work situation?

Predicting the Extent of Resistance

- Anyone facing a change might react with resistance.
- In confronting a change each person's feelings and attitudes might differ considerably from those of the others involved.
- Each person's behavior might also differ from that of the others.
- Individual behavior might vary even among those with similar feelings and attitudes toward the change.
- The extent to which one actually resists the change (or vents hostility on the lecturer) depends in part on the extent of conflict between individual expectations about the effects of that change and personal needs and desires at the time.
- The action that anyone would *like* to take depends on the intensity of feelings and the kind of person s/he is.
- The action that one actually takes is influenced both by his or her *desired* action (see above) and by the reaction to pressures exerted by the group and by the seminar situation. These pressures would encourage mannerly and polite behavior, both with respect to the seminar lecturer and to the others in the group. If they were strangers, this pressure towards polite behavior might be stronger than if the group consisted of colleagues (because there might be less concern with the latter's reactions). In any event, pressure encouraging socially graceful behavior would probably cause each member of the group to modify desired behavior. In this way each person's actual behavior would tend to be a rationalization of the desire to behave in a certain way and the desire to conform to the norms of the group and situation.
- Suppose that a person resists this change (which is but a trivial aspect of the seminar as a whole). As a result, that individual would benefit less from the seminar than might otherwise have been the case, even though its content might have been of value. Thus, from the lecturer's viewpoint, a brilliantly conceived presentation of considerable potential benefit would fail to achieve its intended result. This failure would be caused by the poor handling of a relatively trivial detail, the changing schedule. Thus, any change with sound and justified objectives can fail if the manner in which it is introduced and implemented is mishandled.

How comparable is this experience of change at the seminar with the experience of any change at work? The two situations are quite analogous, except in one important respect. In the seminar, if the conflicts created by the change were sufficiently intense, one could always have the option of walking out of the situation with little concern for the consequences. At work this method of solving the problem would create new problems far more serious than those presented by the change. Therefore, because the option of walking out is not one that can readily be used by anyone facing a change at work, and because s/he would probably feel somewhat trapped, feelings of frustration, hostility and aggression would tend to be even more intense than they would be at the seminar.

Organizational and Group Influences on Behavior

In the above case, certain group pressures probably had a significant influence on actual behavior. Just how these pressures appear to fit into the relationship between feelings and behavior with respect to a change is suggested in figure 3.

Although a person facing a change might want to act in a certain way, the way s/he actually behaves may in fact be quite different. That person is reacting not only to the change but also to the pressures exerted both by the group(s) of which s/he is a member and by the organizational environment. Just as the nature of the individual's personality affects some of the factors influencing initial feelings about the change, so too does the nature of the organization and the group affect other factors influencing initial attitudes. Note that anyone's attitudes toward a change after it has been implemented may differ from how s/he regarded it beforehand. The new attitude will derive from actual experience of the change, and from rationalizations about actual behavior with respect to that change.

What, then, generates these organizational and group pressures? There is considerable evidence that both the organization and the group create a number of forces. These combine to modify the actual behavior resulting from the variety and range of individual desires to act in particular ways in any given set of circumstances.[22] A number of objective realities interact to form one or more operating systems in any organization.[23] These include the strategic business units (SBUs), the organizational and group structure (its size, design, shape, function, etc.), the kind of performance measures and managerial controls in force, the technology and organization of the work, how job and tasks are structured, the information and communication systems, the organizational policies, procedures and practices, and the nature of the reward and compensation systems. All these together require people with different personalities, needs and goals to behave in a similar manner.

Predicting the Extent of Resistance

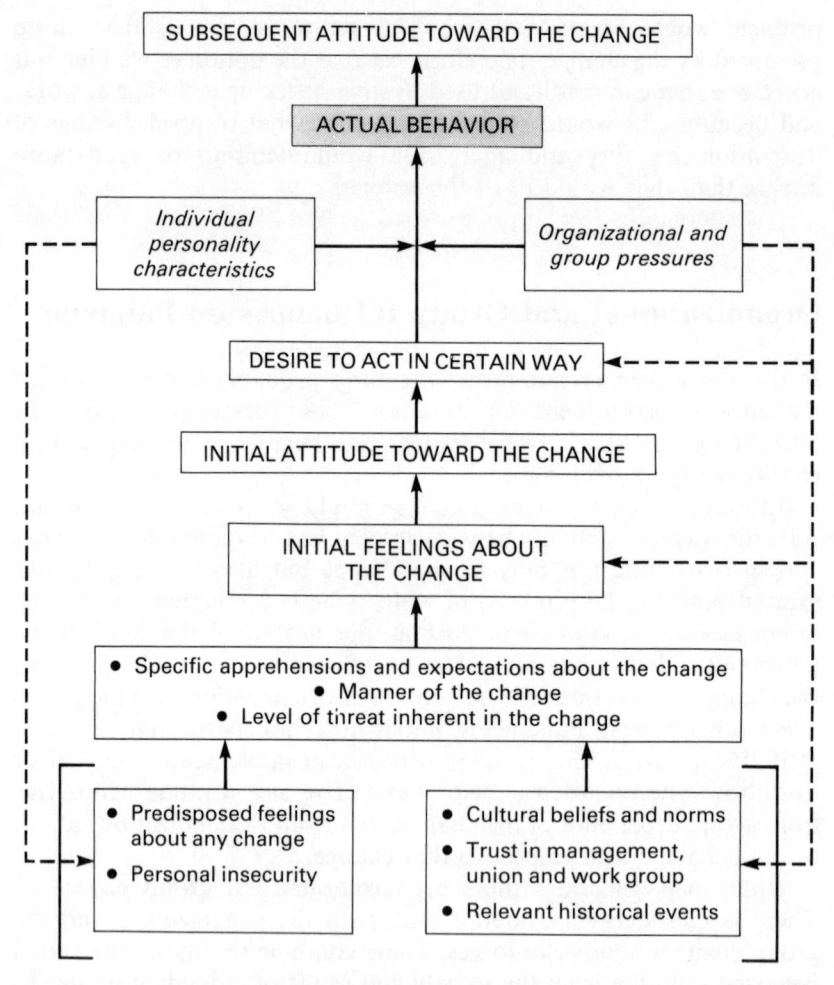

Figure 3 Feelings, organizational pressures, attitudes and behavior with respect to a change

For example, in one research study, ten supervisors with markedly different personality patterns were found to behave similarly when they were in the plant manager's office. In another study, it was found that there were apparent similarities in behavior of more than 200 work groups doing the same type of work in the same technological environment in different plants and companies.

The nature and extent of group resistance to a change are determined in part by some of these organizational forces. From the research noted above,[24] it has been hypothesized that when a work group is undifferentiated as to the tasks performed, the pay received and the working conditions, the problems faced by any one individual will often be similar to those faced by others. This is especially true during a change that affects the entire group. In such a case, any voiced sentiments would soon be echoed by other members of the group. This would cause any individual to feel reinforced in his or her own sentiments. It has been suggested that this phenomenon of "resonance" seems to facilitate the formation of a cohesive work group acting in a unified fashion towards management or the union.

Some researchers concerned with the development of theories of organizational behavior[25] have suggested that changes threatening the stability or equilibrium of an organizational or operating system will tend to be resisted by the system as a whole. Consider the following two examples.

EXAMPLE

The president of one of the largest trade unions in the USA became very frustrated after many unsuccessful efforts to improve the effectiveness of the union's geographically dispersed staff of 150 organizers and field representatives. These full-time employees of the union had themselves organized into a staff union which bargained collectively with the union's national executives.

National union leaders were elected to serve two-year terms by two different constituencies among the union's 600,000 members. Ten national officers were elected by the entire membership; each of 12 district executives were elected only by those members in the district. A third tier of leadership was the officers of each of some 1000 locals distributed across the USA. Each local officer was also elected for a two-year term.

The role of the union's field staff representatives was to serve as a link between the national headquarters and the locals. They worked out of district offices. They had a fourfold function; (a) providing consulting assistance and advice to local officers on matters such as the handling of grievances, the selection, training and organization of stewards, the conduct of meetings, committees and local organizing efforts, etc.; (b) encouraging local implementaion of national programs; (c) supporting district officers in their re-election efforts; and (d) collecting and feeding back information to national headquarters.

The national president had founded the union and had been its top leader for more tham 30 years. For the most part, he regarded his

Example cont.

Example cont.

employee staff representatives with disappointment. Repeated attempts to change their behavior in order to increase their "productivity" failed. The president explained these failures by blaming his employees. They lacked the motivation, work ethic and commitment of their predecessors who established the union, he said. Furthermore, by organizing their own union, they were "biting the hand that fed them."

But in actual fact, these staff representatives were as highly motivated, committed and filled with ideals as any of the union's leaders. The staff's failure to respond to the national officers' change efforts was not a personal phenomenon. Rather, it was systemic. The entire operating system of the union was resistant to change.

Within the union there were major differences of interests, expectations and priorities between headquarters and the districts, between districts and locals, and between locals and headquarters. These differences were partly a function of geography and of the characteristics of the companies and their managements where the union's members worked. They also reflected differences in the agendas of local, district and national officers. The politics of the union made it essential for these differences to be addressed.

There were major problems in the structure of the jobs of field staff representatives. The diversity of functions served required a wide range of abilities and skills. It was unusual for anyone to be able to act effectively as the "man for all seasons" that the job required. The structure of the territories served often required substantial travel and limited the amount of time any staff person could devote to each problem. Staff representatives had no power; they had to rely on persuasion and process skills. The union had great difficulty in defining performance standards and holding their employees to these standards. Staff representatives typically worked alone in isolation in a sink-or-swim mode. Union leaders were very ambivalent about acting as managers and about dealing with the staff union. The union found it virtually impossible to set and keep to priorities for the more than 15 items on their agenda. Everything was important.

Thus, staff representatives were highly frustrated. Their behavior was often nonproductive or counterproductive. Some were angry or bitter. Some were just "going through the motions." Others became active in the staff union. Some simply focused on those activities they felt most comfortable doing, regardless of official priorities. A few tried to work harder and more hours. There was so little interaction among them that each staff person found his or her own "solution." Any attempt to improve this situation would require a major effort to change the way the entire system operated.

Predicting the Extent of Resistance

EXAMPLE

In a manufacturing organization, it was found that both skilled and nonskilled employees had several "high-potency predispositions" in common: the need to experience (a) togetherness in relation to fellow workers; (b) wages which ensured a fair standard of living and a secure job; (c) noninvolvement in the formal activities of the organization, and concern only for their own specific jobs; and (d) control over their own immediate work environment. Supervision in this organization realized that the best way to achieve high productivity, a low rate of grievances and low absenteeism was to maintain the informal employee culture and not to behave in a way that violated its norms. Thus, most supervisors tended to adopt roles that were not directive but rather passive. They concentrated on keeping everyone busy with work that was fairly distributed and that ensured them a fair take-home pay. Otherwise, they left the employees to themselves as much as possible. As a consequence, both morale and productivity were considered to be very high by senior management. At the same time, however, because of the supervisors' passivity, management tended to evaluate them as being of a rather low caliber.

Management then introduced a new control system so that costs could be monitored and managed more rigorously. The introduction of this system caused new pressures to be applied by management to the supervisors so that production goals would be raised, piece-rates tightened, informal employees' activities with regard to the incentive system eliminated, etc. These pressures forced supervisors to increase their interaction with both employees and more senior management, with the aim of "tightening up" control. Because the resulting increase in supervisory direction would have disturbed existing cultural norms, the supervisors, realizing this, resisted passing the pressure from the control system along to their employees. But they could not openly resist the control system and their management. Instead, they complained about the difficulties and complexities of the control system, and excused their failure to implement it.

Because management held these supervisors in low esteem, they tended to delay the effective operation of the new system, thereby making the change easier for the employees. Thus, any excuses offered by supervisors about the complexity of the system and the need for more time to introduce it were generally accepted by management. This, in turn, tended to lower supervisors' aspiration levels as to the time for instituting the change, as well as to the extent of change necessary. In this way, the entire organizational system tended to resist a change that was threatening to disturb its equilibrium.[26]

Because organizational and group forces are important influences on individual behavior, how can we take them into account in anticipating reactions to a change? Where should we focus our attention? On behavior? On feelings? On attitudes? Or on something else?

Feelings, Attitudes, Behavior and Managerial Influence

At this point, there may be some confusion about the picture presented here of the complex, dynamic relationships among individual and group feelings, attitudes and behavior, and organizational forces. How can a manager apply an understanding of these relationships (figure 3) to the way a change is introduced and implemented? More specifically, how can this understanding help anticipate people's reactions to a change so that these can be taken into account in planning an approach, thereby improving the probabilities for minimizing resistance?

From the discussion in chapter 3 of how feelings and attitudes toward a change are formed, it should be evident that predicting these attitudes is far from simple. But to predict the kind of *behavior* that might stem from these attitudes is even more difficult, because this requires an understanding of the impact of any relevant organizational influences.

From the relationships shown in figure 3, we can see that an initially resistant attitude may result in a *desire* to resist; yet the individual might actually behave in a way apparently inconsistent with the intensity of his or her desires. This will occur if certain organizational influences cause a suppression or diversion of feelings, thus modifying actual behavior. In my earlier example of the change introduced at the seminar, some members may have desired to leave or react in a hostile way towards the lecturer. Yet, they would have modified the way they actually behaved because of the organizational pressures to act in a socially graceful manner. Still, their negative feelings might have been expressed more subtly through resistance to the ideas presented by the lecturer, and by awkwardness in any discussions. Thus, the underlying resistant feelings, although suppressed, might nevertheless have had an adverse effect on the final outcome of the seminar.

Clearly we cannot conclude that resistant feelings lead directly to resistant behavior. We can, however, anticipate at the outset of a change, that if resistant feelings are slight, then there is little support for

Predicting the Extent of Resistance

any subsequent resistant behavior. It is unlikely that resistant behavior will occur when underlying attitudes are not resistant.

But after all, a manager's true objective is not predictions of feelings, attitudes or behavior. These are but means to the real objective, that of *minimizing resistant behavior*. If there can be little resistant behavior without any underlying resistant feelings, then the manager should focus on trying to *minimize resistant feelings*. But first, the manager needs to estimate the intensity of such feelings. How, then, can this be done?

Estimating Resistant Feelings

Estimating possibly resistant feelings or attitudes is an important early step in any manager's planning for a change. From efforts to forecast such feelings, it should be possible to spot any potentially serious problems that might arise from the proposed change or from its manner of institution. With such foresight, the manager can then reconsider plans, develop alternative means for accomplishing objectives, or find ways to solve these problems. What approach can one take to forecast how those who are about to be affected by a change are likely to feel about it?

Suppose that you were confronted with an impending change. You might be concerned that as a result of the change you would lose certain things that you had previously enjoyed. Also, perhaps, you might expect certain new advantages and benefits. You would undoubtedly have certain feelings about the way in which you were being treated during the introduction and implementation of the change.

Assume, further, that you were able consciously to identify and analyze the impact of the change and how you felt about this. The result of such an analysis could be expressed by a list of expected gains and losses. You might then be able to assign to each anticipated gain and loss either a positive or a negative value. A positive value would reflect some degree of "good" feelings about the change, and a negative one would be indicative of some degree of "bad" feelings. Your overall feeling, then, would reflect the sum total of all these positive and negative values. To the extent that this integrated value were negative, you would tend towards a resistant attitude, and to the extent that this were positive, you would tend toward acceptance.

It is unlikely that anyone would or could objectively identify and analyze such innermost thoughts and feelings. It is more possible,

Predicting the Extent of Resistance

however, for a manager to imagine what it would be like to be in the position of those about to be affected by a change. That manager should be able to think about the change in the same way as employees would do. S/he should be able to identify those questions which would most probably arise. From knowledge of each individual, and of the organizational and cultural context in which s/he is working, the manager should also be able to identify many of the more common fears, suspicions and hopes.

Checklists to Aid Estimation of Resistance

The following checklists are intended to help any manager identify some of the possible anticipated gains and losses from a change. When there is intimate knowledge of the situation and of those involved, the manager should be able to select from these lists the responses most likely to occur. Also, s/he should be able to translate them into more specific terms to suit the circumstances.

These typical responses are organized by the principal reasons for resisting and accepting changes.

POSSIBLE REASONS FOR RESISTING CHANGES	POSSIBLE REASONS FOR ACCEPTING CHANGES
(Assumed losses: negative values)	(Assumed gains: positive values)
Feared economic losses	*Anticipated economic gains*
• I am being asked to do more work for the same pay	• I shall be able to earn more money.
• This change will result in a speed-up of the work. My pay will be reduced.	• My opportunities for advancement will be greater.
• Fewer skills will be required of me. My pay will be reduced.	• I shall be able to develop new or additional skills that will enhance my value and increase my opportunities for earning more.
• I shall be losing much of the overtime that I have been getting.	
• My opportunities for advancement will be reduced.	

POSSIBLE REASONS FOR RESISTING CHANGES	POSSIBLE REASONS FOR ACCEPTING CHANGES
(Assumed losses: negative values)	(Assumed gains: positive values)

Fears about personal security

- The new situation requires me to learn a new technology or new skills. I doubt that I shall be able to do it.
- I doubt that I shall be able to meet the new standards of the job that will be required.
- I shall be held responsible for quality defects or for the control of quality which I may not be able to influence.
- The new situation will involve greater safety hazards for me.
- This change will make some people redundant. I don't want to lose my job.
- I shall be more vulnerable to redundancy in the event of future reductions in business activity.
- I doubt that I shall be able to handle the increased responsibility.

Hopes about personal security

- The security of my job with the company will be increased because I shall be in a higher job classification.
- The security of my job with the company will be greater because the importance of my work has been increased.
- The security of my job with the company will be greater because the competitive position of the company will be stronger.
- My work will be safer because my exposure to injury or other hazards will be reduced.

Fears about increased personal inconvenience

- The new conditions of work will be less pleasant (physical environment, location, travel, hours).
- The work will be more difficult.
- I shall have to work harder.
- This change will interfere with my personal life (different hours, more travel, etc.).
- I shall have to change what I have become accustomed to over the years. What is wrong with the way I am working now?

Hopes of increased personal convenience

- My work will be easier.
- My conditions of work will be more pleasant (physical environment, location, travel, hours).
- I shall not have to work as hard.
- This change is an improvement in my personal life (more desirable hours, travel, etc.).

Predicting the Extent of Resistance

POSSIBLE REASONS FOR RESISTING CHANGES	POSSIBLE REASONS FOR ACCEPTING CHANGES
(Assumed losses: negative values)	(Assumed gains: positive values)

Fears about decreased job satisfactions

- This new job will be less interesting.
- There is less (or more) challenge in the new job.
- The pressures on me will be greater (or different).
- I shall have less (or more) responsibility.
- My authority is being reduced.
- I shall be receiving much more (or less) supervision.
- This new job is less important than what I am now doing.
- This new job really does not require my qualifications and training.
- This situation will be very restrictive. I shall have less opportunity to contribute my ideas and suggestions.
- This will not fit at all into my long-range career plans.

Hopes of increased job satisfactions

- This job will be more interesting.
- There will be more (or less) challenge.
- The pressures on me will be less (or different).
- I shall have more (or less) responsibility.
- My authority is being increased.
- I shall be receiving much less (or more) supervision.
- This new job is more important than what I am now doing.
- This new job will make better use of my qualifications and training.
- I shall have more opportunity to contribute my ideas and suggestions.
- This will fit nicely into my long-range career plans.

Social fears

- I shall lose status.
- If I cooperate with this change, others will think ill of me. My future relationships will be affected adversely.
- I shall be less in touch with what is going on in the company (or department).

Social anticipations

- My status will be enhanced or improved.
- My opportunities for social contacts with others on the job will be increased.
- I shall have increased access to information about what is going on in the company (or department).

Predicting the Extent of Resistance

POSSIBLE REASONS FOR RESISTING CHANGES	POSSIBLE REASONS FOR ACCEPTING CHANGES
(Assumed losses: negative values)	(Assumed gains: positive values)

Social fears (cont.)
- I don't like working by myself. I enjoy working as part of a team.
- I'm worried about have Y as a supervisor. S/he has a poor reputation. I doubt that we shall be able to hit it off very well.
- This change will damage my relationships with my customers (or suppliers or other persons outside the company).
- I shall be establishing precedents by cooperating with this change. I shall be committing other people to follow my example.
- The union will take a dim view of my involvement in the change. I shall be affecting their relationship with the company.
- I shall have to leave my old workmates. I like it where I am. I have no desire to have to make new friends.
- I don't want to cause others to be made redundant.

Social anticipations (cont.)
- I shall enjoy working as part of a group.
- I shall like working for X. S/he is a good supervisor.
- My contacts with suppliers (or customers or other persons outside the company) will be improved.
- I shall enjoy having that group working for me.

Irritation with manner of handling the change
- Why are they picking on me? They must have something against me.
- No one asked my opinion. I could tell them a thing or two.
- If we go through with this, there's no turning back. I don't like the idea of burning the bridges behind us.

Satisfaction with manner of handling the change
- I'm quite flattered that I was selected to try out this difficult task.
- It is satisfying to know that my ideas and suggestions are being sought and are welcomed.
- This change is really pioneering a new method (or field of endeavor). It is exciting to be a part of this effort.

Predicting the Extent of Resistance

POSSIBLE REASONS FOR RESISTING CHANGES	POSSIBLE REASONS FOR ACCEPTING CHANGES
(Assumed losses: negative values)	(Assumed gains: positive values)

Irritation with manner of handling the change (cont.)

- This is being done in too much of a hurry. I would like an opportunity to think this over for a time.

- This change is really unnecessary. I see no reason to change.

- Misunderstanding of the reasons for the change and ascribing incorrect motives.

- I don't like having things rammed down my throat.

- This idea is no better than what we are now doing. How is it that s/he is such an expert? How can s/he know better than me, s/he doesn't even work here.

- S/he has a nerve implying that we've been having an easy time of it up to now. We've been working hard and doing a fine job.

- This change comes as quite a shock. It has come so suddenly and unexpectedly.

Satisfaction with manner of handling the change (cont.)

- It is gratifying to realize that we are being given the full story on this change and that we shall be able to get answers to our questions.

- This change is obviously important, and I'm proud to be a part of it.

Cultural beliefs

- This change goes against what I know to be true. Such a change is inconceivable. It will never work

- This change is inconsistent with what I believe in.

- Why should I cooperate with management anyway? This is the thin end of the wedge.

Cultural beliefs

- This change reaffirms what I know to be true.

- This change is consistent with my beliefs.

Estimation Balance Sheet

When one integrates all positive and negative values of the potential gains and losses resulting from a change for those affected, it is possible to forecast the nature and intensity of resistant feelings. Any manager can do this by projecting him/herself in the positions of those about to be affected and applying the preceding checklists to the particular change at hand. For ease of analysis, the relevant potential gains and losses can be organized in the form of a balance sheet, as shown in figure 4.

RESISTANCE		ACCEPTANCE	
Estimated losses	*Importance*	*Estimated gains*	*Importance*
Economic		Economic	
Security		Security	
Inconvenience		Convenience	
Satisfactions		Satisfactions	
Social		Social	
Manner of change		Manner of change	
Cultural beliefs		Cultural beliefs	

Figure 4   Balance sheet of estimated losses and gains from a change

Such a balance sheet can be constructed for either an individual or a group, depending on how many are impacted by the change. For this approach to be useful in forecasting individual attitudes, the manager would need considerable knowledge of each person, together with information about his or her reactions toward previous changes. Constructing a balance sheet for a large group is more feasible because there is an increased statistical probability that certain kinds of reactions are likely to occur.

In either case, a balance sheet is useful only as a tool for planning. It is no substitute for face-to-face discussions conducted with the people affected to get their reactions firsthand after the change has been announced (as is discussed in the following chapters). As a planning tool, however, any manager who develops such balance sheets will be able to anticipate and prepare for how people will probably react to the change. Forewarned and forearmed, s/he will be better positioned to conduct meaningful and productive discussions. More important, perhaps, the results of such a preliminary analysis might encourage the manager to reconsider the change itself, the approach being taken to its institution, and perhaps even the objectives for the change, and to make whatever modifications seem necessary or desirable.

In constructing a balance sheet, managers should first list as many of the possible gains and losses as can be imagined from knowing the situation and those affected. Next, they should identify which possible reasons for resistance and acceptance might be most compelling. This could be defined in terms of the greater possible frequency of occurrence in the group affected. If only a few people are involved, "compelling" would be defined in terms of individual attitudes and values. A manager might classify each reason listed according to an estimate of its probable importance (i.e. its intensity, strength or extent shared); any attempt to differentiate among more than three levels – very important, moderately important, of minor importance – would probably be fruitless. These levels of importance could then be used to "weight" each "gain" and "loss" on the balance sheet. The manager could then determine the extent of overall balance or imbalance of losses as compared with gains. S/he could also identify which losses or gains appear to be most significant in shaping attitudes.

Any tentative conclusions suggested by such an overall analysis of a summarized balance sheet must be tempered by a consideration of three other factors. First, the manager must consider how much trust seems to exist in his or her relationships with those affected, and their relationships with management as a whole and the union. The manager must also try to identify any relevant historical events that might prejudice people either in favor of or against the change. The manager should also consider the intensity of any threat inherent in the change as it relates to the hierarchy of needs. All three of these factors will tend either to increase or to lessen the intensity of resistant feelings.

Using the Balance Sheet in Planning to Minimize Resistance

Before discussing a proposed change with anyone affected, a manager can use this balance sheet analysis to get ready. With such preparation, the manager will know what actions can be taken to lessen the effects of more salient problems. The manager will also know what can be done to develop "gains" that will counterbalance any unavoidable "losses." With this planning the most persuasive case possible can be put to the people affected.

How valid will be such efforts to anticipate people's reactions to a change? Clearly, anyone's processes of thought and motivation are far too complicated and subtle for others to predict their nature accurately. At best, any predictions can be made only in terms of probabilities, with a considerable margin for error. No manager should have more than modest expectations from such predictions.

Nevertheless, forecasting people's probable responses can be a productive exercise when a manager plans to introduce and implement a change, provided that the following three conditions are met:

1 There is a clear and specific definition of the existing situation (including organizational forces, the extent of trust in relationships and relevant historical events), as well as the nature and extent of the intended change.
2 When only a few people are affected, the manager's knowledge of them and their behavior during previous changes is considerable. However, as the number affected increases and the laws of statistical probability begin to apply, the importance of this condition diminishes.
3 The manager takes a systematic and thorough approach to estimating and analyzing probable attitudes toward the planned change.

On balance, it is worth the effort for any manager to attempt anticipating likely reactions to an intended change before it becomes known to anyone affected. This estimate will often be more comprehensive and useful when subordinate supervisors are involved in this exercise (see chapter 10). When such a systematic analysis is an integral element in planning for the change, management will be in a position to develop the most effective approach to presenting their proposals and for discussing them with those affected.

Summary

Management can attain their objective of minimizing resistance most effectively when they first focus attention on trying to anticipate the reasons for and intensity of resistant feelings and attitudes.

By constructing and analyzing balance sheets for individuals and groups, a manager can develop a more complete understanding of the following:

- What is likely to be regarded as both potential losses and expected gains from a change.
- The extent and significance of these losses and gains.
- The relative intensity and importance of the various reasons for both resistance and acceptance.
- The extent to which expected losses outweigh gains.
- Any probable differences in individual reactions to the change.

However, even when particularly perceptive managers make such analyses, the resulting forecasts cannot be regarded as having a high degree of accuracy and reliability. No one can possibly anticipate every question and feeling that might occur. Nevertheless, there are two reasons why the development of such analyses as preparation for instituting changes is a useful exercise for managers, especially when their supervisors are involved:

- All managers and supervisors concerned will be better positioned to anticipate the reactions of those involved. They will then be able to plan and prepare their approach both with individuals and groups. They will be able to marshal their arguments in the most persuasive manner possible. They will know what facts are needed to dispel any unrealistic fears.

Predicting the Extent of Resistance

- Management will be able to identify those effects of a change that would probably stimulate such negative reactions that these could not be dissipated by any explanations or persuasive arguments. They could then either modify the change so as to minimize negative reactions, or develop alternative means for solving the problems created by the change.

Thus, such preparation should be one of the first steps in any manager's plan to minimize resistance to a change.

6

Minimizing Resistance to Change: Concepts

No great improvements in the lot of mankind are possible, until a great change takes place in the fundamental constitution of their modes of thought.

John Stuart Mill

Resistance to change by those affected is often the single most formidable obstacle to its successful realization. I have already described this obstacle and how it is formed. Also, I have suggested how some of its characteristics might be anticipated. To what extent can management influence this obstacle? How can they reduce or minimize it?

Earlier, I suggested that although there are many forces that influence resistance to a change, management can have the greatest influence on only two aspects of the situation: (a) the extent to which people may be apprehensive about the change; and (b) the manner in which the change is introduced and implemented. To a considerably lesser degree, management might also have some influence on the impact of conflicts with established cultural beliefs and with relevant historical events. Now I want to postulate more specifically which factors are present in every changing situation, significant in their influence on resistance, and susceptible to management's influence. Each such factor offers managers a kind of "lever" that they can use to enhance their degree of control over the change process in the interests of achieving desired outcomes. Once these levers have been identified, it should then be possible to describe how managers might use them in order to achieve a more successful change. In this chapter, each lever is identified and described. The following chapter is devoted to a discussion of how each lever can be used.

77

Overall Concepts

It should be recognized at the outset that resistance to a change is not the fundamental problem to be solved. Rather, any resistance is usually a symptom of more basic problems underlying the particular situation. To focus attention on the symptom alone will achieve at best only limited results. This is like taking medication to relieve temporarily the ache of an infected tooth. Until the tooth is treated by a dentist, that ache will continue to recur with increasing severity. Thus, for effective solutions one must look beyond the symptom that is resistance to its more basic causes.

I have already suggested that it would be fruitless for management to attempt influencing people's fundamental feelings about change, security and trust. No manager can or should try to deal directly with matters that are so deeply personal. It is unlikely that even a highly skilled therapist would be able to change these deep-seated feelings without months of intense work. Clearly, even if a manager had the requisite psychological knowledge and skills, it would nevertheless be impracticable to attempt changing even a single person's basic attitudes. To try this with a group would be out of the question. Moreover, there are serious moral and ethical issues involved.

It is quite appropriate and practicable, however, for a manager to focus on those *situational* and *environmental* factors that might cause resistance. Many of these are directly within management's power to influence or control. Often, they can be shaped and modified quite readily by using certain levers. In the end, modifying these contextual factors can have a profound effect on the behavior of many in the situation.

What, then, are these contextual factors and levers? Which levers will offer managers the greatest opportunity to influence resistant behavior?

Compulsion

Compulsion is one way in which an individual can attempt to influence or control the behavior of others. In its most primitive form, it involves physical coercion. In a more sophisticated form, it involves the use of threats to an individual's needs or goals. In business organizations, compulsion is represented by the use of authority. What, then, is the effect of the use of authority as a lever when changes are being introduced and implemented?

First reconsider some of the traditional concepts of authority. The classical approach to organization and management is founded upon the principal assumption that authority is the central and indispensable means of managerial control. Furthermore, the concept of authority is generally regarded in absolute rather than relative terms.

Both of these concepts are incorrect.[27] Authority is only one of several means of influencing or controlling the behavior of others. I have already mentioned physical coercion. Another method is persuasion. Finally, there is the form of influence implicit in professional "help." This is based on specialized and expert knowledge. A doctor, architect, consultant or engineer, for example, can offer help to a client. It is understood that this help is being placed at the client's disposal, to be used or ignored. Nevertheless, such help can have a decided influence on the client's subsequent actions.

Furthermore, it must be realized that all these methods of social control are relative, not absolute. In the final analysis, the success of any method depends on altering the ability of others to achieve their goals or to satisfy their needs. A manager can influence or control an employee only when that person is to some extent dependent on either the manager or the organization. When there is no dependence, there is no opportunity to control. Thus, both the nature and extent of dependence are critical factors in determining the effectiveness of any method of social control, and of authority in particular.

The effectiveness of authority as a means of control depends in large part on the ability to enforce it. It also depends on the established framework of cultural beliefs and norms. In cultures where deference to authority is the "normal" response (as in many Eastern societies), the use of authority may still be an effective managerial technique. In fact, the failure to use authority would probably create many more serious problems than its use. In Western societies, especially the USA and the UK, however, this discussion of the limitations of the use of authority is particularly relevant. Nevertheless, attention should be given to the particular culture of the organization in which changes are intended. The extent to which the use of authority should be avoided depends somewhat on the established attitudes towards its use in the cultures of both the organization and its wider social environment.

Punishment is the means of enforcing authority. In business, the forms of punishment are limited: compulsory termination of employment, curtailment of compensation and other rewards, and limiting opportunities for personal development and advancement. However, when unemployment is low in an economy, "the sack" loses its threat. Also, the use or threat of punishment, actual or implied, can result in countermeasures. Employees are often well protected by the power of their union. They can also act directly by limiting their performance or by refusing to accept responsibility. Young people and members of some minority groups are likely to be more militant than older employees. Employees today are far less dependent on their managements than they were prior to World War II. This fact tends to place a considerable limitation on the usefulness of authority as a contemporary method of social control.

There is another problem caused by the use of authority in changing situations, especially when these are complex. When a change is being instituted and implemented, there is an unusual demand for creative thinking, ingenuity and initiative from everyone involved, if the maximum benefits are to be realized. Later I discuss the many valuable contributions that can be made both by operating personnel and by lower levels of supervision. But in order to elicit such contributions, a climate must be established that encourages and empowers subordinates by providing them with both support and freedom to act. The use of authority, however, tends to restrict freedom to act. It also discourages the generation and contribution of ideas by subordinates. The use of authority, therefore, tends to produce results that are in direct conflict with what is desirable in changing situations.

Authority is no longer the central, indispensable means of managerial control. Instead, it is the fact of *interdependence* that characterizes contemporary relationships in business and other organizations. It is still true that subordinates depend to an extent on their managers for the satisfaction of their needs and the achievement of their goals. But it is also true that managers at every level likewise depend on subordinates for achieving both their own goals and those of the organization. Furthermore, interdependence also characterizes the relationships between managers and staff specialists, between "line" departments, and among any group of individuals who report to a common supervisor. Interdependence becomes especially important during periods of change, when cooperation and teamwork become essential for success.

Another problem associated with the use of authority as a method of influence and control in changing situations is dependency itself. People's emotional responses relating to dependency are very complicated. Everyone's development from the moment of birth involves changing from total dependence on parents for life itself, toward a state of independence as an adult. But at no stage of this development can anyone be entirely satisfied. Although dependency can be satisfying in the security it provides, it is at the same time frustrating in the limitations it imposes upon the freedom to act as one wishes. Likewise, although independence is satisfying in that one can make decisions for oneself and lead one's own life, it can also be frightening because of the risks involved. Thus, everyone tends to have conflicting emotions about dependency. Many people, when placed in situations which emphasize their dependency, become frustrated and rebellious.

In any changing situation, the problem of dependency increases and often becomes acute. The familiarity and relatively comfortable security of the individual's work world disappears. In its place is an unknown future filled with fearful possibilities. To the employee, the principal point of reference that remains constant is the organization as a whole, and often, but not always, the manager. It is inevitable that dependent feelings increase under such circumstances, because people feel a loss of control over their work situation. Resentment, frustration and resistance are often the consequences.

Thus, in most organizations operating within a Western cultural framework, compulsion through the use of authority as a method for instituting and implementing changes inevitably increases the frustration of those involved. This occurs because of the additional pressures imposed on them. Their frustration mounts also because of increased limitations on their freedom to act, a consequence of increased feelings of dependency. The result of this heightened frustration is increased aggressive and hostile feelings. In many instances, the end result is intense resistance toward the change. Because compulsion and the use of authority in managing any change serve primarily to increase resistance, these levers are to be avoided in most circumstances.

Persuasion

If authority and the threat of punishment are undesirable ways to manage a change, what about the use of persuasion and rewards as a means of gaining acceptance and cooperation?

Certainly, persuasion is a familiar means for influencing people's behavior. In selling, for example, persuasion is the primary technique employed. The essence of this approach is to convince a person that if s/he behaves in the manner desired, certain gains will follow, gains which will outweigh any losses. To be successful, persuasion depends on one's ability to perceive a situation from the other's viewpoint. A correct analysis of personal needs and goals is fundamental. Only after this is done can potential gains be emphasized and potential losses be explained away.

In a manager's hands, however, persuasion is often not as attractive and effective a lever as it might seem. In selling, the salesman has no further recourse than persuasion. But in employee's perceptions of management, there is often the expectation that authority, or even coercion, might be resorted to if persuasion should fail. Thus, people often view managers' use of persuasion as something more than simply straightforward "selling." When attempts at persuasion are perceived as manipulation, resentment can quickly follow.

Just as the use of authority depends on actual or implied threats of punishment, so does persuasion depend on the actual or implied promise of rewards. The most commonly perceived rewards are financial. The offer of financial rewards is particularly important when the reasons for resistance are primarily economic.

For example, an impending change might lead one group of employees to believe that they will have to work harder. Another group, facing a different change, might believe that they will have to produce more. A third group might believe that they are in danger of suffering a reduction in earnings. In each situation, assume that those involved believe that the change requires them to increase their efforts and contributions to the job. It is probable that in each case the change would be unacceptable unless there were a belief that there would be just compensation for any increased effort or output. Compensation would take the form either of increased earnings, or possibly of changes in the system of wage payment. Thus, when reasons for resisting a change are primarily economic, financial rewards must be offered if resistance is to be lessened.

When, however, the reasons for resistance are primarily noneconomic, or when there are both economic and noneconomic reasons, the use of financial rewards as the only lever for minimizing resistance can *create* problems instead of solving them. Indiscriminate offers of rewards can often cause serious conflicts for those involved. Consider the following example. John is a skilled machinist working in an engineering firm. In this job, he enjoyed the varied work of operating lathes, milling machines, screw machines and the like. He also enjoyed his association with workmates. The company purchased an automatic, computer-controlled milling machine and installed it in a special air-conditioned room, constructed in a corner of the machine shop. John was selected to become the operator of this new machine. To ensure his acceptance, he was offered a substantial pay rise. Although his feelings about the new job were mixed, John felt that he could not afford to refuse the increased compensation. Once on the new job, however, John's feelings about his work changed. He missed the variety in his prior job. He longed for the frequent and friendly interchanges with his associates. He began to feel that his past knowledge and skills were being wasted on his new job. Yet, he felt compelled to remain in his new situation because of the high rate of pay. As a consequence of his increasing frustration, the quality of his work began to decline. In this instance, the use of a monetary reward resulted in a change that was initially successful. But failure to consider other problems arising in the situation eventually caused this success to miscarry.

Conversely, the use of noneconomic rewards to persuade people to accept a change that may adversely affect their earnings is unlikely to succeed. It is also immoral. G. Strauss and L. Sayles comment on this point:[28]

> True, an employer may successfully manipulate an employee into acquiescing to a change that is not in the employee's best interest. But in the long run in a free society such attempts at brain-washing tend to backfire against their instigators. We emphasize this point because there are employers who feel that if proper "human relations" are applied, employees will be willing to do without a fair wage. Such misuse of human relations is, in our opinion, highly immoral; fortunately, it is rarely successful.

When the reasons for resistance are primarily noneconomic, the successful use of persuasion depends on offering noneconomic rewards. These can take many forms. For example, a change might present opportunities for aquiring new knowledge and skills. These might enhance one's worth to the company, or improve advancement and/or career opportunities. Other noneconomic rewards might be opportunities for increases in employment security, and enhancement of satisfactions derived from work. Certain aspects of work might become more convenient and pleasant. There might also be improvements in status and in the nature of the social relationships associated with the work.

When the prospect of any such rewards is used deliberately as a lever to persuade others to alter their behavior, it can often be as effective as the offer of economic rewards. Noneconomic rewards are persuasive when the nature of the reward is made relevant to the specific reason for resistance, and when the promise of the reward can be realistically fulfilled.

Minimizing Resistance to Change: Concepts

Thus, both the extent and nature of any persuasion used as a lever in a changing situation are key to determining the success of the change. The effectiveness of persuasion as a lever to influence behavior depends on the extent to which the rewards offered are both relevant to, and counterbalance and outweigh, the reasons for resistance.

Security

How much one's security is either threatened or ensured in a changing situation is another factor that both has a great influence on resistance and is susceptible to management's use as a lever.

I have already described some of the reasons why anyone might be apprehensive about personal security when facing a change (see the checklist in chapter 5 and the discussion of feelings of insecurity in chapter 3). Some of these apprehensions may be sheer imagination. Others, however, may be based on a realistic appraisal of the situation. The most significant fear is often that of redundancy.

Fear of redundancy can result from any one of several assumptions that a person might make when facing an impending change. Elimination of the job might be one assumption. Or there might be a belief that vulnerability to redundancy will be increased. Or one might fear redundancy because of an inability to learn or meet any new required performance standards. Often, the individual's own past experiences of redundancy, together with the history of redundancy in the organization, the community and the region, will be important influences on any fears.

Whatever assumptions may drive fear of redundancy, intense resistance to the change can result. Such resistance rests on the belief that it will protect personal interests and preserve the job. Or one might resist in an effort to preserve the jobs of workmates.

Fear of redundancy can cause not only intense resistance to a change, but also a general deterioration of both morale and work performance. Such fears can be highly infectious and can affect many in the organization who are not involved in the change. These fears must be allayed if resistance is to be minimized. Frank Cousins, while he was leader of the Transport and General Workers' Union (at that time, the largest union in Great Britain), once made the following comment:[29]

> When workers are told to accept new methods and not be modern Luddites, we have to consider how right in the short run the Luddites

were. Machine looms destroyed the jobs of thousands of handloom weavers. They were introduced without consultation, without any regard to human values, and they had dire consequences for the men directly concerned. We can look back 150 years and say there should have been a rapid step into machine operation, but for the people involved they were absolutely correct to resist it, because no one did anything about their side of the problem. We must make it unnecessary for modern workers to think in the same terms and there is some of that thinking still existent. We must give a degree of security which will enable workers to welcome new methods, to allow a degree of flexibility in industry which cannot come until real security is present.

When any perceived threats to security are effectively addressed by management, a potentially powerful reason for resisting a change is removed. Doing so is crucial, and often requires a safeguard against redundancy. It should be recognized, however, that the leverage offered by providing such safeguards accomplishes only the removal of a major obstacle to instituting the change. It does little to transform resistance into support.

The reason for this can be found in Maslow's hypothesis about the hierarchy of human needs[30] (see chapter 3). He postulates that once a person's most basic needs are satisfied (security needs are one of the most fundamental), these no longer remain important motivators for human behavior. Once fundamental needs are met, satisfying higher-order needs such as those for love, self-esteem and self-actualization becomes the prime driving force for motivation.

Thus, often a change may threaten the security of those affected. Fears of redundancy, either for oneself or for others in the work group, are often the result. These fears must be dispelled if resistance to the change is to be minimized.

Understanding

How much those involved understand about a changing situation is another lever that is both significant and controllable. In this discussion, I consider both *what* must be understood and *who* must have this understanding.

The briefest answer to the question of "who" is everyone involved in the change. Just as the manager must understand what is going on and why, so also must those affected understand. Likewise, any supervisors

Minimizing Resistance to Change: Concepts

and staff specialists who are essential to implement the change must have this understanding. If there is a union involved, its officials must understand. "Who" should be defined as broadly as possible. The more widespread the understanding of all aspects of the change, the less likely there will be resistance.

What, then, must be understood? Everyone involved should know to the fullest possible extent the answers to the following questions:

- What specific long-term objectives are to be accomplished?
- What specific short-term objectives are to be accomplished?
- What need is there for these objectives to be accomplished and why?
- Why is there any need for change? For this change in particular?
- What is to be changed?
- How is it to be changed?
- When is the change to be initially introduced?
- How long will it take for the change to be fully implemented and made operational?
- Who is to be involved?
- What will the situation be after the change?
- What are the potential benefits that might be gained from the change, and who will benefit?

Several points about the above list are important. An understanding of the reasons for the change may require a detailed and specific demonstration that there is indeed a genuine need for change. To accomplish this, management may need to furnish documentary evidence.

Another point is that, whenever possible, it is desirable that the particular means intended to accomplish the change should be perceived by those affected not as a final, fixed method with an inexorable and inflexible schedule, but rather as an initially proposed approach, open to modification. It should be made clear that, with sufficient justification, there is ample latitude for alterations or modifications to be made later on to the method. It should be widely understood that the door is constantly open so that new information and ideas can be incorporated into the change process, provided that these are relevant to the accomplishment of the desired objectives.

Another point concerns information and security. Certain factors in a situation might limit the amount of information that can safely be revealed. One such factor is security, whether it be related to the company, to its marketing and business practices, or perhaps to military or governmental information. Management might believe, for example, that certain information must be kept secret. For instance, knowledge of an impending replacement of an executive might prove disruptive and damaging to morale. Or, knowledge of some new product, marketing strategy, or business performance might cause the company's competitive position to be endangered or weakened. Or, the leakage of some information might be detrimental to the national interest or security. Sometimes, classifying and treating such information as secret is fully justified. Often, however, expectations of damage resulting from sharing such information judiciously are exaggerated.

Management should view matters of security realistically as a trade-off issue. They should compare the risks that might be incurred by a leakage of information to the wrong parties, with the risks that might be incurred by treating this information as secret. Excessive secrecy can easily lead to misunderstandings which in turn can cause increased resistance to the change. From a careful analysis and consideration of these comparative risks, possible consequences and trade-offs, management should be able to decide how much information they can share in advance.

Yet another point is that managers and staff specialists also need to develop some understanding of the specific personal attitudes and social arrangements that would tend to be both sustained and threatened by the change and its method of realization. With this knowledge, they can enhance their consideration of these factors in both planning and implementing the change. As I discuss further in chapter 9, managers and staff specialists often regard changes quite differently from the people affected. When managers and staff specialists are unaware of or insensitive to the effects of a change on existing attitudes and social arrangements, they tend to overlook certain elements of the change which might affect these adversely. The result will be greater resistance to the change.

Finally, if a particular change is in conflict with certain prevailing cultural beliefs and norms (see chapter 3), it is important to try resolving this conflict. Resolution depends first on an awareness that some conflict actually exists. Because cultural beliefs are based on implicit assumptions that certain priorities, practices and behavior are necessary, their validity is rarely, if ever, examined or challenged. These assumptions must first be identified and made explicit. Their validity should then be questioned and reappraised in the light of the existing and the future situation. Through such a process, any potential conflicts between the effects of the change and the prevailing cultural beliefs can be averted.

EXAMPLE

In the early 1960s, a breakthrough productivity agreement was achieved at the Fawley refinery of the Esso Petroleum Company in England. Employing an innovative strategy called productivity bargaining, management at the refinery, with the help of the Emerson Consultants, bargained with the union to achieve the elimination of many traditional restrictive practices, thereby opening up opportunities for improving productivity (subsequently productivity improvements of the order of 20 per cent were achieved). The new agreement was known as "the Blue Book." A key factor in the success of this change was the modification of a number of deeply rooted cultural beliefs. Allan Flanders, in his book *The Fawley Productivity Agreements*,[31] describes how this was achieved:

> We have seen how the production of the Blue Book depended on [the consultants'] questioning of some of the beliefs that had common currency with Fawley management.
>
> This was partly a matter of patient reasoning, where the beliefs were based on faulty deductive or inductive arguments, partly a matter of teaching people to think about their more intractable problems and building up confidence that they could solve them. But it was also due to the consultant acquiring an authority, as did those who were associated with him in management, which was used to undermine the authoritarian foundations of some of the rival beliefs.
>
> The beliefs held by management were paralleled by another set among the stewards and their constituents, some in contradiction, others identical. Thus, while management believed it to be undesirable for first-line supervisors to belong to trade unions because this placed them under the thumb of those they supervised, stewards believed this to be necessary otherwise the supervisors would tyrannize their subordinates. On the other hand, both sides shared the belief in the inevitability of overtime. The changing of the beliefs of management, however, presented less difficulty than changing those of the union-organized employees, above all the strongly-held traditional beliefs of craftsmen about the conditions under which they should exercise their craft.
>
> When a boilermaker refuses to accept orders from someone who is not a member of his trade, he is not just upholding a union rule. He is observing a principle which he would sincerely defend as right and proper by arguments he firmly believes to be valid. Offer him a few more pounds a week to abandon this practice, and in the highly improbable event of his doing so it would only be at the cost of a guilty conscience and a loss of self-respect. The most

Example cont.

Example cont.

intransigent resistance to change springs from this source, when the change offends the morality of the social group concerned. This kind of obstacle is rarely recognized in its true light. Opposition so motivated is frequently dismissed as stupid and misguided – as an irrational resistance to change for its own sake – because that is how it appears to those who do not share the same values.

That workers in general have their own moral code, which among other things places a high value on group solidarity, should be evident to any unprejudiced observer. Trade unions depend upon it for their strength and vitality as much or more than they do on their membership contributions. In the craft unions especially, or those which have most retained their craft character, we find the most stringent and rigid systems of beliefs influencing their members' behaviour. This stands behind the seeming triviality of many craft job demarcation disputes. The extent of the actual work involved in any dispute over "who should do what" may be very small. The trouble is that any slight change may create new precedents which, apart from affecting the larger issue of job and union security for the groups, raise moral questions as well. There is the principle of not letting down one's fellow craftsmen, not only those on the plant, but those who are unemployed. There is the belief that this is *our* work, work to which we are by right entitled. When a union says that a matter of principle is at stake it usually means two things that are practically inseparable: that the long-term institutional interests of the union are threatened; and that what is being proposed runs contrary to the beliefs of its members.

The consultant at Fawley, because of his earlier training in anthropology and the other social sciences, was fully aware that cultural change was a necessary prerequisite to institutional change. The Blue Book was a list of proposed institutional changes – changes in practices that had become institutionalized either through the rules and traditions of craft unions or more recently in established refinery procedures and conventions. These institutional changes had economic implications which were likely to furnish an inducement for their acceptance, since both the company and its employees could reckon on benefiting from them. But institutions, though upheld in the first instance by the sanctions attached to them, do not exist in a cultural vacuum. Their perpetuation depends on beliefs about their value or necessity, so that neither the active will to change them, nor, for that

Example cont.

> *Example cont.*
>
> matter, the passive consent to their being changed, is likely to be forthcoming as long as the underlying beliefs remain unshaken. Admittedly they may not be held with the same degree of conviction by everyone, but among the older men, who have been reared industrially in such traditions, departure from them is looked upon not merely as inexpedient, but as wrong and impermissible on any grounds.
>
> The consultant, therefore, deliberately set out to prepare the minds of the men and their union representatives for change, just as he had previously tackled management in a similar fashion. The difference was that among management he had enjoyed a standing that supported his authority; among the stewards this was more likely to arouse suspicion and distrust. Being an American proved an advantage. It allowed him to act as an interested inquirer into British trade union practices, which indeed he was. That he should want to query assumptions that were alien to his own culture was natural enough. In the latter part of 1959 he was involved in regular and at times almost daily discussions with some of the senior stewards, in which the ideas behind the Blue Book were introduced and argued about in terms of justification, long before there was a money offer and the formal negotiations started.
>
> Those members of Fawley management who by now were fully committed to the new approach were also activity engaged in the same endeavour. Both formal and, to a greater extent, informal consultation were being employed for the purpose of changing beliefs.

In an attempt to define an "ideal" organization that performs at a consistently effective and high level, R. Likert has suggested that such an organization must have

> conditions that lead to full, candid communication. To give relevant information to others and to be interested in and receptive to the relevant information which they have is to behave in a supportive, ego-building manner. To withhold relevant information or to show no interest in information others seek to give us is to behave in a threatening and ego-deflating manner. To give information conveys trust and confidence in others, and increases their sense of personal worth. To withhold information does the opposite.[32]

Ensuring that everyone involved in a change understands everything about it is a powerful lever for managers to transform resistance into support.

Minimizing Resistance to Change: Concepts

Thus there is a direct relationship between how much those involved in a change understand about it and all its implications, and their resistance to it. When as many of these people as possible understand as much as is possible about the change (and in particular about how it will affect them), their resistance to it will probably be lessened. When, on the other hand, little information is made available, a vacuum will be created by the lack of facts. This vacuum will be filled by conjectures and assumptions. In such circumstances, resistance to the change is likely to be great. Developing understanding is a key lever in achieving changes in behavior.

Time

Time is a significant and controllable lever in any changing situation. Three periods of time are important because almost all changes require three distinct phases: (a) the interval between the first inkling that a change is to occur and its actual start; (b) the interval between the start of the change and the completion of its initial installation; and (c) the interval between the initial installation of the change and its institutionalization into day-to-day operations. What is the relationship between the length of these intervals and resistance?

Consider first the period of time between the moment when the people involved first hear about an impending change and its actual start. Is it better in terms of lessened resistance for this period to be long or short? The answer depends in part on the extent to which management are willing to share and discuss information about the change before its introduction.

Generally in this initial phase, slow movement is less threatening than rapid progress. This is so because we often "get used to an idea" when we have sufficient time to think about it. Our capacities for adjustment to changing circumstances seem almost limitless. Throughout our lifetimes, for example, most of us have to make continuous adjustments in our way of life as a consequence of changes brought about by science and technology. These changes are made available, and when we are ready we adopt them. Initially, many may have rejected as outrageous or absurd the ideas of riding in automobiles, or flying in aeroplanes, or eating frozen food, or wearing clothes made from synthetic fibers, or having a computer in our offices and homes, or traveling to other planets. Yet, in time, most of us have come to accept these enormous changes. Why is this?

Minimizing Resistance to Change: Concepts

When a new idea is first introduced, we begin to think about and consider it from many different viewpoints. In time, its novelty and strangeness disappear. Eventually, it becomes familiar. If we are able to observe how this idea impacts and is taken up by others around us, we can then anticipate how it will probably affect us. If our initial fears are dispelled, we become reassured. We then can absorb the idea and regard it as our very own. Eventually, the idea no longer is regarded as something imposed on us by external forces. Instead, it becomes something we have though about ourselves. This process of self-adjustment has been named "accommodation."[33]

Another psychological mechanism for adjusting to the idea of a change is the process of rationalization. Most of us when faced with the inevitable can be quite inventive in finding a variety of reasons to justify why we should comply with a change. We do this to protect ourselves from the discomfort of conflict and anxiety. Through rationalization, we convince ourselves of the necessity for and soundness of the change.

When people have some time to think about a change before it affects them, they have opportunity to voice their questions and fears. Many of their problems can then be resolved in advance of the change, in a leisurely atmosphere that is both relatively free of pressure and dispassionate. It is also likely that in this process of discussion some useful suggestions will be offered to improve the approach to the change. Through such discussions people will come to know what to expect. They can then adjust their thinking and attitudes, and become more receptive toward the change.

In general, the longer the interval between initial communication about a change and its date of initiation, the greater will be the opportunity for accommodation by those involved.[34] The shorter the interval, the more resistance there is likely to be. Most people tend to react in a strongly negative way when they feel that they are being compelled to do something before they have had even the opportunity to consider it and to ask questions. However, after management have discussed the intended change at some length with those affected and any suggestions have been taken and considered, there comes a point where it is dysfunctional for management to prolong the dialog. Once management believe that people have been given a reasonable amount time to prepare and contribute, the change should be instituted without further delay. Employees can be invited to make further contributions to making the change successful during the final phase of institutionalization (see chapter 10).

It should be noted that a relatively long time to consider a change before it occurs is desirable only when management can both reveal and discuss freely information about the change and its consequences. When this is not possible, and only the fact of the impending change is made public, a long period between the announcement and the change can actually cause difficulties. People then have more time to worry and build up hostility and resentment. They also have more opportunity to organize resistance.

For example, a large insurance company was moving its principal office from its original, somewhat antiquated building into a modern steel-and-glass structure. About six weeks prior to the move, an announcement in writing was circulated to all those secretaries assigned to individual managers. From this single sheet of paper, the women learned that after their move to the new building they would no longer be private secretaries. Instead, they would be grouped together into a "pool" to serve any manager requiring secretarial services. No reasons were offered for this change, and there was no discussion. By the time the move was made, more than 70 per cent of the secretarial staff had resigned for "better positions" in other nearby offices.

Once a change has been initiated, how desirable is it to carry out the next phase – initial installation – over an extended period of time? Certainly, resistance to a slow change will be less intense at any one time than it would be to a more rapid change. Nevertheless, there are several dangers in prolonging the process during phase two. A slow change causes those affected to make a continuing series of adjustments over an extended period, often accompanied by personal and social disruption and turmoil.

During the initial installation phase of a change, management would have difficulty in ensuring that those involved sustain a clear understanding of the overall scope of the change, together with an understanding of the answers to all the questions listed in the previous section. People tend to view each increment of a change in isolation, and not as part of a grander design. When those involved lose sight of the ultimate objectives and their rationale, they will probably not understand the significance of each increment of the change. Thus, their questions and apprehensions will tend to multiply.

A change carried out in a piecemeal fashion often yields diminished benefits because it is difficult for management to consider at any one time all the implications and ramifications of the change as a whole. They are less able to plan effectively. Also, they will probably have increased difficulty evaluating its results. For all the foregoing reasons, the second phase of introducing and installing the change should be carried out briskly and not prolonged unnecessarily.

In the final phase of a change, from its initial installation to its institutionalization into day-to-day operations, the time required can vary widely, depending on the nature of the change. In fact, many more complex changes may require many months or even years before the change is made fully operational. In this phase, management's focus should be on providing employees with the encouragement and support necessary to ensure that they are motivated to work toward realizing the full potential benefits of the change. This can be achieved by defining performance in context of the change and establishing and applying appropriate performance measures that will drive continuous improvement.[35]

Thus, in making any change, management can use time as a lever to minimize resistance. The length of time between the announcement of an impending change and its initial initiation tends to vary inversely with the extent of resistance, provided that information about the change can be shared and discussed freely. That is, the longer the time, the lower the resistance. On the other hand, the length of time it takes for the change to be initially installed tends to vary directly with resistance: the longer this period, the greater the resistance. Once installed, full realization of the potential benefits of the change may take a long time. Management can ensure that employees are working to make the change successful by installing performance measures that encourage continuous improvement.

Involvement

Another significant and controllable lever in any changing situation is the extent to which management can encourage those affected to feel actively involved in making some of the decisions about the change. I am assuming an environment where the cultural values are such that the use of authority is generally undesirable and personal needs for self-actualization are relatively strong. Most of us gain considerable satisfaction from exercising some control over our working environment. We gain further satisfaction from the feeling of success that results from having accomplished something by ourselves.

As a consequence, most of us welcome opportunities to take part in making decisions that affect us directly. By taking advantage of such opportunities, our interest in the work is heightened. Furthermore, we would probably be more accepting of a change to which we might otherwise have objected. Our perception of this change would be altered. We would no longer feel that something was being done *to* us. Instead, we would feel that this change was being accomplished *by* us, at least in part. Thus, the lever available to management is the offer of opportunities to participate actively in shaping both the nature of the change and the manner in which it is carried out.

Consider several examples of the effects of personal involvement in making changes. First,

> Industrial engineers in a metal-plating department had been trying for a long time to figure out an equitable way to dividing up the girls' work. The operation was unusually complex and erratic, and every time the engineers made a suggestion the girls were quick to prove that it was unfair to someone. The engineers were about to give up in disgust when the girls asked "Why not let us decide?" In a short while they had worked out job allocations that even the engineers agreed were superior to theirs.[36]

In a second case, an experiment was made with women who were learning machine-paced work and who were failing to keep up with the required pace. In discussions with their foremen, the women requested that they be allowed to determine the pace themselves. A dial was installed that allowed them to set their own speed. It was discovered that the women established a pattern of work which varied with the time of day. Nevertheless, the average speed was considerably higher than the constant speed previously set by the engineers. Yet, the women reported that their work was easier. Their total output was between 30 and 50 per cent higher than expected.[37]

In another example,

> The superintendent of a machine operation was convinced by his safety department that long-sleeved shirts were a safety hazard even when rolled up. So he posted a notice that, beginning the next Monday morning, wearing long-sleeved shirts on the job would be prohibited. Monday morning, four men showed up with long sleeves. Given the choice of working without shirts or cutting off their sleeves, they refused to do either and were sent home. The union filed a sharp grievance, asking for back pay and for time lost. Then the Personnel Department stepped in. The rule was suspended for a week and a special meeting was called with the union grievance committee. The safety director explained that if a worker got his sleeve caught in a machine his whole arm might be ripped off. The union agreed to the rule providing that it was extended to include management (who had originally been exempt on the grounds that they didn't get close enough to the machines). Next

Monday, the rule went back into effect. A few men, forgetfully, arrived in long sleeves. The other men handed them a pair of scissors and insisted that the offending sleeves be cut off on the spot. Later in the afternoon, a union vice-president and a company time-study man were treated in the same way.[38]

Another result of personal involvement in making some of the decisions about a change is that the individual feels some commitment to carry out the decision. There is a feeling of shared responsibility. When a group is so involved, even if an individual member has reservations about the decision, s/he is under strong pressure from others to implement it. This is dramatized vividly in a case which illustrates what happened when workers engaged in the maintenance and repair of furnaces were encouraged to establish their own production goals:

> Groups that participate in setting goals for themselves often make higher demands for themselves than their supervisors and methods engineers consider to be practical. A furnace-cleaning job was cut from four to two days; tardiness was set at less than 3% when formerly it was 10%, service calls were reduced from one in fourteen to one in twenty-one... repairs per man per day rose from 8.5 to 12.5 when the crew planned the service; and over a period of three years, men worked more days when they decided whether or not the weather was inclement than when the supervisor made the decision.[39]

Thus, an especially powerful lever that management can use to minimize resistance is the offer of opportunities for employee involvement in contributing to decisions about a change. The greater the extent of personal involvement in making some of these decisions about a change, the less will be any resistance.

Criticism

Another significant and controllable lever in a changing situation is the extent to which those involved feel criticized as a consequence of the change.

In any change, there is an implied criticism of the past or current situation. Any intention to change carries with it a clear implication that there is something wrong or inadequate about the existing circumstances. Otherwise, why change? Sometimes that criticism is perceived as being levelled at lower levels of management and supervision. They may feel some guilt because they did not initiate the change. When it is introduced by their seniors, these managers and supervisors at lower levels may feel that higher management will regard them as lacking in both ingenuity and initiative for not having taken action themselves.

In other instances, the employees may feel criticized. They may believe that the change was introduced because their work was of an insufficiently high standard, either of quality or of quantity. Or, they might perceive a change as an expression by management of little trust in their ability to perform their jobs properly.

Still another case is the new manager or supervisor who introduces changes in operating procedures. Subordinates might interpret her or his actions as a criticism of their previous boss. Often, their loyalty to the prior manager is stronger than it is to the new one.

Management's lever in this area is the deliberate avoidance of any appearance of criticism.

Thus when anyone feels criticized, s/he becomes resentful and defensive. This resentment and irritation is naturally directed toward the source of the criticism, either the change itself or its originator. This irritation and resentment can readily become translated into resistance to the change. Therefore, the greater the feeling of being criticized, the greater is the resistance. Management must exercise great care in avoiding any actions that could trigger perceptions of criticism.

Flexibility

The eighth significant and controllable lever in a changing situation is the extent to which those involved perceive the change and its method of accomplishment to be open to modification.

I have already stated that most people want opportunities to exercise some control over their environment at work. When they feel they have no control and are at the mercy of external forces, their feelings of dependency and frustration are likely to increase. The interrelationships among dependency, frustration and resistance to changes have already been described.

When most people are confronted by an impending change which they regard as inexorable and irrevocable, their feelings of helplessness increase. They may feel that it is futile to voice any fears or reservations. Their frustration may be further increased by their view that management have little apparent sensitivity toward or concern for their needs and desires. Their only recourse is to resist.

On the other hand, when a person believes that s/he has some influence on the course of the changing circumstances, there is a constructive outlet for any fears or questions. The individual feels that s/he has some measure of control over the future.

Management's lever in this area is their actual and perceived openness to modifying both the nature of the change and its manner of institution.

Clearly, therefore, an inexorable and rigid implementation of a change, that permits no allowances for modifications to the methods of its realization, will inevitably provoke resistance. This reason for resistance will evaporate when those affected by the change believe that there is sufficient latitude in management's approach for their suggestions and contributions, as well as for any unforeseen factors, to be considered and possibly incorporated.

Summary

There are eight levers in any changing situation that can be used by management to influence resistance. By the way in which they use the levers for compulsion, persuasion, security, understanding, time, personal involvement, criticism and flexibility of approach, management can remove or reduce the influence of many factors that cause resistance to changes. In the following chapter, I discuss some methods of using these levers.

7

Minimizing Resistance to Change: Methods

> It is not true, as a good many industrial psychologists assert, that human nature resists change. On the contrary, no being in heaven or earth is greedier for new things. But there are conditions for man's psychological readiness to change. The change must appear rational to him; man always presents to himself as rational even his most irrational, most erratic changes. It must appear an improvement. And it must not be so rapid or so great as to obliterate the psychological landmarks which make a man feel at home; his understanding of his work, his relations to his fellow-workers, his concepts of skill, prestige and social standing in certain jobs and so forth.
>
> Peter Drucker

Managers can minimize resistance to any change by focusing on the eight factors discussed in chapter 6 and using the levers described to influence each of them.

Preferably, efforts to minimize any resistance should be undertaken while it is still potential rather than real. Managers can do this by incorporating into the plan for accomplishing a change whatever methods and levers they want to use to influence these eight factors. Even should potential resistance become an actuality, however, managers can still influence these factors to reduce resistance. What are the methods and levers that managers can use to influence each factor?

Compulsion, Threats and Bribery

Fundamentally, there are only two strategic options available for minimizing resistance. One is to increase the pressures that can overcome resistant behavior. The other is to reduce the very forces that cause resistance. In the first strategy, the act of resistance itself is attacked directly. The causes or reasons for resistance are ignored. Thus, only the symptoms are addressed.

For example, managers using their authority can threaten subordinates with disciplinary action or even with "the sack" if they do not comply with a change. But I have already pointed out that such compulsion could result in immediate countermeasures that would prevent or delay the change from taking place. The change could even be sabotaged to such an extent that no benefits would be realized.

Furthermore, I have cited cases to illustrate how indiscriminate offers of pay increases to bribe subordinates into accepting change can also fail to produce lasting benefits. This can happen when the reasons for resistance are primarily noneconomic. Such bribes attack the resistance rather than it causes. In these instances, bribery often creates new problems which can eventually nullify any potential benefits from change.

Therefore, the strategic option that aims directly at overcoming resistance itself, whether by threats or bribery, is both unwise and undesirable. The consequences of such an approach will be to reduce rather than increase the possibilities for successful implementation of a change. Any manager should reject outright the use of either threats or bribery as methods for reducing resistance.

Persuasion, Rewards and Bargaining

The second strategic option of reducing the forces that cause resistance is more promising. The offer of appropriate rewards, together with other methods for addressing the causes of resistance, are discussed in this chapter. By attacking root causes rather than symptoms, managers can improve the probabilities for bringing about changes successfully. This is because root causes offer far better leverage than do symptoms for solving resistance problems.

The concept of appropriate rewards has already been introduced in chapter 6. Offering a reward that is relevant to a specific reason for resistance can be a powerful lever in providing employees with an incentive to accept a change. Before introducing the change, a manager can identify many of the probable reasons for resistance, and then develop a specific balance sheet of estimated losses and gains for those affected (see figure 4, in chapter 5). From this, it can be determined which of the probable losses might be offset or counterbalanced by the offer of appropriate compensatory rewards. Also, the manager can identify which of the possible gains should be emphasized in discussions with those involved. Used in this way, the offer of *relevant* rewards should reduce, if not remove, some of the causes of resistance. The lever of appropriate rewards can act either as an incentive and positive motivator, or as compensation for perceived losses or unfair treatment.

Rewards can be either monetary or nonmonetary. Monetary rewards result in greater annual total compensation. Often when a change alters the content of individual jobs (e.g. in terms of increased responsibility, mental and physical effort required, education and experience needed, etc.), an increase in the rate of pay can be justified. Increased compensation may be justified if the change causes an individual or group to enhance contributions to company profits. A monetary reward can also take the form of an altered system of wage payment that permits higher earnings, or earnings that are perceived as more equitable (e.g. the introduction or elimination of individual or group incentives). Alternatively, the monetary reward can be in the form of "fringe benefits" such as an improved pension scheme, a better holiday or sickness protection plan, or an enhanced medical insurance program. When the people affected believe that an intended change will somehow increase the value of what they are being asked to do, they are more vulnerable to feelings of unfair treatment. Whatever their form, all monetary rewards are useful in offsetting such feelings.

A broad variety of nonmonetary rewards can be offered because the needs they might satisfy range widely. For example, concern about threats to status might be met with an offer of: (a) a more impressive job title; (b) better "perks"; (c) changing the pattern of personal interactions (i.e inclusion in certain meetings and/or distribution lists, etc.); or (d) education and training. When the way the work is done is reorganized or the relationships within a work group are restructured, the relevant reward might be more satisfying social relationships in the work situation, and/or the opportunity to gain greater satisfaction from the work itself. Opportunities for education and training might be perceived as ways to enhance one's opportunities for personal development within the organization. As with monetary rewards, the particular nonmonetary reward offered must be carefully matched to meet an anticipated need.

The technique of bargaining is a variation of the use of persuasion through rewards. Bargaining is a process based on discussions between management and those affected by a change and/or their union representatives. In this process, management's objective is to gain acceptance of their proposals. Management in no way are committed in advance to accept any proposals made by the group with whom discussions are held. There is, however, an implicit understanding that management might accept some of the proposals put forward by the group as a *quid pro quo* in exchange for the group's acceptance of some of what management want. In a sense, then, any concessions or compromises made by management in bargaining can be considered as similar to the offer of rewards.

There is, however, an important difference between bargaining and persuasion through rewards. In bargaining, rewards typically are not initiated at the outset by management. Instead, they are management's response to proposals made by employees. Thus, bargaining is also related to the processes of discussion and participation, which I discuss later in this chapter.

Increasingly, much of what actually goes on in any organization among its members is the result of *implicit* if not explicit bargains. Actual negotiations or "understandings" occur not only between management and employees, but also between various levels of management, between staff, and between management and staff. Such bargains can be quite powerful. When these are threatened by prospective changes, the resulting resistance can be intense.

EXAMPLE

The chief executive of a large American regional bank brought into the organization five young, talented and aggressive managers from other companies (many of which were not banks) to head up five newly established divisions. Each division was structured as a separate business such as retail banking, business lending, individual trust and the

Example cont.

> *Example cont.*
>
> like. A generous incentive bonus system was instituted to motivate and reward the top managers in each division, who were granted considerable latitude and autonomy to conduct their businesses. For several years, each division grew substantially with good profitability.
>
> Yet, the bank's chief executive was dissatisfied. Believing that the bank's overall performance could be improved considerably, he engaged a consultant to help the management group improve the productivity of the bank as a whole. The consultant's initial study of the bank's operations revealed a number of promising opportunities for significant improvement. These opportunities were inter-divisional rather than intra-divisional. To capitalize on these opportunities would require the divisions to collaborate in certain areas in addition to conducting their separate businesses. For example, there was a major opportunity to cross-sell clients. This would require the divisions to share client lists and collaborate in the development and execution of cross-selling strategies.
>
> The chief executive and most middle-level managers in the divisions were enthusiastic about addressing these inter-divisional opportunities. But the five division heads became intensely resistant to going forward. Efforts to improve productivity collapsed.
>
> The culture that had developed in this bank in some respects resembled medieval England and France. The five divisions functioned as dukedoms, each quite autonomous and run by a powerful leader. To a considerable extent, the chief executive "king" was dependent on his "dukes" to deliver the performance which resulted in steadily increasing stock prices for the bank. The dukes had arrived at an implicit bargain with one another, and with the king as well: "Don't mess with me and my territory, and I'll stay out of your way, and we'll all do nicely." Although threatened by the changes urged by the consultant, this bargain was sufficiently strong to defeat the efforts to improve the bank's productivity.

The essence of bargaining is compromise. To maximize the achievement of their goals and the satisfaction of their needs, both management and those affected by a change must give way on some of the points on which they would have liked to secure agreement.

Often, a change will bring into focus some issues where management's interests conflict with those of emloyees. Management can identify some of these issues before anything is actually changed (see chapter 5). Other areas of conflict will become apparent when complaints and grievances will identify directly the issue in dispute. In

Minimizing Resistance to Change: Methods

other instances, the complaint will be merely a symptom of the conflict.

It is crucial that management give careful and open-minded consideration to every complaint and grievance. In doing so, they must recognize that the employees' and the union's perceptions of the change are often distinctly different from their own. Typically, such differences are based on the fact that management, the union and employees have different priorities, values and concerns.

Once a complaint or grievance is known, and the issues and areas of conflict of interest are identified, management can then entertain possible concessions or compromises. In cases where those affected by a change are likely to sustain economic, personal or social losses that are both real and unavoidable, management should consider concessions or compromises seriously. The cost of each concession or compromise must be estimated. The cost must be compared not only with those of alternative courses of action, but also with the cost of failure to implement the change as intended. In comparing these costs, management should estimate the total effect of both making and not making the compromise or concession. They must consider not only what would be the direct financial effects, but also the influence on such factors as precedent, employee morale, quality of products and services, and public relations. In effect, I am suggesting a classic trade-off analysis. Often, management will discover that the cost of compromise will be more than offset by the increased probability that the change will yield the anticipated benefits.

Bargaining is facilitated and is often more successful when a union is representing the employees. With a union, there is an established mechanism for bargaining. Also, bargaining is recognized and accepted by both management and the union as the normal method for reaching agreement.

For bargaining with a union to be successful, management must be aware of and willing to consider the union's institutional needs for involvement in all matters concerning its members' welfare (see chapter 4). Management must be willing to inform the union well in advance of any impending changes. They must also be willing to listen to the union's objections and take them seriously.

But if the union's objections consistently prove to be fruitless, the mere gestures of notification and listening are not enough for management to gain the union's support for a proposed change. It is essential that the union perceive management as willing to make concessions and accept suggestions. The prospects for fruitful outcomes are the greatest when management begins bargaining with the following premise: it may be necessary to accept certain suggestions and make certain compromises that are not entirely desirable from management's viewpoint, because a reasonably adequate solution supported by the union is better than an ideal solution opposed by the union.

> EXAMPLE
>
> The top management of one of the largest electric utilities in the US wanted to institute a program to improve both the quality of life at work and productivity. To launch this program, an elite group of highly skilled "Troublemen" was selected. This group was responsible for restoring power after "outages" caused by storms, manhole fires and explosions, and the like. A quality-of-work committee was formed with representatives from the union membership and their supervisors and managers. This committee was invited to generate and submit suggestions to senior management that would improve both the quality of life at work and productivity.
>
> At first the union representatives were highly skeptical. Although they doubted that much would come of it, they were willing to make an effort. Their first suggestion was a test of senior management's good faith and intentions. If management responded well, the union members would be willing to take the quality-of-work program seriously.
>
> The committee's initial suggestion recommended changing the place where the Troublemen first gathered at the start of each shift to receive their work orders. They wanted to move from the "cage" to the "chateau." The cage was a dreary, interior space enclosed by wire mesh located in an old warehouse. The chateau was a second floor space with windows in an old office building that was considerably more cheerful than the cage. The committee's recommendation included a detailed estimate of the costs required to "fix up" the chateau along with a discussion of the benefits that would result.
>
> After receiving the committee's proposal, senior management failed to respond. After two months, the committee was informed that management were studying the proposal. After another eight weeks passed with no action, the committee threw up their hands in disgust. Their initial assumptions about management's commitment to the improvement program were confirmed. The program collapsed.

There may be increased difficulty in bargaining with nonunion groups because the process itself is not formalized. Nevertheless, management might deal with informal leaders or with committees selected by employees. For bargaining to be successful in this context, the above-listed principles of early notification, open-minded consideration and willingness to compromise also apply. In addition, participants in any bargaining discussions must feel free to express their opinions and objections openly. They must have confidence and trust in the fairness of their management because they have no union whose power can protect their interests.

Thus persuading employees to accept a change depends on the offer of rewards as a lever. This can be done either unilaterally or within the framework of bargaining. The success of the approach depends on how effectively management:

- Match rewards offered (both monetary and nonmonetary) to their employees' needs and goals.
- Give serious consideration to all complaints and suggestions.
- Give some concessions in order to achieve the major portion of their objectives.

Security and Guarantees

The most effective means for management to minimize feelings of insecurity, and in particular fears of redundancy, is to guarantee that such fears are groundless. Management can use as a lever a pledge that there will be no redundancy as a consequence of a specific change. This can often make possible its acceptance.

Implementing such a pledge can be a challenging task for management. Essentially, there are only six ways in which a pledge of no redundancy in a changing situation can be redeemed:

- Not replacing by engagement from outside the company anyone who leaves the organization in the natural course of events (e.g. people who retire, are sacked, die, and resign voluntarily).
- Reabsorbing work being done by subcontractors and reassigning any surplus employees to that work.
- Retraining redundant employees and transferring or upgrading them to other work.
- Reducing or eliminating any overtime work.
- Absorbing additional work resulting from business growth with no new additions to the workforce until all those who are surplus have been productively re-employed.
- Inventing and implementing new areas of business activity.

Minimizing Resistance to Change: Methods

Fulfilling a pledge of no redundancy can be both difficult and expensive. Management may have to spend some of the savings from the change. Also, they may have to wait longer for these savings to be realized. Nevertheless, the cost of guaranteeing employees' security must be compared with the costs of their resisting the change. Here again, there is a trade-off. As I have already noted in the prior discussion of rewards, in most instances management will probably discover that to provide such guarantees makes sound economic sense.

There is no alternative so effective as a guarantee of no redundancy for eliminating fears of insecurity. It is conceivable, however, that a management might be unable to apply any of the above methods for solving the problem of a surplus of labor created by a change.

In such circumstances, management might consider another lever. This is a guarantee of continued income for each surplus employee until s/he is working in another comparable job, either within or outside the company. In this approach, management undertake to help each surplus individual find another suitable job. If this cannot be accomplished with the company, assistance with "out placement" can be provided. Until this occurs, the employee's income would continue to be maintained by the company as a supplement to any unemployment benefits from the state.

I believe, however, that the lever of maintaining income is inferior to guaranteeing no redundancy. Although employees might feel secure about the continuity of income they would nevertheless feel uneasy about the impending changes in their personal lives. They would undoubtedly have many unanswered questions and apprehensions about new jobs and new environments. Because of these questions and fears, they might still resist the change, although perhaps less intensely than if they were to be made redundant with no guarantees of any kind.

Here is an example of how a declining industry handled the unavoidable threat to the security of the employees involved:

> A notable example of how to avoid industrial strife is the old tinplate industry of Wales. Here the employers realized soon after the war that there would be a decline in the industry. They went to the unions and predicted the closure of many of the small tinplate handmills and that unless something could be done this would cause redundancy and hardship in a few years. As a result of these talks, beginning in 1946, there was time to do something about the situation and to find alternative employment for the men. It was also agreed to set up a fund, so that by the time of the final closures in 1958 there was almost £1 m. available to compensate the men who became redundant. Throughout this decline there were few restrictive practices.[40]

A person's feeling of insecurity can also be heightened if there is fear about inability to perform adequately in the new situation. Management can do much to reduce this fear by using the lever of training. A carefully designed program of training can often help to make a change successful. This means matching the training provided to the true needs of the people involved. It also means providing the training in a way that engages and motivates.

For such a training program to be effective, it must be designed to help people discard those attitudes and working habits that might impede their ability to perform well in the new situation. Only after this has been accomplished can new knowledge and skills be developed. There must be some unlearning before any new learning can take place.

Training programs can yield another benefit as well. The very act of establishing one provides evidence that management are doing everything possible to help those involved cope with the change. Such a reassuring demonstration of management's support should reduce the feeling of insecurity so often associated with feelings of inadequacy.

To lessen any feelings of insecurity from factors other than fears of redundancy or inadequacy, management can engage their employees in discussions. Those involved in discussion can develop a realistic understanding of the change and its probable consequences. Such understanding can do much to dispel any fears resulting from misunderstanding or lack of information. Discussion as a lever is discussed in the following section.

Thus, the strongest cause of insecure feelings is fear of redundancy. This can best be minimized by management's pledge that no redundancy will result from the change. As a less desirable alternative, management might promise to maintain the incomes of those who become surplus until they find other work. To reduce feelings of insecurity resulting from fears of inadequacy, management can offer training programs tailored to employees' needs. Management can deal with the remaining reasons for insecure feelings by developing an understanding of what are likely to be the consequences of the change.

Understanding and Discussion

Earlier I suggested that when as many as possible of those people involved in a change understand as much as possible about it and its

Minimizing Resistance to Change: Methods

consequences, resistance is likely to be reduced. It is management's job to develop this understanding.

> Resistance will be prevented to the degree that the changer helps the changees to develop their own understanding of the need for the change, and an explicit awareness of how they feel about it, and what can be done about their feelings.[41]

Such understanding will occur only when the information provided is sufficient, factual and accurate. Management can transmit information about a proposed change and its probable consequences to those affected or concerned in a variety of ways. Fundamentally, there are only three practical media for communication: written material, audio-visual, and oral. Here is a list of the variety of media that can be employed.

Written media

Notices on bulletin boards.

Brief, scheduled newsletters specially composed and individually addressed.

Articles in the company newspaper or magazine.

Special memoranda delivered to each individual either at work or at home.

News releases for general publication in community newspapers.

Messages on electronic mail.

Posters and signs.

Specially designed and constructed visual displays such as models, mock-ups, etc.

Audio-visual media

Films, filmstrips, videos, overheads, slides, and other audio-visual presentations.

Self-administered programmed instruction.

Fax.

Minimizing Resistance to Change: Methods

Oral media

Formal orientation, indoctrination and training meetings.

Announcements and messages on company public-address systems.

Group discussions (face-to-face).

Individual discussions (face-to-face).

All these media can be used to transmit information. Each can be employed effectively. No single means, however, should be relied upon exclusively. The more complex the change, the greater should be the variety of media employed. The broader the range of media used, the greater will be the possibilities that everyone involved is being reached with a maximum of information.

All but two or possibly four of these approaches, however, have severe limitations. When transmission of information is only one-way, there is no assurance that people will gain understanding Several conditions must be met for understanding to be developed in a changing situation:

- Information must be readily accessible, factual and accurate.
- Information must be communicated in language or in a form that is readily understandable.
- Information must answer the questions that are being asked – not only what is to happen, but also how, why, when, where and to whom.
- There must be a way to test and confirm that real understanding has in fact been achieved.

All of the above media can fulfill the first two conditions. But the only means of communication that can readily achieve all four conditions and are suitable levers for management are those that depend on face-to-face discussions conducted in a climate where a free interchange of ideas is encouraged. Two other media, although not face-to-face, provide capabilities for very rapid interactive exchanges of information. These are electronic mail and fax. In such discussions (and to a lesser extent, electronically assisted interchanges), employees can ask questions directly of managers. Sensitive and observant managers can learn a great deal about employees' unexpressed fears from the nature of their questions and from the manner in which they are asked. Also, managers can raise questions to test how accurate are any predictions of reactions to the change and confirm the existence of any fears. These fears can then be reduced by supplying additional information. Managers can also test and estimate how widely particular questions or fears are shared within the group. Managers can also ask questions to test and evaluate how much understanding has actually been developed. Only in give-and-take exchanges that are possible in a discussion or in electronic exchanges can managers be certain that the needed information is being provided and that understanding is in fact being achieved.

Through discussion or electronic exchanges, any who may have pent-up feelings of irritation and anger from the frustrations about the change can find a ready outlet to release hostile feelings People can "blow off steam" by voicing their fears and by giving vent to these feelings in words. Such a release or "catharsis" can in itself be a valuable by-product or discussions or electronic exchanges. Through such safety-valves, aggressive feelings that might otherwise have been expressed in restriction of output, in "mistakes" or in sabotage can be released with little harmful effect.

It matters little whether a discussion is carried out in a formal and structured manner (e.g. orientation and training meetings and conferences), or in an informal and unstructured way. What does matter, however, is that a supportive climate be established by the manager. It is vital that participants feel free to raise any questions or to make any comments they wish, without fear of reprisal.

A manager can do this first by encouraging people to raise questions and explain their meaning. The manager must also respond freely and openly with honest answers. Care must be taken to distinguish among facts, opinions and speculation. There must be no appearance of judging the questioner for voicing fears or queries that might appear ridiculous or suspect in their underlying motivation. Finally, there must be sufficient time allowed for the discussion to develop, and for as many that so desire to speak.

At first, a manager's success in establishing a supportive climate for discussions will depend almost entirely on the nature of her or his past relationships with the participants. However, if, over a long enough period of time, a manager persists and is consistent in doing everything possible to establish a supportive climate, and if the participants learn from experience that they can in fact speak up with no distasteful consequences, that manager can to some extent overcome a past history of mistrust and suspicion.

Whatever medium of communcication is issued, the language must be readily understandable. The problem of language often arises when a

Minimizing Resistance to Change: Methods

change is being explained by a staff specialist. Such "experts" often believe that the reasons for a change are so complicated and particular that it is impossible to explain them to operating people whether they be supervisors or workers. True, many operating personnel might have difficulty understanding some of the analytical techniques used by staff specialists. When specialists make no effort to translate their ideas into language that can readily be understood by supervisors and operatives, they may conclude that the specialist is deliberately either confusing or misleading them with technical jargon and complicated formulas and figures. Such a conclusion can be harmful to the successful implementation of a change.

> A staff specialist was temporarily successful in "selling" a change based on a complicated mathematical formula to a foreman who really did not understand it. The whole thing backfired, however, when the foreman tried to sell it to his operating people. They asked him a couple of sharp questions that he could not answer. His embarrassment about this led him to resent and resist the change so much that eventually the whole proposition fell through. This was unfortunate in terms not only of human relations but also of technological progress in the plant.[42]

Clearly, it is unnecessary for operating personnel to understand the reasons for a change in the same terms or to the same level of detail as does the staff specialist. They must, however, be able to visualize the proposed change and its rationale in terms of their own work experience. When employees fail to understand the basis for the change and the change itself, it reflects a failure by both management and staff specialists to provide adequate explanations.

When a change and its rationale are complex, the use of imagery can be helpful in gaining understanding. Often, if suitable analogies and metaphors can be developed, these can make complexity more accessible to everyone involved. In chapter 5, I describe how organizational systems can generate resistance to changes. This concept and its dynamics are subtle and complex. But the idea can more readily be grasped if the analogy is introduced of antibodies attacking "invaders" to the body. Systemic resistance to change can begin to make sense when an analogy or image is evoked of antibodies swarming all over change efforts and killing them (however imperfect this may be).

A lack of understanding can result in heightened anxiety about the possible consequences of a change. This, in turn, can result in resistant behavior. In addition it is likely that, because of this lack, those performing the work will derive less satisfaction from their jobs. This should be of concern to management, particularly during a change. When people do not understand what they are doing, those abilities which are uniquely human cannot be exercised. These abilities are the application of informed and intelligent judgments to the performance of work. When anyone is deprived of the opportunity to make meaningful judgments, the result is increasing frustration. Not only will both the person and the work suffer, but so also will the organization.

During a change, therefore, many of the normal mechanisms and channels of communication are often disrupted and impaired. To compensate for this, management must devote special attention and make an extra effort to communicate a full understanding of every aspect of the change and its probable consequences. They should use every practicable technique of communication. The language used must be related to the frame of reference of those to whom the communications are addressed. Of all the possible communication techniques, management should make the greatest use of face-to-face discussions, both with individuals and with groups. Electronically assisted exchanges may also be useful. These techniques are the most effective methods for ensuring that answers are being given to those questions of genuine concern to the people involved. Also, these methods are the most effective means for determining how much true understanding is being achieved.

Time and Timing

Previously, I noted that when management are willing to discuss openly with their employees all aspects of an impending change, it is desirable that ample time be planned between the initial mention of the change and the start of its actual initiation. Management should use this interval as a lever to ensure that all involved attain maximum understanding of the change and its probable consequences.

Management should plan the length of this interval by working out a trade-off between two considerations. Often these will be in conflict with one another. The first of these is the question of how long it takes for the processes of accommodation and rationalization to occur for most people involved. The second consideration is an evaluation of

Minimizing Resistance to Change: Methods

those situational factors which determine when the change must be instituted and implemented and when the benefits must be realized.

First, management should question and re-examine the reasons and premises on which they based their original schedule. Must the change really be completed by date X? How much of it must be completed by date X? What would be the consequences of postponing the completion of the change to dates Y or Z?

To achieve the best trade-off between these two considerations, management need to evaluate the relative costs of two alternatives: (a) delaying the introduction of the change to gain more preparation time in the interests of realizing optimum benefits; or (b) conforming to the intended schedule with the possibility of an increased risk of resistance, and the resultant probability of reduced benefits. In many instances, management may discover that it will be economic to delay the change until the possibility of its acceptance is enhanced. If management decide not to delay, resistance may cause not only a reduction in the possible benefits but also probable delays in their realization. In the end, it might not matter which of the above approaches management choose because there will be little difference in the completion time for the change. The resultant benefits, however, might be very different. It might prove worthwhile, therefore, for management to plan sufficient time during the early phases of the change for accommodation and rationalization to occur and for understanding to be developed.

When management are establishing the timing for a change, they should also consider the relationship of that change to other events both in the company and in the community. Several questions should be answered. First, is the change being timed so as to coincide with any other events that may jeopardize its successful implementation? Contrast two examples. In one case, the management of a worldwide manufacturer of photographic products were planning to automate one of their manufacturing operations. Concurrently in a nearby facility the workforce were being reduced as a consequence of a drop in consumer demand for the company's products. The resultant redundancies caused the entire workforce to become increasingly aware and fearful of losing their jobs. This was not an opportune time to introduce a new process that could result in further redundancies. In the other case, in a community of moderate size, company A introduced extensive office automation in its headquarters' offices. Because of inept planning and poor management, this change was handled badly. The employees' reaction to the change was unfavorable, and the company received some poor publicity in the local press. Company B in this same community was also about to introduce similar tech-

Minimizing Resistance to Change: Methods

nology into its offices. Company B's management decided to delay the introduction for several months and to devote the time gained to improving their plans for the change and to conducting numerous preparatory discussions with the employees to be affected.

Another question that should be examined is whether or not the contemplated change could be so timed as to coincide with other events that might improve the chances for its successful implementation. For example, Acme Products PLC completed a major study of its distribution operations throughout the UK. If certain improvements were made in methods of operation, the company would be able to distribute its products with about 800 fewer employees. The company had been subcontracting many of its distribution operations to its smaller customers. From the study, it appeared economic for Acme to handle directly about 75 percent of its total distribution activities. Contracts with most of the subcontracting firms were scheduled for renegotiation in 12 months. Management decided to time the improvements in distribution operations to coincide with the break-points in these contracts. Thus, most of the employees who would otherwise have been redundant were retained by the reabsorption of the work that had been subcontracted.

Consideration should also be given to the question of whether or not the change is timed most opportunely from the standpoint or management's bargaining position. For example, in a peak period of production of a moderate-sized machine tool manufacturer, a bottleneck developed in one manufacturing operation involving a small group of highly skilled men. After studying this operation, management concluded that it could be streamlined and improved to the extent that the existing workforce should be able to cope successfully with the greatly increased but temporary flow of work. This, however, would require the men's cooperation. After further analyses of the situation, management decided to postpone introducing the changes until after the production peak had subsided. They could deal with the immediate crisis by subcontracting some of the work. This decision was made because management realized that while the bottleneck existed the skilled operatives were in a particularly strong bargaining position. Their morale could not be permitted to deteriorate when high productivity was crucial. Also, they were likely to be fearful that some of their number might become redundant later on when their workload decreased after the peak of activity had subsided to a more normal level. At that time, these fears could be handled more effectively when the problem of redundancy would be immediate and clear, rather than being somewhat vague and in the future.

Thus, management should use the timing of a change as a lever, basing their decisions on several carefully considered factors. In so doing, they must compare the costs of alternative courses of action and make a trade-off decision. In most cases, they should discover that the cost of devoting more time to preparing their employees for the change will be less than the cost of increased resistance and decreased and perhaps delayed benefits. Also, management should time the change so that it is coordinated with other relevant and significant events occurring both within and outside the organization.

Involvement and Participation

Involvement and participation are perhaps the most powerful levers management can use to gain acceptance of a change. An old Chinese proverb states: "Tell me and I'll forget; show me and I may remember; involve me and I'll understand."

I have already noted that personal involvement in making some of the decisions about a change often has several beneficial effects. Commitment to carry out these decisions is intensified. Personal satisfactions derived from the job are increased. Resistance is decreased. I have already described how face-to-face discussions can help to develop understanding of a change and its probable consequences. The process of participation is the lever management can use to conduct discussions and increase the probability that the change will indeed yield the desired outcomes and gains.

The objective of participation is to achieve acceptance by a group of people that they are taking an active part in planning, initiating and implementing a change rather than being the passive recipients of its effects. Participation tends to empower people. They feel more in control than victims of events. Participation is most likely to be effective when applied to relatively small groups, and when it concerns changes that are essentially local in nature.

A manager can use participation as a lever in a variety of ways. These can vary according to how much personal involvement in decision-making management or individual managers want to achieve or permit. The extent of personal involvement can range from merely being informed, to discussing problems and voicing opinions and feelings, to actually making and implementing decisions (see figure 5).

At its most superficial level, some participation occurs when one is

Minimizing Resistance to Change: Methods

```
                    Management action              Employee action

Active         Delegating decision-making    ┌─ Making and implementing decisions
  ▲                    authority             └─   — Task assignments with accountability
  │
  │              Group consensus             ┌─ Formulating proposed plans and solutions
  │                                          │    to problems
  │                                          │      — Planning groups
  │                                          └─     — Task forces
  │
  │                                          ⎧─ Group suggestions and recommendations
  │                                          │      — Formally established councils or
  │                                          │        committees
  │                                          │      — Informal groups
  │              Soliciting inputs           ⎨─ Analysis of problems and alternatives
  │                                          │      — Task forces
  │                                          │      — Formally established councils or
  │                                          │        committees
  │                                          ⎩─ Individual suggestions
  │
  │                                          ⎧─ Face-to-face discussion of problems
  │              Consultation                ⎨─ Face-to-face invitations to voice opinions
  │                                          ⎩─ Electronics exchanges
  ▼
Passive          Inclusion                   ⎧─ Attendance at briefings
                                             ⎩─ Inclusion on distribution lists
```

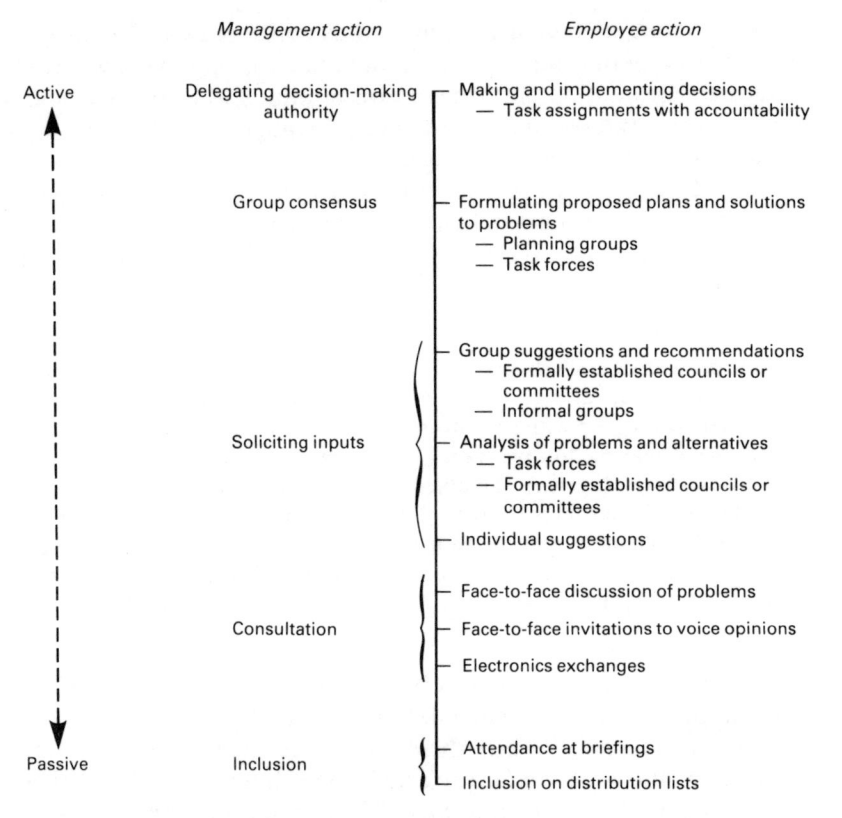

Figure 5   Spectrum of levels of participation

designated to receive information either written via distribution lists or in face-to-face briefings. At a slightly more intensive level, participation can be gained through individual or group consultation. This process is no more than an extension of the face-to-face discussions that I have already described. In a discussion, the manager typically describes some proposed or intended courses of action. Those present are then invited to raise questions and voice their comments or feelings. In the process of soliciting inputs, the manager carries this approach a step further. Those present are asked to make suggestions about how the change might best be accomplished. Alternatively, a problem might be assigned to a group for analysis and recommended actions.

When inputs are solicited, there is an implicit or explicit understanding that management are under no obligation to accept any of the ideas offered, so long as they are given serious consideration. If, however, over a period of time all suggestions are rejected, employees will come to regard consultation and solicitation of inputs as a pretense and a fraud. If this attitude should develop, a manager's relationship with employees can be severely damaged.

When employees are invited to contribute their thoughts, many valuable ideas often come to light. The person actually doing the work on a day-to-day basis is usually more knowledgeable about it than anyone else.

> Management in a small steel plant was facing an unusually stubborn problem. Product quality had fallen off and none of the engineering staff was able to come up with a solution. Expensive consultants also failed to stem the increasing flow of scrap. Finally, the plant manager called some of the old-timers together, explained the problem, and told them the firm would face bankruptcy if the problem wasn't solved. After a few minutes' discussion, one of these workers suggested the cause of the trouble and how to solve it. When asked why he hadn't produced this important information before, he answered, "I wasn't asked."[43]

Employees take pride in and derive satisfaction from knowing that their suggestions or recommendations are being considered. These feelings are intensified when their inputs are actually adopted and acted upon. But if inputs are rejected, then those who offered them must be made to understand why. When managers are effective in explaining why certain inputs were rejected, consultation and solicitation can still be productive. There are three reasons for this. First, the very fact that employees have opportunities both to express themselves and to be given serious attention can, in itself, be beneficial to attitude and morale. Also, by understanding why a suggestion was not acceptable, an employee may reach a better understanding of the change. Third, the employee may be encouraged to offer better suggestions in the future.

EXAMPLE

The Arcturus Company employs about 3,500 employees in research, development, manufacture and sale of a complex series of consumer products. All personnel policies and procedures evolve through a system

Example cont.

Example cont.

of consultation with and solicitation of inputs from all members of management and supervision, and a representative Employees' Committee. Suggestions for new policies or modifications to the existing policies and procedures are submitted to a Personnel Policy Committee made up of members of top management. When so ordered by this committee, a *First Draft* of a proposed new policy (or modification to an existing policy) is issued on yellow paper. This is circulated to about 700 members of management and to the members of the Employees' Committee. These individuals are invited to discuss the proposed change with as many other employees as possible, and to return their written comments to the Personnel Policy Committee. If there is no adverse reaction of significance, the policy is then reissued as a formal *Instruction* on white paper, to be included in the personnel policy manuals maintained in each department.

If, on the other hand, there is a significant response to the *First Draft*, the comments are evaluated in terms of both their content and their frequency of occurrence. A *Second Draft* (also on yellow paper) of the proposed policy is then issued to the same group. This is a modification of the *First Draft*, with the changes reflecting the comments. Again, comments are requested on the *Second Draft* and the process described above continues until a formal *Instruction* is issued. Occasionally, when the responses are strongly negative, the proposed change in policy (or new policy) may be dropped altogether. Sometimes a proposal will be reissued in as many as four separate and different drafts before it is finally accepted as a formal policy. This process has the disadvantage of taking a long time between the introduction of a new proposal for a change and its formal institution as a policy. On the other hand, this disadvantage is offset by the fact that all changes in personnel policy are introduced smoothly. By the time they become official practice, these changes are well understood and accepted, not only by all levels of management, but also by the employees as well. This is because the change has been thoroughly discussed, and is familiar to everyone.

In order to engage employees even more actively, the participative process should include some involvement in actual decision-making. Going beyond the solicitation of suggestions and recommendations from those involved in the change, managers should also encourage them to share, to some defined extent, in making and implementing the decisions related to that change. This approach to managing has received considerable attention in recent years, and is becoming more widespread.

EXAMPLE

An early fundamental research study in the participative process involved a pyjama factory in the United States.[44] In this pyjama factory, there were constant changes in the style of the product and in methods of production. These changes were often opposed strongly by the female workers. Opposition was expressed in several forms. For instance, when employees were transferred from one job to another, they often took a longer time to learn the new job than did those entirely new to the company. Also, 62 percent of the transferred employees either failed to achieve satisfactory levels of production of else quit altogether. Some of the groups restricted their output and engaged in aggressive behavior against management. Their resistance was caused by frustration over loss of status, the difficulties in learning new methods, and the fear of not being able to regain their earlier levels of proficiency. Economic fears were less significant, because the women received a liberal learning allowance during the period of adjustment to make up for any losses in piecework earnings.

As an experiment, four groups were established. Each was subjected to changes in their methods of work. These changes affected less than 10 percent of their total work. For each of these four groups, a different method was used to introduce the change. The results were carefully recorded to determine what, if any, resistance occurred.

The *control group* followed the traditional routines for instituting changes. They were gathered together and told in general terms that the new method was made necessary because of competition in the pyjama business. The new piecework pay rate was announced, and the members of the group were given an opportunity to ask questions.

The *partial-participation* group attended a meeting at which the need for change was explained in a dramatic manner. Management emphasized that as a consequence of the change, the company could produce pyjamas more competitively and gain a greater share of the market. As a result of this, the employees would enjoy better working conditions and have greater job security. The members of this group agreed in principle to the change. They elected a committee to assist management in developing the necessary plans and in establishing the new piecework pay rates.

Two *total-participation groups* were formed, each smaller than the partial-participation group. These groups followed a procedure similar to the partial-participation group, except that all of the operatives participated in planning how the change was to take place. The groups discussed how existing work methods could be improved. When the new methods were agreed, all were trained and then observed by the time-study men so that the new piecework pay rates could be established.

Example cont.

Minimizing Resistance to Change: Methods

Example cont.

The most striking difference in the resultant behavior was between the control group and the two total-participation groups. The output of the control group dropped immediately to about two-thirds its previous level. Production remained at this lower rate throughout the period of 20 days after the change had been introduced. The researchers reported that:

> Resistance developed almost immediately after the change occurred. Marked expressions of aggression against management occurred, such as conflict with the method engineer... hostility toward the supervisor, deliberate restriction of production and lack of cooperation with the supervisor. There were 17% quits in the first 40 days. Grievances were filed about piece-rates; but when the rate was checked, it was found to be a little "loose."

In contrast with the control group, the total-participation groups (and almost to the same extent the partial-participation group) were very cooperative. After a small initial drop in their output, they soon achieved a production level 40 percent higher than that of the control group. There were no signs of aggressive behavior toward management and there were no quits during the experimental period.

From this study, the researchers concluded that when people affected by a change became involved in making the decisions which determined how it was to be implemented, they tended not to resist it. This conclusion, however, is valid only in certain instances. The problem of how a manager can achieve genuine participation in a changing situation is more complex than one might realize from this research.

EXAMPLE

In a later study, C. Argyris[4,5] found that the 30 employees affected were apparently unconcerned with their management's failure to use participation with them in implementing a change.

Management decided to mechanize production to cut costs and prices. No opportunity was given to the employees to become involved in planning this change. Management simply made an announcement of the change beforehand. There were no other communications until the process was ready for installation. Then,

Example cont.

Example cont.

the men were shown the new process, briefed about it, and given a demonstration. The new process required little skill and meant that there would be a significant reduction in the skill required of the men to do the work.

Through interviews, it was determined that in the culture of that organization the men's most important needs were for job security, for fair wages, for control over their immediate work environment and for comfortable social relationships. They apparently had no interest in becoming involved in the organization's activities, except for their own immediate jobs. Management purposely set loose piece-rates so that wage levels were maintained. With the change, job insecurity was increased somewhat because of increased dependency on the success of the particular product (and on the Sales Department). Nevertheless, 83% of those affected stated that, "They did not care that they were not included in the planning of the changes. That is management's worry." Ninety-two percent viewed the changes as necessary if the company were to remain competitive. Although there was concern over possible reductions in quality, there was no apparent concern about the de-skilling of the jobs.

A typical comment by one of the men was, "I think management introduced the merry-go-round (nickname for the new process) correctly. There's no need in calling the people in and wasting a hell of a lot of time. You tell them what you plan to do, you guarantee their job security, and then let them think about it. When you're ready, you put it in. Sure they complain a little bit, but it's quieted down now."

The results of this research can perhaps be better understood by applying Maslow's theory about the hierarchy of needs (chapter 3). Opportunities to participate and be involved meet people's higher-order needs for esteem and self-actualization. When their more fundamental physiological and safety needs are not being satisfied or threatened (as was the case in this situation), these tend to take precedence in their thinking. Participation is thus of little interest.

The concept of "participation" or "employee involvement" has become quite loosely understood and rather fashionable in some management circles.[46] Many managers now think of it as a "good thing" in the same way that they regard other techniques currently in vogue, such as organization restructuring, just-in-time, and total quality management (TQM). Interest in participation has been heightened by study of Japanese management methods.[47] Yet, there is reason to question how genuinely participative Japanese management's approach to decision-making is in actuality. Recent accounts[48] suggest that what we in the West have interpreted as participation is in fact ritualistic manifestations of Japan's highly autocratic cultural traditions.

In actuality, participation means different things to different managers. To some, it is a device for "masterminding" and manipulating people to share a viewpoint already held by the manager. To others, it is merely a ritual to be observed so that there will be an illusion created that the employees have some voice in what is happening to them. This is intended to create "a sense of participation." Such views differ widely from the true meaning of participation:

> Participation does not mean winning friends and influencing people. Rather, it is analogous to the good salesman's sincere concern for the potential customer. Even more basically, it is a means for the company to exercise its responsibility to the people who work there – to provide its people with a sense of belonging based on human dignity.[49]

Participation can be applied to a broad range of problems. Consider these examples.[50]

> A company planning an expansion invited help from the foreman group in deciding where to locate the new plant and which foreman to transfer to it. The foremen joined in a study of alternatives, recommended a new location and drew up a list of their number to be assigned there. At that point the layout of the plant came up for discussion. The participation of the employees of the department which was to be expanded into the new plant was requested. The group pored over drawings, made three-dimensional models, and recommended changes in facilities, equipment, layout, parking areas, services and other matters that reduced the bill for the new plant considerably.

> A company wanted to introduce a rating and evaluation program for middle-management people as a part of its executive development program. Rating systems from consultants were available, but the problem was turned over to the group to be rated and the members developed their own system, which was more stringent than any proposed by outside firms.

> A distribution company put the problem of territory boundaries, quotas and commissions before a representation of its salesforce. This group made recommendations to management which showed real insight into the problem and also an understanding of its intricate detail. The group also suggested that it administer and review the matter at regular intervals.

In the office, groups have reviewed records, reports, forms, methods, procedures and equipment; hundreds of examples of improvement in paperwork through participation are known. For example, one office group found a lengthy report that had been compiled by it for some time and distributed monthly in a large quantity, but which was no longer used or needed in the company. It was quickly eliminated and the women released to more meaningful activity.

True participation cannot be created simply by management decree. It is not possible to find and appoint managers or staff specialists with an inherent ability to "get participation." Even if a well-meaning manager ordered subordinates to "get back to your section and start participation," the result would probably be a far cry from the genuine involvement of employees in making decisions.

Real participation depends on the feelings and attitudes of the people involved. It also depends on the manager's competence in applying process skills (chapter 8). The mechanistic act of assembling a group for discussion provides insufficient motivation for effective participation. What, then, are the prerequisite conditions necessary for true participation to take place? The five conditions discussed below are relevant to employees as individuals or in groups (whether or not they are members of management), and to union leaders and staff.

A basic reqirement for participation is that the people involved *want* to participate. In the cultural beliefs and behavioral norms of the organization (and to some extent of the society as a whole), people must feel some need to be involved in the planning and organizing of work. As can be seen from the Argyris study cited earlier in the section, when this need is absent or subordinated to other more pressing needs there would be few benefits, and possibly even some disadvantages, to be gained from attempting to achieve participation.

It is quite possible, however, that an apparent lack of concern about involvement is a defensive rationalization developed by employees because they suspect that management are not genuinely interested in real participation. Instead, they believe that management want to use participation as a manipulative device to "mastermind" them into accepting a change about which they are doubtful or fearful.

Fundamentally, employees who are asked to participate must believe that the intentions of their manager or supervisor are sincere and honest. Furthermore, they must believe that if their ideas have merit, there will be a reasonable possibility of their adoption and implementation. For these beliefs to exist, the relationship between manager and employee must be based on some degree of mutual respect, confidence and trust. When these elements are absent, then any attempts to generate participation will be regarded with suspicion and mistrust. When managers attempt to use participation for "masterminding," their true underlying motives would soon be perceived. The result would be further deterioration of the management–employee relationship.

A second prerequisite condition for successful participation is that the manager or supervisor must feel reasonably secure in his or her position and role. Some managers may be reluctant to attempt developing participation with employees because of certain preconceptions about their role and status. For instance, a manager might believe that to ask for advice or opinions from subordinates would be a sign of weakness. This would be based on a belief that by inviting participation, s/he would be revealing to subordinates a lack of omniscience or potency (see chapter 11). Thus, managers might feel that any involvement of subordinates in making decisions that were their prerogative alone would endanger their managerial status. Anyone with these beliefs would be surprised to learn that when employees are permitted and encouraged to participate, their esteem for their manager often tends to increase rather than decrease.

When managers can bring themselves to risk their status in the eyes of subordinates by involving them in some form of participation, they may find the consequences startling.

The manager who wishes to get participation started should logically begin with a situation that is not too complex, political or emotional. If possible, it should be obvious, both to him and to the group members, that he could benefit from the advice of those around him. A slow, easy start is better than a sensational beginning, for this is a great change.

He may come out in the open and state the change and ask the group to help, on the basis that confession is good for the soul and prompts sympathetic cooperation; or he may want to get his feet a bit wet before commiting himself to the change since, being human, he like everyone else resists being pushed into the new. In the latter case he might start asking people for ideas and then listen them out. This technique is perfect for breaking up yes-men conferences and developing constructive ideas. Here is the kind of thing that happens:

A plant superintendent who had become conscious of his tendency to run the meeting decided to change his tactics; he would ask for ideas and suggestions and then shut up. After a painful silence during which time the yes-men were moving their heads the other way looking for someone to speak up, two supposed incompetents quietly but definitely took a long-standing situation apart, called a spade a spade, and laid out a possible solution as neatly as a trained surgeon performs an appendectomy. The superintendent listened goggle-eyed and amazed.[51]

A third prerequisite condition for participation is an absence of commitment by a manager to any single course of action. S/he must be open-minded to possibilities for alternative approaches. When others are invited to participate in making decisions, some of their suggestions will probably be different from those of the manager. They may also be as valid. Some of these ideas may even be superior. If the manager is convinced from the outset that her or his method is the best and only means of accomplishing the change, then s/he would be wise not even to try involving others. Any such attempt would soon be perceived as meaningless and essentially dishonest.

When managers consider the objectives of a change to be of primary importance, whatever method is used to accomplish these objectives will be of secondary importance (chapter 1). When managers value ends above means, there will be ample latitude for the adoption and use of any worthwhile ideas generated through participation.

However, even when a manager is committed to a particular method of approach, there will inevitably be some elements of the change that can be accomplished in a variety of ways, any one of which would be acceptable. The manager can select one or more of these elements and offer them as a menu for participation. In this way, the areas for participation can be controlled while gaining some degree of personal involvement among those affected by the change.

For example, a manager is moving her manufacturing department to a new location. This move involves a number of changes in the location and interrelationship of individual operations, as well as changes in the methods of handling materials. These changes have been predetermined by industrial engineers. The manager agrees fully with these changes, and is convinced there will be significant reductions in operating costs. Nevertheless, the manager is quite open-minded about other elements of these changes: the placement, design and decor of the employees' lounges and other facilities; the decor of the entire department; and some details of the specific arrangements of individual work stations. The manager designates these areas as problems for her employees to solve. Because the manager allows them to decide some elements of the change, the employees become personally involved in the change as a whole. As a result, they are cooperative about many aspects of the change that they might otherwise have resisted.

Again, a manager decides that his secretary should have a new and better computer. He defines the objectives and constraints of this change to his secretary (e.g. performance, cost, features), and then suggests that she decide on the particular computer that she would like. Thus, the final decision to purchase will be a joint one.

A fourth condition necessary for effective participation is the manager's willingness to give credit and recognition openly to all worthwhile contributions made by others to the realization of the change. Also, if impracticable ideas are offered, the manager must ensure that the contributors receive full explanations about reasons for rejections. Such explanations must be both understandable and acceptable.

By now it should be evident that a manager's self-concepts, attitudes, and particularly feelings of self-confidence and personal security, are crucial to achieving effective participation. Managers must be able to admit to themselves, as well as to others, the possibility that their subordinates (even if they are unskilled operatives) might have suggestions about the introduction of changes as valid as their own. Such an admission requires considerable self-assurance and self-concept not distorted by excessive concern with role and status.

> The fact that participation is not used in our business rests with the managers on every level. I have long felt that they are deterred largely because of their preconception. The thought of the manager asking for advice goes against the administrative grain. As the boss, he thinks that he cannot show those under him that he does not know all the answers. He cannot ever let them take control away from him for he will lose his managerial position, or at least his status.[52]

The fifth condition necessary for effective participation is the employees' willingness to voice their comments and to offer suggestions once they have been encouraged to do so. Participation will not work with people who are passive or apathetic. Such attitudes are usually a result of their responses either to the previous behavior of management or to prevailing cultural beliefs and behavioral norms.

If *all five* of these conditions are not present in a changing situation, a manager should be very cautious in trying to use participation as a lever. When all these conditions are met, the use of participation in managing a change can yield at least eight significant benefits:

1   Participation helps to develop a better and more complete understanding of the change, its causes and its probable consequences.

2 Participation is a powerful way to unfreeze fixed attitudes, stereotypes or cultural beliefs which are held either by management or by the workforce, and which conflict with the accomplishment of the change. Through participation, these beliefs can be re-examined in a more objective light. Thus, participation can help open up one's mind.
3 Participation helps to increase employees' confidence in management's intentions and objectives.
4 Often, as a consequence of participation, firsthand ideas are contributed that result in better methods of introducing and implementing the change.
5 Through participation people involve themselves in the change. They "buy into" and become more committed to the decisions in which they took part.
6 Participation sometimes serves to prevent poorly-conceived changes from being made.
7 Through participation, staff specialists tend to broaden their outlook.
8 Through participation, employees at every organizational level gain a broader perspective and develop their capabilities.

An example of point 2 - the re-examination of beliefs - occurred in the pyjama plant previously discussed.[53] During World War II, the company's staff psychologist attempted to persuade management (because of the shortage of manpower) to abandon their policy of not engaging workers over 30 years of age. Management immediately opposed this idea, insisting that older women required a long training period, were absent more, and never worked at top speed. When the psychologist referred to the good performance of those older women currently employed, management dismissed these examples as exceptional cases. Then the psychologist tried another approach. He involved management in a research project to determine how much money the company was losing by employing older women. Management themselves determined the criteria to be used and decided how the data were to be collected. Management became actively involved. To their surprise, the data showed that older women were better in every respect. Because of their findings, management changed their policy and urged other companies to follow suit.

An especially effective use of participation is the involvement of those employees concerned, in diagnosing the particular problems giving rise to the need for a change. Diagnosis can result from participation in gathering the relevant facts. Because these indivi-duals participated in developing the data that later led them to identify the problem requiring solution, they would tend to support the change intended to solve that problem.

> A number of high-level supervisors in an electric utility came to feel that the workers had many negative attitudes about their jobs which were due to poor supervisory practices. Each supervisor, quite naturally, felt that other supervisors were at fault. Top management set up a number of study groups in which the supervisors first learned how they could diagnose the cause of these negative attitudes. Each supervisor then returned to his own work place and gathered facts that would be necessary for him to analyze the causes of negative attitudes he could spot among his workers. Later the supervisors came together to report their findings. At this meeting their enthusiasm for change in their own practices was high because they had participated in gathering the facts which best described their problems. People will be more likely to act in terms of information they gather themselves than in terms of information gathered by others and delivered to them.[54]

Thus, participation is probably the most potentially effective managerial lever for transforming any possible resistance to a change into active support. It is, however, a lever that must be used skillfully and carefully, and only when certain prerequisite conditions are met.

Criticism, Ceremony and Building on the Past

In a changing situation, managers should avoid any actions that would lead those involved to feel criticized. At least two courses of action are possible as levers. Positive and constructive use of the past can be made in all communications about the change. Also, managers can make deliberate use of ceremony and ritual.

Anthropologists have long known that in order to work effectively with any group of people it is essential to learn their customs, ceremonies and symbols and their expected ways of doing things. Changes can be introduced far more easily when adjustments are made to the past. One way of making such adjustments is to retain in the changed situation certain elements of past rituals and symbols. For example, the chief psychiatrist of Nigeria's most important mental hospital was describing the application of European and American psychotherapeutic techniques in the treatment of some of his patients who were still rooted in a tribal culture. At the conclusion of a successful course of treatment, the patient could not feel wholly cured until he had sacrificed a goat to appease the gods responsible for his mental illness. Such a sacrifice is retained by the hospital as an essential part of the person's treatment.

Another way of adjusting to the past is to position past practices in proper perspective to the proposed change. The value of these traditional methods of doing things should be acknowledged. But their value should be related to the way in which they fulfilled the requirements of past situations and circumstances. It should be made clear that the reason why such traditional practices are no longer adequate and must therefore be changed is because the present or future situation and circumstances require new and different practices and methods. Everyone involved should understand that although traditional methods might have been appropriate in the past, they are now no longer appropriate because conditions have changed. Full credit should be granted to the appropriateness and legitimacy of past practices. But the difference in today's conditions must be emphasized. Clearly, no individual or group can be blamed for changes in conditions.

A smooth transition from an established state to a new one can also be facilitated by the deliberate use of ceremony as a lever. Through ceremony, one's loyalty can be focused on the organization as a whole rather than on any particular individual. Also, ceremony helps people think in terms that are broader than their own immediate personal needs and desires.

It is not by chance that ceremonies are an important element in the conduct of affairs of such long-lived institutions as the Church, the State and the universities. In our personal lives, ceremonies are a means for making such major changes as birth, coming of age, completion of education, marriage and death. At these occasions, gathering together relatives and friends and giving gifts and flowers help symbolize friendship and the unity of families. When we become involved in the ritual of the ceremony, we are able to lessen some of our own fears and pains that result moving from one stage of life to another. The heightened emotional atmosphere of such ceremonies help us to prepare for significant changes in our relationships with others.

Furthermore, a ceremony can be regarded as a public statement that, although changes are taking place, fundamental values remain constant. In England a new sovereign is hailed with, "The King is

Minimizing Resistance to Change: Methods

dead; long live the King." In France, it is, "Plus ça change, plus c'est la même chose." In the USA, every new President is inaugurated by swearing to an oath of office.

EXAMPLE

Consider an illustration of how both an adjustment to the past and ceremony were used as levers in introducing a new supervisor into a large restaurant.[55] The old supervisor had developed warm relationships with her subordinates. Therefore, the restaurant manager feared that her departure might affect adversely the morale of the entire organization. He therefore made careful preparations for introducing her successor. First, he discussed the problem of a replacement with both the old supervisor and her assistant, the chef. The chef proposed a candidate for the job. Although this candidate had to be rejected, the reasons were explained to the chef.

Finally, a new supervisor was selected. She was introduced to her subordinates at a general meeting. The manager announced that the old supervisor was leaving. He noted how much she meant to the restaurant, and how she would be missed. The old supervisor then spoke emotionally about her regret at leaving her associates. Next, she introduced the new supervisor. She voiced her warm approval of the new supervisor, and asked her employees to cooperate with the new woman in the same way they had worked with her. The new supervisor then promised to do her best to follow in her predecessor's footsteps.

During the next few days, the new supervisor accompanied the old one, acquainting herself with the employees and with the old supervisor's routine and methods of dealing with people. On the old supervisor's final day at work, the kitchen staff gave her a farewell party.

The new supervisor planned to make certain changes in the operation. Nevertheless, she was careful during her first several weeks to follow the pattern of human relations that her predecessor had established. Soon she was fully accepted by the group. Only then did she begin to introduce changes.

Thus, both the meeting at which the new supervisor was introduced and the farewell party for the old supervisor served as ceremonial functions. These gatherings helped to make the change an accepted fact. They also helped the new supervisor acquire some of the prestige held by her predecessor. In her care to learn the existing routines and the old supervisor's methods of dealing with people, the new supervisor made it clear that she was not rejecting past practices or suggesting any criticism of her predecessor.

A manager may be tempted to be impatient with past practices and traditions, and to be cynical about the use of ceremony. Yet, by rejecting these, two useful levers for reducing resistance to a change are being ignored.

Flexibility and the Tentative Approach

So that the people involved in a change can feel some control over what happens to them, it is often desirable to introduce the change initially as a tentative trial effort. A trial can be defined on the basis either of a specified period of time or of a designated segment of the operating system (e.g. group of people, section, department, facility, etc.). The particular basis chosen should depend on the particular circumstances.

There are several advantages of using the lever of positioning the change as a tentative trial:

- Those involved are able to test their reactions to the new situation before committing themselves irrevocably.
- Those involved are able to acquire more facts on which to base their attitudes and behavior toward the change before it becomes final.
- When those involved have strong preconceptions about the change beforehand, they will be in a better position to regard the change with greater objectivity during the trial. As they gain experience with change during the trial, they will be able to reconsider their preconceptions and perhaps modify some of them.
- Those involved are less likely to regard the change as a threat because they will feel some ability to influence what happens.
- Management are better able to evaluate the method of change and make any necessary modifications before carrying it out more fully.

All these advantages accrue from the opportunity to gain some limited experience of the change while the situation is still fluid and susceptible to further revision or modification.

Thus, introducing a change by positioning it as a tentative trial tends to reduce its threat to those affected. Consequently, their resistance to the change in its final form will often be lessened.

The Scanlon Plan

To illustrate most of the levers available to management for reducing resistance to change, I discuss a strategy based on sharing any gains that result from successful changes aimed at improving operating effectiveness. This strategy has often produced some rather spectacular results for those managements with the courage, wisdom and opportunities to implement this approach. A gainsharing strategy is designed to improve the productivity of an entire organization. The original version is known as the Scanlon plan.[56] It has been gaining acceptance in the past several decades.[57]

The Scanlon plan has been known primarily as a company-wide group incentive plan, based on sharing any gains in productivity. However, its scope and implications have considerably greater breadth. The gainsharing aspects of the Scanlon plan are very important, but they are but the means to an end: that of transforming both the attitudes and the capabilities of the entire organization toward carrying out changes intended to improve operating effectiveness and productivity. Successful applications of the Scanlon plan have resulted in dramatic improvements in labor-management relations, better organizational teamwork and integration, more motivated employees, and an environment where changes are accepted and supported rather than resisted. It is in this last context that the following discussion of the plan is presented.

Briefly, the Scanlon plan consists of two basic elements: a wage formula which provides a group incentive; and a means for ensuring that all employees have an opportunity to participate in improving the effectiveness of operations.

The objective of the wage formula is to permit all employees to share any gains resulting from increased productivity. Because each company develops its own formula, there is no "standard" approach. Typically, however, the wage formula provides that every employee of the organization (with the possible exception of the managing director or chief executive officer) receives a monthly bonus. This is based on month-to-month improvements in total company productivity as compared with a specified "base period." This improvement is usually measured in terms of the ratio of total payroll cost as to the sales value of whatever is produced. The ratio, specific wage formula, and base period for each company (or facility) are developed through union-management negotiations. When there are no unions, other methods for reaching agreement with employees are established. The monthly bonus not only serves as an incentive for better operating effectiveness and higher productivity, but it also provides employees with continuous information about the extent of the plan's success.

Employees' participation in improving operations is achieved through a number of "production committees": one in each department, and a single company-wide committee. The departmental groups meet at regular intervals to discuss and evaluate suggestions submitted from individual employees and groups, and to formulate general plans for improving productivity. Rejected suggestions, or suggestions affecting the plan or company as a whole, are referred to the company-wide (or plant-wide) committee. This group consists of members of top management and the union leadership. They consider suggestions that relate to the company's operation as a whole.

Under the Scanlon plan, what happens to proposals that result in changes? Consider the following examples:

> At the LaPointe Machine Tool Company, their best and most experienced form grinder was enjoying high earnings under the original piecework system. He had no incentive to share his knowledge and skill. After installing a Scanlon plan, this operative reorganized his work, took on two helpers, and taught them his skills and methods of doing the job. He also increased his productivity by about 300 %.[58]

> At a printing plant, management tried to introduce a conveyor system. The engineers had developed the plans without consulting any of the employees. The system failed to work properly from the start, and there was no interest from the employees in making it work.
>
> After instituting a Scanlon plan, management decided to try to introduce a conveyor system again, but to handle its introduction in a different manner. A small-scale model of the proposed layout was constructed and shown to the employees. They were encouraged to make criticisms and suggest improvements. From these comments, the joint production committee made modifications to eliminate problems that the engineers had not anticipated. The new system was installed successfully, and was supported with enthusiasm by the employees. [59]

> Later on, we discovered the reason why one of our grinding departments was continually running low on work. We were not able to compete against other broach[60] companies. This problem was taken up with the workers in the department involved, and the union asked the company to set their prices at a competitive level in order to bring work in. The company was a little reluctant to do so as they showed us some of the large losses which this department had taken. Nevertheless, we still maintained that if the company would go out and get some of this business, we would do all that we could to make it a profitable job.

Minimizing Resistance to Change: Methods

Finally, the company agreed to take another order for these tools and had to bid substantially below our former manufacturing cost. The order was for 1,000 broaches. All workers concerned with this job got together and came forth with their ideas on how the job should be run. Consequently, on the first 100, there was only a slight loss. The remaining 900 were made with a profit of better than 10 %. [61]

One of the pressroom employees pointed out that waste paper was now being crumpled up and thrown in a basket in preparation for salvage. Everyone conceded that, if this paper could be salvaged in flat form, its value would be much higher. Management had been aware of this possible saving but had been unable to enlist the cooperation of the employees in keeping the stock flat. A committe member pointed out the reason for the lack of cooperation: workers felt the foreman was trying to check on them to see how much paper they wasted. Consequently, through various subterfuges they made it impossible for him to police his system. With the suggestion and impetus coming from the employees themselves, however, there was no trouble in getting the waste paper placed in flat form on pallets located at appropriate places in the pressroom.[62]

I [a foreman] was in engineering today and they gave me a blueprint of a job coming into the department about two months from now. There are some tough problems on it. I gave a copy to the operators who will be working on the job and asked them to look it over, suggest methods and tools. You'd be surprised at the number of things they can suggest that you'd probably never think of. Then, when the job comes in, I'm ready for it and so are the operators. Besides, doing it that way lets the operator know he is important. And he is important.[63]

There is a surprising quantity of proposals for increasing efficiency and eliminating waste which has come from the productivity committees. Over 1,000 suggestions have been made so far, and although at the beginning many of the proposals were really disguised complaints, recent months have shown a rise in the proportion of worthwhile ideas. Many of these have been adopted. For example, the line workers in one part of the plant suggested that maintenance holdups would be avoided if the craftsmen did their work during the normal dinner hour. The craftsmen agreed after the management had said that they could take their dinner break at a different time.[64]

Why does a Scanlon plan create a climate of acceptance and support rather than resistance to change?

Minimizing Resistance to Change: Methods

1. There is no compulsion or threat.
2. Employees both suggest and accept changes because they share in the benefits. The opportunity to share any gains lubricates the entire suggestion and change processes. There is an easily understood and direct reward for implementing changes that result in improvements.
3. The adoption of the plan itself and the particular wage formula are arrived at through the process of bargaining.
4. A mutuality of interest is developed and sustained between employees (and their union) and management. The company's continued success is perceived by everyone as the most effective guarantee of their personal security.
5. Because of improvements made in operating effectiveness, the company can compete more successfully in the marketplace. The resulting increases in revenues and organizational growth provide an excellent means for absorbing any potentially redundant and surplus employees.
6. An environment is created and sustained where most employees are highly motivated to expand their knowledge and to increase their skills. Hence, training can be carried on in a climate of enthusiasm and acceptance.
7. Discussion and the sharing of all information relevant to the company's operations and business is an essential element in the success of a Scanlon plan. These discussions are carried on at all levels in the organization.
8. Typically, the timing of change is determined jointly between employees and management.
9. Full participation and involvement in making decisions is another essential element in the success of the plan. The entire operation of the plan is based on such participation. Workable suggestions are rewarded by the monthly bonus. Suggestions are rejected only after careful consideration by a group. Rejections are accompanied by full explanations.
10. A Scanlon plan can work only when managers and supervisors abandon their traditional prerogatives and attitudes. There is no place for the autocratic or authoritarian manager in a system based on free and open criticism, discussion and consultation. Moreover, management must be willing to share all information openly, and discuss and act upon any topics raised by their employees and by the union.

Minimizing Resistance to Change: Methods

Douglas McGregor has summarized effectively the introduction of changes in a company with a Scanlon plan:[65]

> The Scanlon plan is a philosophy of organization. It is not a program in the usual sense; it is a way of life of life – for the management, for the unions, and for every individual employee. Because it is a way of life, it affects virtually every aspect of the operation of the organization. In this fact lies its real significance.
>
> A fair amount of research has pointed up the fact that resistance to change is a reaction primarily to certain methods of instituting change rather than an inherent human characteristic... The Scanlon plan minimizes such resistance because it involves people in the process of creating changes rather than imposing it on them. Improvement management is the Scanlon way of life because everyone is interested in improving the ratio.
>
> Significant examples of worker-generated changes in the organization of work are common in Scanlon plan companies. Ironically, these are frequently changes that management tried unsuccessfully to introduce in pre-Scanlon days. Resistance becomes, instead, active instigation. In fact, the Scanlon plan company experience with the change process is one of the most clear-cut examples of the way in which the research-based predictions of social science are fulfilled in practice.

Summary

Management can minimize resistance to change and often generate support by actively addressing the eight levers described in chapter 6. The key factors for success are management's skill in making use of rewards, bargaining, safeguards or guarantees, discussion and other media for communicating, timing, participation, ceremony and building on the past, and trial periods. For substantial changes, management should apply these key success factors in a planned, integrated approach.

8

Process Skills

> *The productivity of people requires continuous learning, as the Japanese have taught us. It requires adoption in the West of the specific Japanese Zen concept where one learns to do better what one already does well.*
>
> Peter Drucker

In chapter 7, I discussed two levers available to managers that are especially powerful in minimizing resistance to change. One is discussion to develop understanding about a change and its implications. The other is participation to gain employees' involvement in and commitment to the change. In order for both these levers to be used effectively, managers must be competent in applying what is known as process skills. As the terse phrase "process skills" encompasses a rather complex group of concepts about attitudes and behavior, I want in this chapter to describe these in some detail.[66]

Process Skills

"Process" has to do with *how* things are done or the *ways* in which managers interact with each other and with their subordinates. It is different from – but no less important than – "content" and "objectives," which have to do with *what* is being done and *why*. A given objective and the substantive actions required to accomplish it can be dealt with in a variety of ways or processes – some more effective than others.

One approach might cast everyone except the most senior accountable executive in passive, "obedient" roles. Another might encourage broad involvement in a debate (or a series of discussions) on overall approach or strategy and then allow considerable individual latitude with respect to specific detailed tactics. In either case the goal or objective might be the same. The substantive actions taken might even be very similar.

The differences in managerial process, however, could lead to very different outcomes. The first approach might be far more effective in one type of situation, and the second one far more productive in another. The differences in process would manifest themselves in such dimensions as motivation, learning and understanding, conviction and commitment, speed of decision-time, flexibility, success of implementation, and ability to generalize in future situations. Process aspects of decision-making can also affect greatly several of the important nonrational dimensions of cooperation and coordination – things like trust, mutual esteem, tolerance and loyalty.

Process skills rest on a knowledge of how results can be enhanced by careful attention to the ways in which they are pursued. This knowledge in turn grows out of a heightened awareness of what takes place in the realm of attitudes, expectations, feelings, and perceptions when two or more people interact either face-to-face or through written communications. Process skills also encompass the application of certain techniques and the creation and maintenance of certain conditions in the organizational environment that facilitate and support interactions that enable people to air and discuss their disagreements openly and to reach agreements more readily.

Since the mid 1960s, managements in the US and then in the UK and in Western Europe have been demonstrating a steadily increasing interest in developing process skills. Their interest stemmed from a growing need for enhancing their ability to win organizational consent and support for decisions and programs that could no longer be successfully carried out by relying solely on traditional mixtures of authority and expertise.

Why Process Skills are Important

Effective use of process skills contributes in five important ways to overall organizational effectiveness and productivity, especially when changes are being carried out.

Process Skills

First, the effectiveness and productivity of an entire organizational system depend to a large degree on every relevant employee understanding what is to be done, and why it is to be done this way rather than that. To build this kind of understanding requires skills of the kind that make it easier for one to confess a lack of understanding, to introduce alternatives, to challenge and debate rival propositions, to get past parochial barriers, and to uncover obstacles and opportunities before plans have jelled. This point is especially relevant to managing any change when the development of understanding and discussion of alternative options in carrying out a particular change is a key lever in achieving successful outcomes.

Second, process skills can improve the quality of solutions to problems, particularly those calling for innovative ideas. It takes a carefully nurtured climate to draw out people's ideas (particularly specialists with varying backgrounds, skills and viewpoints) and to alter and combine their contributions. Discussion must be open, mistakes must be permissible, and ego defenses must be relaxed.

Third, process skills can help elicit comments which lead to early identification of emerging problems before such problems become severe and complex. Thus, pitfalls can be avoided when embarking on a new course of action (especially in cases of change), and provision can be made in advance to deal with a wider range of possible eventualities.

Fourth, managers, supervisors and other employees who participate in the solution of problems and the formulation of how to implement these solutions are more likely to feel "ownership" and responsibility for ensuring that these solutions work. Because of their direct involvement in the process, these managers, supervisors and other employees are likely to feel more strongly motivated and committed to ensuring successful implementation than they would be if they were passive recipients of some directives. The intensity of anyone's personal motivation and commitment to accomplishing an objective and implementing a course of action when carrying out a change, is often the single most imortant determinant of how many of the potential benefits from that course of action are achieved. The use of process skills can thus be of central importance to the successful outcome of management's decisions when they are making changes.

Fifth, process skills can help managers and supervisors to resolve major differences of opinion. When they are able to make explicit their concerns (including personal and parochial ones), these concerns can be more easily accorded their proper weight than if they remain latent and unexamined. Thus, the way can be cleared for more objective discussions of issues on their merits. Consensus, rather than compulsion and compliance, can then be made the basis of planning and subsequent implementation of changes.

Key Aspects of Process Skills

Clues and Responses

When managers, supervisors and other employees come together for business purposes each brings with him or her certain expectations, preconceptions, attitudes, feelings and personal history. These elements combine in complicated ways to form motivation, the outward manifestation of which is behavior. Often only the overt behavior is observed, and clues regarding motivation and its foundation are overlooked. Typical clues are tone and loudness of voice, facial expressions, hesitation, signs of discomfort, argumentativeness, silences, passivity, aggressiveness, etc. When such clues are ignored, what appears to be a purely rational discussion ensues, in which resistance increasingly comes to be seen as obtuseness or stubborness. In fact, this resistance may derive from other factors.

By paying greater attention to the behavioral clues they pick up in their interactions with one another (and with other members of their organization with whom they interact), and by acting on these clues to encourage more open discussions, managers and supervisors may overcome obstacles to the unity of vision, purpose and action they wish to achieve. Otherwise they must fall back on invoking sheer power or charisma to carry people with them, or suffer half-hearted support from dutiful but unreconciled colleagues.

To act on a suspected clue, a manager or supervisor can test his or her suspicion by inviting the other person to make explicit her or his attitudes, perceptions and feelings and to explain why, with respect to the subject matter at hand. The manager or supervisor taking the initiative can facilitate this process by sharing with the other individual his or her own attitudes, perceptions and feelings so that these are also known.

Involvement and Participation

The development of process skills is especially critical to the success of participation. The object of participation is in some way to involve managers, supervisors and other employees in planning, initiating and implementing decisions (especially those having to do with changes), rather than being passive recipients of their effects. To the extent that managers, supervisors and employees feel they have had a part in developing a plan or program, in making a decision, or in carrying it out, they will support actively that decision, program or change. Because they contributed to its formulation, they feel some ownership and are thus committed to making it successful. Participation does not mean communal rule. It does not mean abdication by the executive, manager or supervisor, nor does it require concessions as proof of good faith.

Participation is a way to mobilize intelligence and illuminate choices. This is accomplished by soliciting comments, suggestions and data, and by making clear one's assumptions, needs, constraints and criteria. The top manager asks and listens and gives serious consideration to what s/he hears but is under no obligation to accept any of the ideas offered.

The extent of participation can vary, according to both the needs of the executive, manager or supervisor, and the situation. At its most superficial level, participation consists of individual or group consultation. After describing her or his proposals and intentions, the executive, manager or supervisor then invites those involved in the discussion to voice their comments and feelings, and encourages them to make suggestions as to course of action and method of approach. In consultation, there is an implicit understanding that the executive, manager or supervisor is under no obligation to accept any of the ideas offered, so long as they are given serious consideration. If, however, over a period of time all or even most suggestions are rejected, consultation will be regarded as a pretense and a fraud.

At a deeper level, participation includes some involvement in actual decision-making. Not only does the executive, manager or supervisor elicit suggestions, but s/he also encourages those involved to share, to an explicitly defined extent, in making decisions related to the issue at hand.

For a participative managerial process to succeed, the executive, manager or supervisor must feel secure in her or his position and role. If deep down s/he believes that asking for advice or opinions from subordinates is a sign of weakness, or that their involvement in making decisions endangers her or his power and status as a manager, any efforts to encourage participation will most likely be perceived before long as fraudulent. Some managers try to have it both ways by offering subordinates "a sense of" participation, when in fact their minds are already made up. If an executive, manager or supervisor is convinced from the outset that his or her ideas are the best and only way to deal with an issue, s/he would be wise not to attempt the involvment of others in a pseudo-participative effort.

The successful participative executive, manager or supervisor takes pride in the way s/he leads and orchestrates, not in always being the wisest or quickest on the team. S/he does not feel diminished when s/he openly gives credit and recognition to all contributions of merit made by others to the organization's decisions. S/he sees unsound contributions as opportunities to clarify rationales and clear up misapprehensions.

Deriving the maximum benefits from participation requires mastering the art of preparing the menu of participation, since the alternative is wide-open, *carte blanche* anarchy. It means posing issues and problems in ways that make it easier for others to contribute their special knowledge and skills. It means listening and asking. It means conceiving of leadership not in terms of generating brilliant ideas and exercising authority, but rather in terms of developing and focusing motivation, energy, consent, commitment and synergy.

Creating and Maintaining a Supportive Atmosphere

Process skills do not flourish out of a simple desire to exercise them. They require a favorable environment. In part this environment can be created and sustained by the members of a participating group. But it must also be established by management. The general organizational environment that is conducive to the exercise of process skills has five characteristics. First, management must be sincere when they invite participation. Simple tests of this sincerity are the availability of time, the significance of the issues involved, the treatment of dissent, the sharing of relevant information, and the response to suggestions.

Second, the context and need for participation must be clearly and widely perceived. Organizational goals and needs for innovative solutions, fresh approaches, resolution of differences and the like must be clearly articulated and understood. Otherwise, "participation" itself may seem to be the goal, when in fact it is the means.

Third, participation must be accorded a high priority and value in the organization. Participation must be seen generally as a part of the management development process of the organization, for testing and challenging younger managers and supervisors and broadening their awareness of the implication of business decisions.

Fourth, specific attention to the development and refinement of

Process Skills

process skills is needed to raise them above the level of intuition, good intention and self-indulgence. (How this might be accomplished is discussed in the following section.) When individual managers and supervisors are selected to work together in working parties or task groups, they should be carefully chosen. Certain personal characteristics are more suitable to the development of competence in using process skills than are others, for example:

- An open, questioning mind and a willingness to learn.
- Interest and competence with respect to the subject matter to be addressed.
- Ability to voice opinions and concerns in the presence of others with higher organizational status.
- Ability to enter into a vigorous exchange of ideas with good parliamentary manners and not too much ego-involvement.
- Sensitivity to and willingness to express personal feelings and concerns.

Fifth, the most important aspect of the organizational environment with respect to its nurturing of process skills, is the managerial style characteristic of the organization as a whole. There is a spectrum of possible managerial styles ranging from authoritarian to adaptive.

An *authoritarian* style of management has the following characteristics:

- The hierarchy is well designed, ordered and understood.
- Responsibilities and resources are subdivided. There is no overlapping. Responsibilities and resources are assigned to subordinates in accordance with the delegation to them of only limited authority.
- Conflict and uncertainties are resolved by appeal to higher level.
- Status is determined by rank in the hierarchy.
- Communication takes place almost entirely between peers responsible to the same supervisor or between a supervisor and her or his subordinates.

The *adaptive* style of management has the following characteristics:

- There is a diffusion throughout the organization of understanding of objectives and a feeling of responsibility for striving toward the achievement of these objectives; thus, local decisions are consistent with the dominating scheme of goals, missions and values. This diffusion must be continuous and dynamic.

Process Skills

- Decisions can be made anywhere in the organization and are based both on the nature of what is to be decided, and on the experience, knowledge and ability of the people involved.
- The locus of decision-making depends on the subject matter.
- The concerted implementation of decisions is a result of consensus among those involved and affected.
- Status and authority are ambiguous, often based in part on personal competence.
- Responsibilities tend to overlap.
- Control and communications flow through a multiply-connected network, instead of a well-ordered hierarchy or channels.

The more the managerial style in an organization tends toward the adaptive end of the spectrum, the greater will be the encouragement within that organization of creative and collaborative activity. The adaptive approach is especially appropriate to changing conditions in an organization's external environment which tend to give rise continuously to fresh problems and unforeseen requirements. If adaptive "cells" are established within an essentially authoritarian organization, careful attention must be given to the interfaces between these cells and the rest of the organization if the cells are to function effectively.

When managers or even managers and employees sit together to define or resolve an issue, their successful collaboration will depend on their meeting the following requirements:

- The problems addressed by the group must appear (and be) real to everyone involved; i.e. they must be relevant, timely and in everyone's best interests to solve.
- Primary orientation should be toward the task or goal, not to particular jurisdictions.
- The leadership of the group should be regarded as a *service* that supports it; leadership is a function to be performed in any given situation by the person best qualified at that time. Thus, leadership could change with the needs of the circumstances.
- There must not be too much pressure for closure before different viewpoints can emerge and be explored and tested.
- There should be a tolerance for unusual or deviant behavior and differing personal styles within the group, as well as for the challenging of "sacred cows" and traditions.
- Group members should cultivate ways of looking at the familiar and the "obvious" as though it were strange and new.
- Group members should be willing and able to share tentative, half-formed thoughts, the precursors of ideas, and to accept the help of the group in building on them.

Process Skills

- The group's members must be willing to deal openly with such interpersonal feelings as hostility, petulance, anger, affection and trust as may emerge in the course of their work.
- There must be a shared belief in the legitimacy of collaborative behavior itself so that this is not regarded as a sign of weakness.
- There should be considerable sensitivity to clues identifying where problems really lie.
- Communication channels between the group and its ultimate sponsor should encourage a two-way flow of information, attitudes and opinions.

Ways to Begin the Development of Process Skills

Once it is agreed that it is desirable to enhance and extend the use of managerial process skills, what are some ways of beginning this process? It is not easy to go forth determined to be aware and sensitive and receptive, feeling collaborative and looking for participation. One had to be able to link up to some situations and mechanisms and occasions designed to evoke and exercise these skills. One must test his or her skills and get some feedback on how s/he did and what were the effects.

Existing situations and mechanisms can be used by setting aside some time during and at the end of meetings (formal and otherwise) to focus directly on questions of process. Those present can question one another to probe the perceptions, attitudes, feelings and reactions involved.

For example, in the course of a meeting did A really feel that he was being heard? Did B get cut off before she could make her point? Did C "drop out" because she felt sure she would be ridiculed or ignored? Did D feel he was being pressured into agreeing with something he really didn't believe in? Was E allowed to "walk the plank" by those he was counting on for support? And so on.

In two-person encounters, other questions can be used to test process effectiveness: How do you really feel about this? Did you feel I was crowding you? Is what we "agreed" on really credible? What help do you/I/we need? And so on.

To help make use of regular occasions to practice process skills, an organization might consider selecting and developing a few managers or staff "professionals" who seem to have special aptitudes in this direction. The observational and consultative skills of such people can be fairly rapidly enhanced by a relatively small investment in specialized training – typically of two or three weeks' duration.

Another approach might be to select a specimen but real problem that requires inputs from more than one operating unit and the central group. Such a problem might be addressed with a deliberate intent to apply process skills, both as a learning experience for the organization as a whole, and as a demonstration of what might be accomplished with such an approach. An outsider to the organization with professional competence in the use of process skills (either an internal or an external consultant) might be engaged to assist the participants in this exercise enhance and apply their process skills. This would enable a nucleus of process competence to be established within the organization for further development when such outside assistance will no longer be available.

Once a few staff members and/or managers have acquired these skills, the organization can use them as process observers and commentators in key situations. Until such a specialist cadre is available, an organization could consider the occasional use of outsiders skilled in matters of process to observe and comment on critical meetings at various levels.

The application of process skills must not be regarded as an esoteric art or mysterious cult. The heart of the matter is to consider one's impact on others – asking about it if need be – and to help and be helped in the search for more options and more innovative solutions, and in the resolution of differences.

Summary

The effective use of process skills is key to the successful use of the levers of discussion and participation in minimizing resistance to changes. Process skills have to do with the dynamics and quality of interaction among members of management and between managers, supervisors and employees. The cultivation and development of effective process skills depend on having a supportive atmosphere in the organization, on personal willingness to take risks in trying new modes of interpersonal behavior, and on personal sensitivity to the behavioral clues offered by others. As with any skill, process skills can be learned and developed through persistent application and practice, with helpful feedback from outside experts.

9

Differences in the Perception of Change

The owner of the axe, as he released his hold on it, said that it was the apple of his eye; but I returned it sharper than I received it.

Henry David Thoreau

A foolish consistency is the hobgoblin of little minds, adored by little statesmen, philosophers and divines.

Ralph Waldo Emerson

I have been discussing changes as they affect two different groups of people: those concerned primarily with introducing and implementing them, and those affected by their consequences. Earlier, I pointed out that in any group affected there will inevitably be a wide range of perceptions of and reactions to the change.

Likewise, there are differences in how a change is perceived by those responsible for its introduction and implementation. Not only do these differences stem from such individual factors as personality and experience, but they also result from the particular organizational role taken by the person in the changing situation. This role often has a considerable influence both on the way s/he perceives the change and on her or his subsequent behavior. The nature of each role is determined by forces that derive from the organizational structure and its context.

Of all those responsible for accomplishing changes, there are at least four distinct and different roles: the originator of the change, the manager responsible and accountable for its ultimate success or failure, the supervisors directly concerned with the immediate problems of implementation, and the staff specialists available to give advice based on their expert knowledge. An examination of these roles in some detail should illuminate how and why each one influences the viewpoint of its incumbent.

Clearly, it would be fallacious to assume that every supervisor involved in a change will perceive it identically, or that all staff specialists will have a similar bias in the way they view changes. Yet, each of these roles tends to foster a certain characteristic frame of reference which often affects how its incumbents perceive and approach any change. It is as if certain biases, constraints and filters distort the way in which the incumbents of each role view what is happening in any change. On the one hand, these biases and filters prevent them from seeing changes objectively. On the other hand, each role has characteristics that often help its incumbents view certain aspects of a change with unusual clarity.

Whether the role be that of change originator, manager, supervisor or staff specialist, each has its own unique characteristics. These can both distort and clarify the way in which different aspects of changes are perceived. I want now to examine more closely each of these roles and their characteristics.

The Originator of the Change

The originator of any change is the person with the initial ideas. S/he is the one who sees the need for a change, defines that need, and devises what s/he believes is the solution to satisfy that need. The originator can be an executive, a manager, a supervisor, a staff specialist or another employee.

Originating a change, like originating any other idea, is a creative act. Creative thought involves a complex fusion of rational and emotional elements. We know little as yet about the mechanisms that underlie creative thinking. We do know, however, that it is often difficult for the originator of an idea to evaluate it objectively.

Like a proud parent, the originator of an idea has a deep emotional attachment to his or her offspring. S/he tends to amplify its virtues. S/he tends to deny or rationalize its faults and limitations. S/he has a deep and compelling interest in the implementation of his or her idea. S/he tends to visualize only success, not failure. S/he identifies strongly with the idea. Its success is his or her success. Its failure is her or his

Differences in the Perception of Change

failure. Any criticism of the idea, whether direct or implied, is often regarded as personal criticism.

It is unreasonable to expect the originator of a change to be dispassionate, objective and detached from the process of that change. S/he can see its beneficial results with great clarity, and may be unduly optimistic about the magnitude of those benefits. On the other hand, s/he may underestimate or not wish to face up to the difficulties and problems which must be solved before these benefits can be realized.

It is natural for the originator of a change to want a deep personal involvement in its institution and implementation. S/he is highly motivated to ensure that success is achieved. His or her enthusiasm and optimism might prove encouraging and stimulating to those directly responsible for making the change a success. This same optimism and enthusiasm, however, might also cause the originator to become impatient and irritable when faced with any obstacles and difficulties that may hinder the progress of the change.

When the originator of a change is involved in its implementation, s/he wants success to be on his or her terms. It is the originator's approach and the orginator's method that must be used. S/he would probably regard any suggestion or adoption of alternative means or modification to the preferred method as an implied criticism of both his or her idea and person. S/he would also tend to feel that any such alternatives would mean a weakening of his or her approach. Such alternatives would therefore be rejected as undesirable. As a consequence, s/he would probably resist any attempts to "dilute" the original plan.

The kind of behavior described above is not based on an objective evaluation and logical analysis of what is happening. Instead, it is often quite irrational because it is based on an emotional involvement and identification with one particular course of action.

There are two ways in which the originator of a change makes a significant contribution. First, s/he identifies the problem and the need to change. Second, the proposed solution often points the direction in which action should be taken. But the particular detailed solution or method proposed to achieve the objectives need not necessarily be followed literally. Certain modifications or alterations may become essential because of subsequent events. Yet, in the originator's mind, the objectives of the change are often inextricably bound up with one particular detailed method of accomplishment. It is difficult for any originator to distinguish between the two.

Herein lies a source of difficulty, especially when the originator of a change is also involved in its institution or implementation. Unlike other members of management, supervision or staff service groups, the originator is often deeply committed to one particular course of action. When the realities of the situation make it desirable or necessary to alter this course, even though the objectives remain unchanged, the originator can become highly resistant to change.

Remember that the role of an originator of change is not a distinct organizational function. There is no such position as "change originator." Instead, anyone who originates a change is at the same time filling another organizational role: usually that of manager, supervisor or staff specialist. Sometimes, the originator of a change is an operative or a clerk.

How much influence the originator's personal involvement and bias has on the way his or her ideas are implemented will depend on what formal position in the organization s/he occupies. The originator's opportunity to influence the process of change will be the greatest when s/he is also the manager accountable for its success. His or her influence will be less when s/he is a supervisor, and less still when the position is a staff specialist. Those at operative level will have the least influence.

Yet, no matter what the formal organizational position, the originator's direct involvement in the implementation of his or her ideas can create problems that can affect adversely the success of the change. This does not apply if the originator can implement the change directly without involving anyone else (e.g. an operative who devises a more effective routine in doing his or her job). But when implementing a change depends on other people for its success, the most effective role for its originator is usually that of an advisor with no direct control over events. As an adviser, s/he can continue contributing ideas while the evaluation of what happens and the taking of decisions are in the hands of those with greater objectivity about the situation.

The Manager

The manager is responsible for instituting and implementing a change, and accountable for its ultimate success or failure. In discussing this role, I assume at first that the manager is not the originator of the change, but rather is carrying out someone else's idea.

When changes must be accomplished within an organization, those with formal management responsibility are the ones who typically

Differences in the Perception of Change

both introduce and implement them. They are directly responsible and accountable for the workforce, and are in the best position to influence their attitudes and behavior. Managers are expected to be in direct control of organizing and accomplishing the work to be done. Only they can make the necessary decisions on which depend the successful achievement of any change. Making changes effectively can be regarded as the most important function of any manager's job.

What are the forces that influences a manager's thoughts and behavior in a changing situation? Unlike the originator of the change, whose first and foremost concern is that his or her ideas are successful, the manager's outlook typically is complicated by several, often conflicting interests. Because s/he does not have the orginator's emotional involvement with the change, s/he is often able to view it more objectively. Managers tend to see problems and difficulties as well as benefits. Their estimate of these benefits may be more conservative than the expectations of the originator.

Managers may have certain doubts or reservations about either or both the objectives of the change and the proposed methods of their accomplishment. These doubts may stem from their more objective evaluation of the situation, or from their greater awareness of the problems and risks involved.

In addition, managers might be influenced by political considerations. They might be fearful about how they could be affected by the change (particularly in regard to status), or they might be concerned about the consequences of failure to achieve anticipated benefits. They might also be highly aware of how their handling of the change might affect their careers.

Also, managers might often be deeply concerned about the effects of the change on the operations for which they are responsible, and most particularly on subordinates. Managers' anticipations of the attitudes and reactions of subordinates would probably have a significant influence on their own attitudes and reactions. Their anticipations would, however, depend on the effectiveness of their communications and interactions with subordinates. If, for example, a manager anticipated that a particular change would be resisted strongly and would threaten the morale of his or her workforce, s/he would be inclined to seek alternative means for accomplishing the desired objectives. If s/he were sufficiently concerned, s/he might even attempt to modify the objectives themselves.

The net effect of all this is that the manager will probably develop an attitude toward the change and its expected benefits that will be markedly different from that of its originator. Managers tend to be more skeptical and questioning about changes and their objectives. Their expectations of any potential benefits will probably be more modest. Finally, they will tend to be more willing to compromise in altering the methods employed for achieving the change, and even in modifying its objectives.

Very few of these characteristics, however, would apply if the manager were also the originator of the change. When this is the case, the manager's thoughts and behavior will tend to be influenced predominantly by those characteristics previously attributed to the originator.

There is another important point relevant to the manager's role. Because any manager's authority and status in the organization is substantial, s/he is in a strong position, while the change is still in the form of a proposal, to influence both its objectives and its method of accomplishment. If s/he has reservations about either of these, the manager has a responsibility to discuss any objections and recommendations both with superiors and with the originator of the change. If s/he believes his or her position is well justified, the manager has a responsibility to do his or her utmost to modify either or both the objectives and the method of accomplishment.

When a manager is in the position of having to institute and implement a change about which s/he has strong doubts and questions, to a considerable extent s/he has only him or herself to blame for being in such a predicament. Such a situation would occur either because s/he failed to try altering the course of events, or because s/he was ineffective in doing so. In practice, such failures often result when the manager decides it would be politically unwise or inexpedient to "make an issue" of the matter. The consequence of such a politically inspired decision is a manager who is left "holding the bag." This "bag" is the requirement to accomplish a change about which s/he may have little conviction and many doubts. Such a conflict can have only adverse effects both on the success of the change and on the manager's future career.

A manager has two important goals with respect to any change. First, s/he must do all s/he can before the change is introduced to ensure that its conception is sound. This means that its goals must be well founded, that the expectations of potential benefits are realistic, and that the proposed method of accomplishment is practical. A wise manager will try to ensure that the method of accomplishing the change remains open and not fixed. S/he would allow for a maximum of flexibility and the freedom to modify or alter the method should this be made necessary by subsequent events.

Differences in the Perception of Change

The manager is well situated to accomplish this first goal, because compared with everyone else involved, s/he is often in the best position to assess the situation and to evaluate matters objectively. How effective s/he can be in accomplishing this first goal depends on the manager's abilities, especially judgment and the soundness of relationships with peers and superiors.

The manager's second goal is to introduce and implement the change effectively, and to achieve optimum results. In this, success again depends heavily on judgment and the quality of relationships. In chapter 11, I discuss in detail those managerial abilities particularly relevant to the successful accomplishment of changes.

The Supervisor

The characteristics of the supervisor's role[67] are not unlike those of the role of managers, but they differ somewhat in several significant respects. Like managers, supervisors are responsible and accountable for instituting and implementing changes. But their areas of responsibility and accountability are more circumscribed than those of managers. When the scope of a change is broad, the supervisor may be concerned only with certain particular aspects. On the other hand, if the change is more limited (e.g. a change in the method of work affecting only a single operation), the supervisor's role may be almost identical to that of the manager.

Another point of difference is that, unlike the manager, the supervisor can often escape much of the blame should a broad scope change be a failure. Although the manager is ultimately accountable for success or failure, it is the supervisor who operates in the front lines. It is s/he who must cope directly with the reactions of the workforce. Although the supervisor can be blamed in part for any failure to achieve the desired objectives, s/he can escape this burden by shifting the blame, in turn, on any resistant behavior by employees. It is often difficult for managers to determine how much any resistance is a consequence of the change itself, and how much it is a result of supervisors' ineptitude. Thus, supervisors can easily mask any personal failure behind such a screen of uncertainty.

Furthermore, a supervisor is likely to be less objective than his or her manager about a change. Because of proximity to both the operations and workers, supervisors cannot escape being influenced strongly by

Differences in the Perception of Change

concerns about the effects of the change on both. Any problems and difficulties which they might anticipate would probably loom larger to them than to managers. Also, supervisors are often limited in the information they receive and are too remote from whatever benefits might result from a change to be impressed with their desirability and importance. Particularly in changes of broad scope, supervisors would probably be more concerned about the problems and difficulties than they would be impressed with any potentially beneficial results.

Such disproportionate concern with the problems associated with a change is likely to distort the way any supervisor regards that change, and often the way s/he reacts to it. Supervisors often are less committed to the successful accomplishment of a change than are managers. Supervisors' expectations are often much more modest than those of managers.

There is yet another point of difference between the roles of supervisor and manager. In any organization, supervisors' status and freedom to act are at relatively low levels. Consequently, they are not in a strong position, while the change remains a proposal, to influence either its objectives or its method of accomplishment.

Certainly, if supervisors have well-founded reservations and recommendations about a change, it is their responsibility to discuss these with their managers. But even if they have the courage to do so, their comments would probably be somewhat discounted because their bias would be recognized and their judgment would be more open to question. However, during implementation of a change, supervisors' objections and recommendations would tend to be taken more seriously because their comments would then be regarded as based on direct experience and facts rather than on apprehensions, predictions and conjecture.

Because supervisors' status is relatively low and because they often feel more insecure than managers in their position, political considerations are frequently a strong influence on supervisory judgment and behavior. For example, they would be less inclined than managers to differ with superiors. Consequently, supervisors are often in the position of having to implement a change about which they have more doubts than confidence.

As a consequence of all the foregoing, supervisors' motivation to achieve optimum results from a change is often considerably less than that of managers, and much less than that of the originator of the change. Of all members of management, supervisors have the greatest predisposition toward compromise and expediency.[68]

Differences in the Perception of Change

The Staff Specialist

One might expect that of all four roles involved in a change, that of staff specialist would enable its incumbents to be the most objective about that change. After all, they have no direct responsibility for results. They are there to give advice based on expert knowledge. Whether or not and how this advice is used is the manager's responsibility. We should expect the staff specialist to view and approach a change with almost Olympian detachment.

Yet in fact, staff specialists often resemble change originators in their lack of objectivity. There are several reasons for this.

Because specialists have expert knowledge about a particular subject (e.g. management information, work study, accounting, the engineering disciplines, quality, organization and methods, human resources, etc.), they often become originators of ideas about how the change should be carried out. These ideas inevitably lead to suggested changes in approach and method. Staff specialists, therefore, are like change originators: either for an entire change, or for particular aspects. Their role is to analyze the situation, identify problems, think creatively and propose solutions. Once they begin offering advice and suggestions, all the characteristics that I formerly attributed to change originators also apply to staff specialists: emotional involvement with and attachment to their ideas; underestimation of any problems and difficulties; and inflexibility about subsequent attempts to modify their suggestions.

Also, specialists are often blind to the social and psychological implications of any change as a whole. It is often difficult for them to conceive or to be aware of the problems that might be imposed by the change on the people involved. They can become so engrossed in the technology of the change (in its many dimensions) that they are oblivious to the things troubling those affected. This problem is intensified when the staff specialist is the originator of major elements of the change. Consider two illustrations of what can happen.[69]

> In one situation the staff people introduced, with the best of intentions, a technological change which inadvertently deprived a number of skilled operators of much of the satisfaction that they were finding in their work. Among other things, the change meant that, whereas formerly the output of each operator had been placed beside his work position where it could be viewed and appreciated by him and by others, it was now being carried away immediately from the work position. The workmen did not like this.

Differences in the Perception of Change

The sad part of it was that there was no compelling cost or technical reason why the output could not be placed beside the work position as it had been formerly. But the staff people who had introduced the change were so literal-minded about their ideas that when they heard complaints on the changes from the operators they could not comprehend what the trouble was. Instead, they began repeating all the logical arguments why the change made sense from a cost standpoint. The final result here was a chronic restriction of output and persistent hostility on the part of the operators.

An industrial engineer undertook to introduce some methods changes in one department with the notion firmly in mind that this assignment presented him with an opportunity to "prove" to higher management the value of his function. He became so preoccupied with his personal desire to make a name for his particular techniques that he failed to pay any attention to some fairly obvious and practical considerations which the operating people were calling to his attention but which did not show up in his time-study techniques. As could be expected, resistance quickly developed to all his ideas, and the only "name" that he finally won for his techniques was a black one.

Specialists often believe that the technical aspects of a change should be the sole or primary determinant for its acceptability. Their view is that, after all, these technical aspects are based on facts and can be analyzed and evaluated objectively. This is, in effect, the job of specialists. It is often difficult for them to understand and to accept the idea that the psychological and social effects of the change are what, in most cases, determine the extent of resistance. For specialists to think in these terms is typically alien to their outlook. They would consider these psychological and social effects to be essentially irrational because they cannot be identified and measured with precision.

Another problem of staff specialists' viewpoint is their inclination to underestimate the contribution that can be made by supervision, as well as by operatives, to improving both the method of the change and possibly even its objectives. It is often difficult for staff specialists to recognize that supervisors and operatives are really specialists in their own right, in their experience with operating problems. Because of their more sophisticated appreciation of the technology of an operation, specialists can often overlook or underestimate the value of the detailed, practical knowledge that these less well-educated men and women possess.

In actuality, anyone with continuous, firsthand experience of operations can assist staff specialists (as well as managers) in two ways. They can often identify practical difficulties or problems with the specialists' ideas, and help to correct these difficulties before they become major

Differences in the Perception of Change

issues. Also, supervisors and operatives can draw upon their knowledge of the existing social arrangements in the work situation, and point out those elements of the change which might adversely affect these relationships. Thus, they can help to develop improved approaches for accomplishing the change, so that any disruption of the social arrangements will be minimized, thereby increasing the probability of acceptance.

A further problem with many specialists is that they often fail to appreciate the complexities and problems that prevent the rapid accomplishment of changes. Because their position is often somewhat removed from operations, and because their interactions and therefore the amount of information they receive are constrained, they are frequently ignorant of and oblivious to the amount of time that must be taken by those involved to adjust to the change and reach solutions to any problems created. Time is also necessary for learning new skills and for absorbing new knowledge. In addition, time is needed to work out any technical difficulties that were not foreseen. Because of their familiarity with the technology of the change, specialists often find it difficult to appreciate why others cannot understand it as readily as they do, and speedily adapt themselves to the new conditions.

When a specialist becomes impatient with the timing of a change, there can be friction with managers, supervisors and operatives. They may feel that the specialist is putting pressure on them. The result can be feelings of frustration, antagonism and increased resistance.

Still another problem common to many staff specialists is their difficulty in communicating with those directly involved in the change. Specialists with this problem may adopt one of two approaches in their communications. On the one hand, they might assume that the bases for their ideas and suggestions are so subtle and complicated that it would be futile to attempt their explanation to others, particularly if their education and experience were significantly different. On the basis of this premise, they would tend to oversimply any explanations and "talk down" to members of management and to operatives. On the other hand, they might try to impress them with their brilliance by dazzling them with a highly technical explanation, replete with complex mathematical formulas and data, and technical jargon.

Either approach creates problems. Those who might receive the oversimplified explanation could regard this as an insult to their intelligence, and become infuriated. Those who might be given the full "scientific" treatment could become confused and frustrated because they were not able to follow the argument. They, too, could become infuriated.

Differences in the Perception of Change

The ability to translate complicated technical material into terms that are readily understandable by laymen is a special skill which few staff specialists possess. The specialist who can do this effectively has patience and understands the frame of reference of his or her audience.

Sometime, staff specialists have additional problems. When they become involved in a change, they expect that everyone concerned will resist it blindly. This assumption makes no allowance for any individual differences in attitudes and reactions. When specialists base their dealings with people on this assumption, they often provoke the very reaction they expect. When people are treated as if they were intractably stubborn, their ire can be aroused to the extent that they conform to this self-fulfilling expectation.

Can managers do anything to broaden the perspective of staff specialists so that they can contribute more effectively to the realization of a change? Certainly, there are no simple and quick solutions to the problems I have described. Many of these difficulties are a consequence of the narrowly focused and circumscribed nature of specialists' education, training, experience and interactions. Adding to these difficulties can be those elements of personality which caused them to become attracted to specialist careers in the first place.

Yet, in time, managers can help specialists to broaden their outlook. Managers can ensure that specialists' relevant interactions with respect to a change are broadened and intensified so that they gain a balanced understanding of the entire problem. If specialists become over-involved in a particular change, the manager might encourage them to develop an interest in one or more other projects. Thus, their energies and attention could be diffused rather than concentrated. By individual "coaching" and through personal example a manager could encourage specialists to become more conscious and appreciative of the contributions and assistance that they might gain from operating personnel. Once a specialist is able to experience directly such help from operatives and foremen, conversion is more likely.

Furthermore, it is desirable that specialists develop an understanding of and an appreciation for those factors which motivate people at work. Specialists should learn that those satisfactions which they themselves derive from being creative and productive are the same satisfactions which most people want to enjoy. Yet, most employees' opportunity to achieve these satisfactions from their work is controlled, in part, by how specialists behave toward them. Specialists can come to realize that there is great satisfaction in helping and encouraging others to enjoy the pleasure of being creative. They can also be helped to realize that there can be a great personal challenge and

Differences in the Perception of Change

reward in winning the acceptance of their ideas. Both this challenge and reward can come through achieving a better understanding of and more productive relationships with others. Accomplishing these can yield satisfactions comparable to those resulting from generating new ideas.

Unifying Management's Approach

From the foregoing discussions, it should be evident that there are substantial differences in the characteristic attitudes and behavior associated with the roles of the key players (the originator, manager, supervisor and staff specialist) when any change is introduced and implemented. These dissimilarities often cause the incumbents of these roles to have significantly different perceptions, expectations and personal stakes in a change and its possible outcomes. The greater and more persistent these differences, the more difficulty management will have minimizing resistance and achieving the full potential benefits from that change.

It is imperative, therefore, that management's approach to any change be unified. This means that all the key players must work together to achieve a shared view about the change – its objectives, its potential benefits and threats, its priority, and what is required to introduce and institutionalize the change successfully. This unified view and expectations must be achieved before taking any steps toward instituting the change.

The responsibility and leadership for ensuring a unified approach to a change rest with the manager responsible and accountable for its implementation. Of all four roles involved, the manager is likely to be the most objective and rational (unless s/he is also the change's originator). This objectivity should help the manager take a more balanced and realistic view of the change and its implications. An effective way to achieve unity among the four roles is for the manager to meet with the change's originator, and all the supervisors and staff specialists expected to be involved in carrying out the change. In this meeting, the manager's objective is to achieve, through discussion, consensus among the group in the answers to the following questions:

1 What are we trying to accomplish with this change? Immediately? Longer term?
2 What gains are we expecting and when?

Differences in the Perception of Change

3 What threats might this change present to those affected?
4 How important is this change relative to everything else going on?
5 What approach or method are we planning to use in making the change? What alternative approaches might be considered?
6 How are those affected likely to react to the change and why?
7 What is it going to take to carry out this change successfully? What does this require of each of the key players?

The greater the agreement among the manager, supervisors and staff specialists in the answers to these questions, the better prepared and strongly positioned they will be to institute the change successfully.

For example, should supervisors' concerns about the practicability of the method taken to institute a change remain unanswered, they are unlikely to be persuasive in dealing with any employee resistance. Also, when the sense of urgency about making the change varies widely among the key players, the priority each of them assigns to working on the change will differ, thus weakening their collective ability to solve the problems that inevitably arise as the change is instituted. When staff specialists are permitted to retain their narrow, biased perspectives regarding the change, the effectiveness of their contributions will be undermined. When those affected by a change perceive significant differences in attitudes and approach among managers, supervisors and specialists, their questions and concerns are more likely to be exacerbated than resolved. Any resulting resistance is likely to be more effective in the face of a management group in disarray.

Summary

By now, it should be clear that each of the four organizational roles present any changing situation has associated with it particular characteristic views and attitudes. These tend to distort and to color the judgments made by the incumbents of each role. When an originator, a manager, supervisors and staff specialists become involved in a change, the expectations and way of looking at and thinking about that change will differ for each role. These viewpoints can be quite different from one another.

The originator will tend to see the change with the least amount of objectivity. S/he will be the most optimistic about the results, the most impatient about timing and problems, and the most resistant to any subsequent efforts to modify or alter her or his original ideas.

Differences in the Perception of Change

The manager will tend to be the most objective. S/he can visualize the benefits and anticipate the problems. Provided that s/he is not also the originator of the change, s/he should be able to evaluate the situation as it develops, and make any necessary changes to the method of accomplishment. More than anyone, the manager determines the extent of success or failure.

Supervisors are likely to be influenced more by whatever difficulties and problems they expect from the change than by any potential benefits. It is not unusual for supervisors to find themselves having to implement a change about which they have more doubts than confidence.

Because staff specialists are generating suggestions and advice about the change, they often have a bias similar to that of originators. The narrowness of their specialization often causes them to be insensitive to the psychological and social effects of the change.

In any particular change, there are likely to be wide differences in the motivations toward success of the originator, the manager, supervisors and staff specialists. Of these four roles, the originator is likely to have the strongest desire for success. If the basis for the change is sound, the manager should have the next greatest interest in achieving a successful result. Supervisors' motivations would tend to be considerably less strong. Unless they were deeply involved, specialists would probably be somewhat indifferent about success.

Clearly, resistance to a change can occur at any level. That is, like the workforce, managers and supervisors too can become resistant. Two factors in particular can cause such resistance. One is the manager's or supervisor's estimates of the political consequences of a change. Their concern is for their status in the organization, both for the present and also for the future. They might also become resistant if they felt pressured into implementing a change in which they had little confidence and much doubt.

Senior executives must understand that when bringing about any change they must consider the feelings and needs of their managers and supervisors in the same way that they would expect the feelings and needs of all employees involved to be considered. Similarly, the manager accountable for implementing the change should also consider the feelings and needs of those staff specialists whom s/he has invited to participate. For any change to succeed, the manager and supervisors directly responsible must first be unified as closely as possible with the originator in their will to accomplish the change with optimum effectivness. Also, they must collectively accept full responsibility for the ultimate success or failure of that change.

10

A Systematic Approach to Making Change

The enterprise's demand for the worker's ability to change therefore requires positive action to make it possible for him to change.

Peter Drucker

In the preceding chapters, I have discussed how people are affected by changes in which they are involved, and how they can react. I have also analyzed resistant behavior and its causes, together with several managerial techniques for minimizing such behavior. I want now to integrate these ideas and suggest a comprehensive and systematic approach that managers can use when they introduce and implement any change.

Clearly, it would be both foolhardy and impracticable to suggest that any rigidly standard approach could or even should be used in *any* area of managerial activity. There are at least two major reasons for this.

First, there are different personal styles of managing. These differences preclude the broad applicability of any single method of approach. Manager A might succeed with the identical method that manager B employed fruitlessly. That method might have suited A's personal style of managing, as well as her relationships with superiors, subordinates and peers, along with the nature of the organizational structure with its cultural beliefs and norms. Because that method might have been unsuitable to B's style, his relationships and the organizational context, B would have felt uncomfortable and unsympathetic toward it. If such were the case, B would have found it difficult to apply that method.

Second, the notion of a standard method for solving any managerial

A Systematic Approach to Making Change

problem is a useless concept because no single approach can possibly take into account the enormous variability of all the factors present in each unique situation and organization. The facts of organizational life are far too complicated to permit the application of "universal" methods and solutions. Just as it is impossible to prescribe the single "proper" method for raising children, so it is also impossible to prescribe managerial formulas guaranteed to produce effective results in every, or even in most, situations.

Yet, although there are no universally applicable methods for managers to use, we can nevertheless offer suggestions to help them improve their ability to institute changes. Any manager can be helped to develop a more systematic and effective approach to this most critical and demanding aspect of managing.

An improved approach must ensure that as many as possible of the significant factors that might affect outcomes are identified and considered before any decisions are made or actions taken. Such thoroughness and forethought cannot fail to improve the quality and effectiveness of such decisions and actions. Managers who adopt a more systematic approach to changes will be more likely to anticipate correctly how those involved will react, and thus will be better able to cope with their reactions. Because any resistance will be thereby minimized, more successful implementation of changes will be inevitable.

I cannot prescribe any set of detailed procedures for managers to follow when they carry out changes. I can, however, suggest which factors they should be concerned about, together with a general sequence for their consideration. These factors should be regarded as a kind of guide or checklist. With this, managers wanting to improve their effectiveness in making changes can ensure that they have overlooked nothing of importance, in either planning or implementation. I can also suggest some specific options for management action that will maximize success in achieving the desired objectives when making changes.

Not every element of this checklist or actionable option will be relevant for all situations. But any manager can use the checklist to decide at the outset what is significant in the case at hand. S/he must then assemble and evaluate the relevant data, applying some of the techniques already suggested. After this analysis, s/he must decide what action to take.

Broadly, there are at least five phases of managerial work in carrying out any change: (1) analyzing and planning the change; (2) communicating about the change; (3) gaining acceptance of the required changes in behavior; (4) making the initial transition from the status quo to the new situation; and (5) consolidating the new conditions and continuing to follow up in order to institutionalize the change. Now consider each of these phases in detail.

Phase 1: Analyzing and Planning the Change

Before taking any action to introduce or implement a change, the manager who is accountable and responsible should first devote some time to developing a strategy and action plan based on analysis. In this initial phase, there are three objectives. The first goal should be to anticipate, in as specific and as detailed terms as possible, what effects the change is likely to have on those involved, and what problems are likely to arise. Such predictions can be framed only in terms of probabilities. The manager's second objective should be to work out, in advance, answers and solutions to some of the more important anticipated questions and problems. The third objective should be to develop a tentative but detailed action plan and timetable.

In order for managers to develop strategies and plans that are both realistic and workable, they must have from the outset a broad understanding of the basis of the change, its objectives, its scope and its implications. They can develop this understanding by answering a number of questions (listed below) about the change. These should be answered in sufficient detail so that a clear and thorough understanding is reached by all concerned members of management. This analysis must be made before any action is taken to introduce the change itself.

When the magnitude of a change is substantial, impacting many employees in a variety of departments and involving a number of managers and supervisors, the task of formulating a strategy and plan for its implementation is most effectively addressed as a group effort. The group should include the senior manager accountable for carrying out the change, all the other managers and supervisors involved, the originator of the change, and all the staff specialists who are likely to be making contributions to the implementation process. The group's objective is to achieve consensus first in understanding the rationale for the change, its objectives, scope and implications, and then in the approach to making the change.

A Systematic Approach to Making Change

There are four important advantages in taking a group approach to formulating a change strategy and plan:

1. The quality of the strategy and plan will be enhanced in terms of comprehensiveness and accuracy in anticipating future events, because a variety of viewpoints and knowledge will have been brought to bear upon the problems. Plans developed in this way are likely to be realistically based.
2. Because all relevant managers, supervisors and staff specialists will have been involved in the discussions from the start, they will develop a thorough understanding of the change and its implications. This will help minimize any reservations or doubts that they might otherwise have had about the change.
3. Because managers, supervisors and members of staff groups will have participated in planning the change, their commitment to it and its objectives will approach that of the accountable manager. Thus, all those responsible will be unified and consistent in their approach to and management of the change.
4. The originator's and staff specialists' typically narrow perspective will become broadened. As a consequence, they will become more flexible and understanding in the way they deal with those affected by the change.

When a group of managers, supervisors and staff specialists convenes to formulate a strategy and plan for making a major change, their agenda should follow the sequence of tasks described in the remaining pages of this section. In most instances, this work should require no more than a day's effort. In my experience such focused analysis and creative thinking by a group of five to ten people is best accomplished away from the work site, free from distractions and interruptions.

Work in formulating a strategy and plan for making a change, whether undertaken by an individual manager, or a group of managers, supervisors and staff specialists, should begin by answering the following questions:

- What are the objectives of the change, in both short- and long-range terms? What is to be accomplished? To what extent are these goals desirable? To what extent are they realistically achieveable?
- What is the proposed method for accomplishing the change? How is it to be introduced and implemented? How can this method be

A Systematic Approach to Making Change

distinguished from the objectives of the change? How strong is the commitment to one particular method? Can other methods be used provided that the objectives are achieved?
- What is the justification for making the particular proposed change? What are the expected benefits to be realized? Who will gain from these benefits? To what extent are these expectations realistic? What are the probabilities for success and failure? Is any change at all really necessary?
- Who originated the idea for the change? What is his or her motivation for proposing the change? Is s/he still motivated by these forces? To what extent will s/he be directly involved in or able to control the realization of the change? What is the nature of the relationship between the originator of the change and the manager accountable for its success?
- Who else in the organization (other than the originator) is active in supporting the change? How widespread is this support? What are the organizational levels of the supporters of the change, and what are their relationships to the manager responsible for its success?
- By what date must the change be achieved? How flexible is this deadline? How complete must the change be by that date? Is it possible first to test the change experimentally with a trial group? How long a period of time is available for the introduction and implementation of the change? How justifiable or valid is that target date of completion?
- What is the scope of the change? What are the short-term and longer-term implications? How far-reaching will be the effects of the change (on the way the work is done and organized, on the organizational structure, on the culture)? Who will be directly affected? Who will be affected indirectly? Who will be involved in the introduction and implementation of the change? Who else should be informed about the change and its progress, even though they may not be directly concerned? What will be the effect on the union(s) and at what point ought they to become involved?
- Who is being held responsible and accountable for realizing the expected benefits from the change? What sources of assistance and other resources can the manager employ in accomplishing the change?

The answers to these questions can be thought out and recorded either by a manager working alone in isolation, or by a management group working together. Many changes are straightforward enough to be handled by a single manager. If such is the case, this process need

A Systematic Approach to Making Change

not occupy more than several hours. In larger, more complex changes, a group approach is more effective as has already been discussed. This process is unlikely to require more than a day's work.

In order for any manager or group to develop reasonably accurate answers to these questions in a systematic and thorough manner, they need to have a broad appreciation of the background and nature of the change. This understanding provides the sound foundation upon which they then build subsequent plans for action.

Once the basis for a change is understood, a manager or group can then go on to estimate its probable effects on those to be involved, together with their probable reactions. This procedure, already described in chapters 3, 4 and 5, is based on the managers' imagined projection of themselves into the position of those likely to be affected by the change. While regarding the change from the viewpoint of those affected, managers can construct two separate lists in the format of a balance sheet.

The first list is made up of all the possible answers that managers can visualize to the following questions:

- If this change were to apply to me, what questions would I want to be answered about my future circumstances?
- What might I have to fear from the change?
- What might I reasonably expect to lose as a consequence of this change?

The second list is made up of all the possible answers that managers can visualize to the following questions:

- If this change were to apply to me, what might I expect to gain from the change?
- How might I benefit from the change?
- What new advantages might I reasonably anticipate as a result of this change?

When only a few people are to be affected, a manager can consider how each individual is likely to react. Thus, s/he can construct separate lists for each one, taking into account any individual differences in needs, goals, attitudes and behavior. When, however, the group to be affected is large, it is difficult and impractical to consider each individual separately. In these circumstances, the lists must be sufficiently comprehensive to include as many as possible of the more likely reactions.

A Systematic Approach to Making Change

Once these lists have been compiled, it is then possible to construct one or more balance sheets of estimated losses and gains (see figure 4 in chapter 5). On each balance sheet, specific fears and questions, together with hopes and expected benefits, can be grouped according to their nature. The intensity of feeling about each loss and each gain can then be estimated. Also, any feared losses which are a consequence of cultural beliefs should be identified and segregated.

These balance sheets can be analyzed by asking the following questions:

- Which fears are primarily a product of individual imaginations and which are more realistically based?
- Which hopes and expected benefits are primarily products of individual imaginations, and which are more realistically based?
- How can those fears and hopes which are imagined and not realistically based be dissipated? What facts and arguments are necessary, and what form should any reassurance take?
- Which questions will require specific and detailed answers? What facts will be necessary so that acceptable answers can be supplied?
- When realistically based fears are compared with realistically based expectations, what is the extent of any imbalance?
- If estimated losses greatly outweigh estimated gains, is it wise to proceed at all with the change in its present form? How could either the change itself or its method of accomplishment be so modified as to restore some degree of balance between the forecasted losses and gains?
- If estimated losses outweigh gains, what action can be taken to minimize the imbalance or, better, to reverse the imbalance? Which losses are likely to be the most significant barriers to the acceptance of the change? Which losses can be eliminated altogether? What offsetting gains can be added?
- Which cultural beliefs are susceptible to being changed? What facts and arguments are required to accomplish such changes?

From analyzing the balance sheets in this way, managers can develop a positive program for action. They can assemble whatever facts and construct whatever arguments are necessary to answer questions and to dispel groundless fears, hopes and cultural beliefs. They can plan how to communicate these facts and arguments with those concerned. They can modify both the change and its method of accomplishment so that the balance between forecasted losses and gains can be improved. They can plan how to eliminate many of the

A Systematic Approach to Making Change

objectionable aspects of the change. Finally, they can plan how to provide rewards to offset those objectionable features of the change which cannot be eliminated.

The final stage of analyzing and planning a change is the development of a tentative but specific time plan for its introduction, implementation and follow-up. First, each distinct task or element of the change should be identified and listed. Next, the dependent elements should be distinguished from the independent ones. Thus, from analyzing such a list, managers will find that some elements must be completed before others are begun. They will also find that other elements can be carried out at any time, because they are independent of the rest.

After this analysis is done, all the elements of the change should be arranged in their proper sequential or parallel relationships. The time needed to complete each element can be estimated. Then, priorities can be assigned to the accomplishment of each task. Naturally, the highest priority should be given to completing those elements which, on further analysis, appear to be critical to the achievement of the entire change. For complex changes with many separate elements requiring long periods of time for completion, the techniques of network analysis (e.g. critical path scheduling or PERT[70]) may be employed to develop the timed plan and to assign the priorities.

It must be recognized, however, that any timed plan constructed at this preliminary stage of the change must necessarily be considered as tentative. Although there must be a general plan for action, its timetable should be sufficiently flexible to enable the incorporation of modifications whenever these become necessary.

There are two ways in which a timed plan is useful to management. Once constructed, it becomes a master plan for action. As such, it must be considered a dynamic instrument, subject to systematic reviews and revisions. Thus, with a timed plan, management can understand at each step of the change its numerous facets, how they interrelate with one another, and what sequence of action is required. Also, the timed plan is a control tool that management can use to measure their progress and accomplishment. From periodic comparisons of the actual versus the planned status of each element of the change, management can develop detailed pictures of what is on schedule and what is falling behind.[71]

In summary, the analysis and planning phase of a change should be completed before any overt action is taken actually to institute it. Thus, management can be prepared beforehand to cope with any resistance. They need to have a clear concept of what is to be accomplished and

A Systematic Approach to Making Change

why. They need to understand how the change is likely to be perceived by the people affected and by the union(s). Because management will have anticipated many of the problems, they will be prepared to meet these difficulties with possible solutions. With such preparation, management can improve the probability of acceptance of the change by those on whom its ultimate success is most dependent. Thus, the time management invest in analyzing and planning the change should pay rich dividends when they implement it subsequently.

Phase 2: Communicating About the Change

The next phase of any change is a period of communication during which management thoroughly discuss it and its implications with those affected and involved (including the unions). Much of this communication should be carried out before any action is taken to introduce the actual changes.

In this phase, there are two objectives. Managers should ensure that all those involved develop as complete an understanding as possible about the reasons for the change and its objectives and anticipated benefits, about the intended method (or alternative methods) of approach, about the proposed timetable and plan for action, and about how they are likely to be affected. Also, managers should try to assess both individuals' and unions' reactions by identifying as many as possible of their specific questions, beliefs and fears about the change.

This process of communication must be two-way. Managers and supervisors must transmit information about the change to everyone concerned with what is to happen. This information should be primarily factual, but it may also contain some realistically based conjecture and predictions. In addition, however, management must do some listening. They must listen so that they can evaluate the effectiveness of their communications by assessing how much understanding has been achieved. Also, they must listen to the comments and ideas expressed about the change. From these can be determined the employees' and unions' true attitudes and reactions, not all of which will have been anticipated. From such two-way communication, both employees and management will learn what to expect.

This process will benefit everyone involved in the change. Management will be able to test the validity of their initial predictions. From

A Systematic Approach to Making Change

employees' feedback in their interactions with management, managers will be able to learn how to improve their preparation for future changes. By understanding what is to happen, employees will be better able to adjust to the new conditions. Also, they (together with the union) can influence the course of events before these actually occur. This is especially important if there are elements of the change which might affect them adversely.

By anticipating employees' and unions' reactions to a change, management can modify those aspects which might otherwise have proved objectionable, or introduce compensating factors. Management can benefit in another way from discussing the change in advance with employees and unions. Because of their involvement in discussions, employees, together with the union leaders, will probably feel less intense about resisting the change. By gaining prior knowledge of what will be happening to them, they will, in time tend to accommodate themselves to this eventuality (see chapter 6). Also, unions' institutional requirements for recognition and continued survival will be in part satisfied.

Clearly, for management, employees and unions to realize these benefits, management must be willing to share as much as possible of the information about the change. True understanding can be based only on full knowledge of the relevant facts. Withholding or distorting information about the change will, in most instances, prove to be more harmful than beneficial to management. If they are apprehensive about sharing certain information in advance, they should analyze and compare risks with potential benefits before they finally reach a decision (see chapter 6).

As a change gets carried out, communication should be maintained with as many of the people concerned and as extensively as possible. Communication must be not only with those directly affected, but also with those on the periphery of the change. For example, members of relevant staff groups should be included. Also, people doing related jobs may regard a change in another area as a precursor to what may later happen to them. In such instances, these persons too should be included. In addition, both national and local union officials should be involved from the outset of the change, if it is at all relevant to matters about which the union is concerned.

Communication with all these people can be accomplished most effectively through discussion both with individuals singly and with groups. However, management should also consider using any other written and oral and visual media that might help improve understanding of what is to happen (see chapter 7).

A Systematic Approach to Making Change

This intensive program of communications should begin at the completion of the analysis and planning phase of the change. The program should be continued throughout the entire change until its objectives are met. No action should be taken to introduce any actual changes until there has been sufficient discussion to reach general agreement that some kind of change is necessary, and that one or more of the approaches discussed will probably produce the desired results. When a change is complex with far-reaching implications, management should plan their timetable to allow sufficient time for communications to be thorough and complete.

Considerable time is required particularly when there is a need to change deeply-rooted cultural beliefs and mistaken notions. It is desirable that such beliefs be altered or at least shaken before the way can be paved for the acceptance of new ideas and practices. Changing fundamental beliefs that are seldom examined or questioned is very difficult. Considerable time is required for repeated, intensive dialog and debate. Often, the most that can be accomplished before any change is actually made, is making particular beliefs explict and opening them up to question. People often want "proof" before being willing to abandon deeply-rooted beliefs. The communications phase of a change is the time to begin the process of challenging and modifying cultural beliefs.

Throughout this period, all references to the particular methods that might be employed to achieve the intended changes should be framed in terms of possibilities and proposals. No doubts should be allowed to persist about the desirability or inevitability of realizing management's objectives for the change. Yet, actual methods for accomplishing the change should at this point be perceived as proposals, subject to further alteration and modification. Such flexibility is essential if those involved are to believe that their comments and suggestions will be considered seriously.

Management can be flexible about their approach only if they are able to distinguish clearly between their objectives and how these are to be accomplished. They should be able to complete the development of the particular method during the next phase of the change, This method should evolve from a proposal toward a more definite plan during the discussions held during the communications phase.

Thus, the principal function of the communications phase is to enable those involved (and the unions) to accustom themselves to the idea that a change is needed, and that it will soon be taking place. Attention should be focused on the objectives of the change and their justification. At the outset of the communications phase, it should be made clear that precisely how the change is to be accomplished has not yet been crystallized into its final form. The method of change is therefore open to discussion and consideration. By the latter stages of the communication phase, all concerned should understand why the change is necessary, what is to be achieved, what are some alternative methods of approach, and what are the more important problems that might result from each of these alternatives. At the close of the communications phase, everyone involved should be close to agreement on the most desirable method for accomplishing the change.

Phase 3: Gaining Acceptance of the Required Changes in Behavior

The next phase of a change is the period during which agreement is reached on whatever specific alterations are required in employees' behavior to accomplish the transition from the status quo to the desired conditions. The behavioral changes necessary for the transition are determined both by the particular method management select to accomplish their desired objectives, and the nature of the objectives themselves. Agreement on these should be reached between management and a significant majority of those affected by the change.

It is difficult to define exactly when phase 3 begins and ends. It starts some time during the latter stages of phase 2 (communications), when many have begun to understand and accept what is about to happen and in particular how they are likely to be affected. Phase 3 ends when a general agreement has been achieved about how much and what kinds of behavioral changes are required to accomplish the transition from the existing conditions to the desired situation.

Managers can secure agreement to a particular method of change in one of several ways. They can apply persuasion and offer rewards. Alternatively, they can reach agreement through negotiation and bargaining. Or, they can invite people to participate in making some of the decisions about how the change is to be accomplished. Any combination of these approaches can be used.

The particular approach chosen should depend on the special circumstances of each case. Persuasion and rewards are appropriate for situations where managers have already decided that the change can best be achieved only by one particular method. They might also negotiate and bargain to gain acceptance of that one method, especially if unions are involved and the change is relevant to the labor agreement. However, if they choose to bargain, they must be prepared to compromise and modify their original ideas.

When it is possible to achieve a change by more than one method, managers may decide to involve the people affected. They may invite them to participate in making some of the decisions about how the change is to be carried out. Participation is effective when managers are open-minded about how the change might be accomplished, and when there is a choice of alternative approaches. Even when managers are committed to a single method of carrying out the change, they can nevertheless combine participation with either persuasion or bargaining, provided that there are some elements of the change that could be accomplished in more than one way.

Whatever approach managers take, its effectiveness depends on how much discussion takes place. Discussions with everyone concerned must be carried on continuously throughout the change. These discussions should begin at the start of the communications phase and should continue until agreement has been reached on how to proceed with the actual transition. Discussion is the best method for developing an understanding of the change and its implications. Discussion is also an excellent means for ensuring that most of the problems that might later have caused resistance are identified and solved.

Whatever approach managers choose to secure agreement, special personal problems will inevitably arise in discussions. These will be individual problems and will not apply to the group as a whole. These problems arise from conflict between a person's own needs and goals and the effects of the change. Managers can solve such problems when they remain sufficiently flexible in their attitude and approach, thus providing for any differences in individual circumstances. Managers must be able to reconcile what is fair to the person with the problem and what is equitable for the group as a whole. In so doing, managers should bear in mind that a uniform approach for all is often neither equitable nor fair. Whenever exceptions and modifications are made to accommodate individual needs, these can be understood and accepted by the group if they perceive these exceptions as reasonable.

Thus, in most changes, managers should begin the transition from the status quo to the new conditions only after a consensus has been reached about the method for this transition. This agreement can be achieved through the use of rewards, through bargaining, through participation, or through some combination of these approaches. If the transition is attempted before such agreement has been reached,

A Systematic Approach to Making Change

managers risk an increased resistance to the change and a lessened probablity that the potential benefits will be fully realized.

Phase 4: Making the Initial Transition

In any change, the next distinct phase is the initial transition from the existing to the new situation. The prior three phases of planning, communications and gaining agreement should all preface the actual start of the change itself. Only after these preparatory phases have been successfully completed should management then begin to introduce the specific changes.

Just before the start of the transition, the timed plan for the change (previously developed in the planning phase) should again be reviewed. Managers should question and re-evaluate the originally established final date of completion to determine whether or not it is still realistic and achievable. They should consider whether or not it might be possible or desirable to test out the method of transition on a trial basis. This may be done either by using an experimental group before involving everyone in the change, or by setting up a specific trial period for all involved before the change is finally established as definite. It is extremely important that the target date for completing the change be set so that managers will not be hindered by any arbitrary deadlines from remaining flexible in their choice of method for handling the transition. Furthermore, there must be sufficient time allowed for finding effective solutions to problems that are certain to arise as the change proceeds.

Once managers have determined how to handle the transition, they must ensure that everyone involved is briefed on what is to take place. Carefully planned presentations should help to crystallize everybody's understanding of what to expect, why it is to happen, and what the effects should be. Furthermore, these briefings should help people establish what their roles will be during the transition period and afterwards in the new situation.

If new knowledge and skills are required by the change, appropriate training should be designed and implemented. The objectives of this training must derive from the particular demands made on those involved by the changed circumstances. Such training should not only prepare each person to carry out her or his responsibilities more effectively, but it should also help reduce any fears and doubts about ability to cope with new responsibilities.

A Systematic Approach to Making Change

Often, managers and supervisors have as great a need for both briefing and training as do operatives and staff. The same can be said of key union members and officials. In complex changes, sufficient time must be scheduled for such training before any actual changes are instituted. Time invested in this way will often yield rich dividends when the benefits from the change are finally measured.

During the transition, more careful and thorough supervision is required than is needed during more stable periods of operation. Many unforeseen problems inevitably arise. Usually, first-line supervisors are the most appropriate people to answer questions, solve problems, and call for any required specialized assistance. They are in the best position to act as the central link for all communications about the progress of the change during the transition period. In order to be effective, they must be on the scene and readily accessible. First-line supervisors should therefore spend the greatest proportion of their time at the scene of the change. They should, however, regard themselves more as sources of assistance to employees than as order-givers. Managers, too, should devote more time than normal to acquainting themselves with what is happening "on the shop (or office) floor" during the transition period.

I have already emphasized that any specialists required should be involved as early as possible during the planning phase of the change. Managers must help them understand the objectives and reasons for the change. They should be kept informed about its progress and about any problems arising as well as about any modifications to the method of change. Because they have probably contributed ideas and recommendations about the methods and even the objectives of the change, they are often as deeply concerned about what happens as are those directly affected. When managers involve specialists in participating directly in formulating some of the decisions about the change, the full benefit to be gained from their contributions will be ensured. By fulfilling specialists' needs in this way, managers will ensure that their cooperation will continue both during the change at hand and in future changes as well.

During the transition period, managers must remain continually informed about what is happening at the scene of the change. Up-to-the-minute information is needed if they are to modify the method of approach. Such modifications may become necessary if unforeseen problems arise, or if it appears that better results are achievable through an approach different from the original.

To ensure a constant flow of timely information about the progress of a change, managers can use several techniques. They can discuss the situation frequently with first-line supervisors. Also, they can seek opinions and comments from any specialists directly involved. They can discuss progress with union representatives. They can visit the scene of action with sufficient frequency to gain a firsthand appreciation of what is actually happening. During such visits, they can chat informally with the people directly concerned with making the changes. In this way, they will be in the best possible position to take immediate corrective action should this become necessary.

Thus, the transition from the status quo to the new conditions should begin only after some agreement has been reached on the method of change. Managers should allow sufficient time to make the change on a trial basis, and to solve any unforeseen problems. Briefings and training for supervision, staff, union representatives and operatives should precede the start of any changes. During the transition, supervisors, and to a lesser extent managers, should spend a considerable portion of their time at the scene of the change so that questions and problems can be resolved without delay. Full benefit can be gained from the contributions of specialists by involving them deeply in the planning and conduct of the change. Throughout this phase, managers must remain well informed about progress so that they can make any necessary modifications to the method of change.

Phase 5: Consolidation and Follow-up

In any change, the final phase is the consolidation of the new conditions and the continued follow-up of events after the initial transition is complete. Follow-up should continue until the success of the change has been ensured.

Simply because the transition period may have been accomplished smoothly, with few difficulties, managers should not assume that the change has been an unqualified success. Many unexpected problems can arise later after the initial changes have been made. The planned change might trigger subtle secondary effects that may not become apparent for some time. Also, what might appear to be a successful change at the outset might later prove to be a failure, either because of the effects of subsequent reactions to the new conditions, or because of other unforeseen factors.

To ensure that the objectives of a change are fully realized, managers must institute systematic and thorough follow-up procedures. They

A Systematic Approach to Making Change

must see to it that first-line supervisors continue to be on the lookout for any signs of difficulty. Managers and supervisors must continue to be at the scene of the change with sufficient frequency to correct any misunderstandings and questions that are certain to arise about the new conditions of work.

Furthermore, managers should ensure that specialists continue their involvement in the change until they can make no further useful contributions. After the initial transition, specialists can continue to study and report on the progress of the change, as well as to submit their recommendations about any further desirable modifications and refinements.

Also, managers should institute procedures whereby they receive regularly scheduled reports, both oral and written, from first- and second-line supervisors as well as from any specialists who remain involved. These reports should draw comparisons between the actual and the planned progress made toward the objectives of the change. The actual accomplishments realized should be described quantitatively with as much objectivity as possible. The prudent manager will supplement this information by conducting informal interviews with key persons directly involved in the change. By chatting with operatives, staff specialists, members of supervision and union representatives, the manager can gain valuable firsthand perceptions of the situation.

Such systematic follow-up procedures will inevitably reveal the existence of additional problems. With an accurate and timely knowledge of the situation, managers can act swiftly and decisively. They can either initiate further detailed studies of the areas of difficulty, or they can modify the relevant elements of the change.

During the follow-up phase 5 of a change, managers will be able to determine the extent to which the anticipated results and benefits have been realized. The effects of the change should be defined and measured as objectively and as specifically as possible. The results can then be compared with earlier expectations. Similarly, any identifiable secondary effects of the change should also be analyzed. A final assessment can then be made of the degree of success, along with the explanation.

From such reviews, management can learn lessons from which they can improve their effectiveness in introducing and implementing future changes. In addition, they may discover that, with further immediate action, increased benefits are achievable from the change just "completed." Productive organizational learning depends on management's ability to conduct systematically, such post-mortem reviews of major changes. The agenda should include an assessment of success, defined in terms of the extent to which the intended objectives of the change were actually achieved. Also, the reasons why a change was more or less successful should be articulated and discussed. These reviews can yield useful insights and guidance for future action if they are carried out in an atmosphere of clinical examination. There should be no attempts at finger-pointing or assignment of blame. Rather, the focus should be only on understanding what happened and why.

Throughout a change, managers must keep clearly in their mind those objectives that justified it from the outset. They should feel free to modify or alter the original plan if a better realization of the objectives could result. Just as a manager would wish employees to remain open-minded and flexible in their attitude toward the change, so also should s/he try to remain open-minded on approaches to accomplishing that change. Such personal flexibility is a major element in achieving success.

Thus, to ensure that full benefits from a change are realized, managers must institute systematic and thorough follow-up procedures. They must be alert to unexpected secondary effects and after-effects. They must continue to give close attention to the progress of events so that they can remain fully informed. They must ensure that both the results of the change and the way in which they were achieved are evaluated completely and objectively so that the organization as a whole can learn and enhance future effectiveness in making changes. Managers can contribute greatly to success so long as they remain personally flexible about changing the methods used for realizing the change.

The Fawley Agreement

In England during the early 1960s, there was concluded a change of extremely broad scope with far-reaching implications. I want to focus on this example for two reasons. One is that it is extremely well documented. The other is that in the accomplishment of this complex change were embodied almost all the concepts I have been describing in this book. I have already referred to this case in my discussion in chapter 6 of changing cultural beliefs.

This change was the negotiation and implementation of a radically different agreement on labor productivity at the largest petroleum refinery of the Esso Petroleum Company Ltd, located in Fawley,

A Systematic Approach to Making Change

England. The development and subsequent implementation of this agreement is described and analyzed in detail by Allan Flanders of Oxford University.[72]

By pursuing a strategy called productivity bargaining and through systematic application of those principles of managing changes outlined in this chapter, a group of managers brought about the acceptance of an entirely different way of working, a way that represented a radical departure from past traditions and practices not only at the refinery but also in British industry. How was this complicated and difficult change accomplished?

First, let me summarize management's objectives. The change was initially stimulated by an economic need: to raise labor productivity as a key element in a more general program to improve operating efficiency. Soon, however, management had formulated two other objectives of a different kind, objectives concerned with the institutional and cultural aspects of the industrial society at the refinery. One of these objectives was to make labor relations more responsible and constructive, and to create an environment that would emphasize the common interests of management and the unions in improved working methods and in organization. The other objective was to change the attitudes of all employees toward change itself. An effort was to be made to modify those prevailing beliefs and values held both by management and by the workers that tended to be barriers in the path leading to the adoption of new attitudes.

During a two-year period devoted to the planning and communications phase of this change, three things happened. First, a series of very specific proposals were developed defining a number of desired changes in working methods and practices. Second, the entire management structure was simplified and strengthened. Third, everyone involved in this change (including the union) had the opportunity to discuss the proposed changes extensively (initially in general terms and later more specifically) and to gain an understanding of what was to take place and why.

The proposed changes in working practices and methods can be briefly summarized as follows. It was proposed that the job of craftsman's mate (or, helper) be eliminated, and all incumbents deployed to other work. Also, it was proposed that a group of existing demarcation practices related to inter-craft flexibility be relaxed so that minor maintenance work could be transferred to process workers, and so that slinging and rigging work could be done by various craftsmen. Furthermore, management were to have greater freedom in their use of supervision, so that craft groups would take orders from

A Systematic Approach to Making Change

any supervisor without regard for his particular craft. In addition, a number of traditional refinery conventions were to be modified. Unproductive time allowances such as those for walking, washing and set tea breaks were to be abolished. Special payments for heat and dirt were to be discontinued. There was to be a dramatic reduction in the number and variety of different pay rates. Finally, the amount of overtime worked on a continuing, regularly scheduled basis was to be reduced from an average of 15–18 percent to 2 percent.

To secure the workers' agreement to these changes, management proposed to offer three benefits and one guarantee. One of these benefits was a reduction in the normal basic working week from 42 to 40 hours. Another was a dramatic reduction in the total hours worked each week from almost 50 to about 41 hours. Third, there was to be a significant increase in basic pay rates so that, even after most of the overtime had been eliminated, employees' take-home pay would be greater than it had been at the outset. In addition to these benefits, a pledge was made that no one would be made redundant as a consequence of these changes. This pledge was possible because it was feasible to reduce the amount of work being done by subcontractors and because the refinery was in a period of expansion.

After a five-month period of hard bargaining, the union (and the employees) agreed to most of the detailed proposals. During the following two years, the provisions of this new agreement were implemented. What were the results?

The economic results are the easiest to define. In the maintenance departments, the productivity of the individual worker rose more than 50 percent over the two years following the negotiation of the new agreement. In the process departments, individual productivity increased about 45 percent. In return for this, the total take-home pay of the workers rose about 21 percent, and their work week was shortened by about 11 percent.

The success with which the institutional objectives were achieved is far more difficult to evaluate. Let me quote Flanders:

> There were certain significant changes in the relations between management and unions at Fawley, which can be conveniently summarized under three heads. First, labour relations acquired a greater formality in that they were governed by more explicit and less flexible rules. Second, the shop stewards' influence on union negotiations was enhanced. Third, rivalry among the three main union groups ... as represented by the CUC [i.e. the group of crafts unions] and the TGWU [i.e. Transport and General Workers' Union] Shifts and Day branches ... was intensified.

A Systematic Approach to Making Change

It is evident that together [the above changes] subjected the relations between management and the unions to new stresses and strains. Growing formality made for less give-and-take and ease of accommodation in daily relations. The stewards' augmented influence tended to make union negotiations more protracted and complex. The intensification of rivalry among the different union groups had the same effect, and in addition produced tensions that hampered consistent settlements for the refinery as a whole. The conclusion is inescapable that the immediate effect of the Blue Book [the local term for the group of specific changes] and its successor was to make labour relations more conflict-prone ... in the sense of rendering them more liable to the confrontation of opposed interests or viewpoints. By enlarging the subject matter of formal collective bargaining, and by disturbing settled relationships and accepted comparisons, they extended the range of possible disagreements between the two sides and among the union representatives themselves.

... Peace in industry is most easily achieved by avoiding change ... at any rate change that is likely to meet resistance. Had this been the supreme consideration for Fawley management, the Blue Book proposals would never have been formulated. Managements that engage in productivity bargaining have to be prepared to devote more, not less, of their time to labour relations and to expect that their tasks will become more onerous and exacting.

Since an evaluation of labour relations cannot be based upon the avoidance of conflict, it follows that its increase at Fawley was not necessarily a sign that labour relations there were deteriorating. On the contrary, the absence of any costly stoppages when sharper conflicts had to be resolved could rather be taken as evidence of their improvement. The ingenuity of management and union representatives in finding the workable compromise that would satisfy their constituents was being subjected to a severer test and, on the whole, emerged triumphant.[73]

Flanders found it more difficult to assess the extent to which management was successful in its third objective of changing attitudes toward change:

The conversion of top management could be directly observed and tested in many conversations. It appeared to be fairly complete. How the middle and lower levels of management viewed the experiment was much more difficult to ascertain. Such evidence as exists points to a good deal of scepticism about its value and to reservations about particular changes in working practices.[74]

As for the accomplishment of any changes in craft and noncraft workers' attitudes toward change, Flanders suggests that only slight inroads were made in modifying their traditional attitudes toward lines of craft or trade demarcation, the central problem in many of the changes that were carried out.[75]

How was it possible for management to accomplish successfully such a radical series of changes, many of which were in direct conflict with prevailing cultural beliefs and traditional working practices and habits? There is no simple answer. Certainly, the nature of the economic climate and the generally good relations which existed between management and the workers were important factors. But perhaps one of the more significant reasons for management's success was that they approached the accomplishment of these changes in a planned and systematic manner. Examine more closely the elements of their approach.

Management's intial attitude was one reason for the success of the changes. Senior management perceived and accepted the view that it was management's responsibility to change the union's restrictive practices and to reduce overtime. Management understood that if any changes were to be made it was up to them to seize the initiative and not up to the union to do so. Also, management believed that any benefits from increases in individual productivity should be shared between the company and its employees. Thus, management were willing to offer the workers a fair reward for their contribution toward higher productivity.

Another element in the success of the change was managment's early appreciation of the concept that cultural change was a necessary prerequisite to institutional change. Thus, if overtime was to be reduced, if the jobs of craftsmen's mates were to be eliminated, and if traditional lines of craft demarcation were to be relaxed, then it was necessary first to challenge and to modify a number of deeply rooted cultural beliefs. Many workers, union officials and even members of supervision had to review their long-held beliefs and question their validity. As a consequence of management's grasp of these concepts, they were able to plan and carry out a systematic and comprehensive attack on these beliefs, prior to introducing any changes and starting any negotiations with the union.

A further factor in the success of the changes was the amount of planning that preceded the union negotiations and the introduction of the changes. About one year was devoted to a series of comprehensive and detailed studies of the original situation, to the design of those changes desired, and to the development of a general strategy and plan for their achievement. During this planning phase, the objectives for the changes were clearly defined. Also, the specific proposals for the

A Systematic Approach to Making Change

changes were developed in great detail. The clear definition of these proposed changes facilitated the subsequent discussions held with both the workers and the unions, and minimized ambiguities and misunderstandings. Management were able to forecast the effects of the change on those involved, and to estimate how people would react. As a result, management were able to identify beforehand the main potential sources of resistance to the proposed changes, and to devise a means for minimizing this resistance.

This means was comprised of three distinct elements. Two of these were in the form of rewards that management offered to persuade their employees to change their traditional work habits. One of these rewards was a dramatic decrease in the total hours worked per week. The other was an equally dramatic increase in basic pay. Not only was this pay rise sufficient to offset any possible losses in weekly take-home pay that might otherwise have resulted from the reduction in the number of hours worked, but it was also designed to result in a significant increase in workers' weekly pay. The third element of management's plan to minimize resistance was to provide positive protection from the workers' strongest fear, that of redundancy. This protection took the form of a pledge that there would be no redundancy as a consequence of the proposed changes.

Yet another factor that contributed to the success of the changes was the amount of communication between management and those involved in the changes, both prior to and during the negotiations with the union, and prior to the actual introduction of any changes. More than one year was devoted to the communications phase of the changes. During this period, management used virtually every possible means to communicate with the supervisors, the workers and key union officials. The means most frequently employed by far was face-to-face discussions both with individuals and with groups. In these discussions, cultural beliefs were identified, held up to examination and challenged. Also, the general nature of some of the more fundamental proposals was suggested and discussed.

Later, once negotiations had begun, the specific proposals were discussed at length with all employees, who were then encouraged to explore their broader implications. In these discussions, consultation, and to a lesser extent participation, took place. By the end of the negotiations with the unions, almost everyone concerned had reached some understanding of what was proposed and why, and what the effects were likely to be. Furthermore, a general acceptance of most of the key proposals had already been achieved prior to the completion of negotiations.

A Systematic Approach to Making Change

Still another essential factor in the success of the changes was senior management's recognition and implementation of a concept: that as a prerequisite to the introduction of any changes, it was first necessary to strengthen management's effectiveness at all levels within the organization. Consequently, during the first year while the changes were being planned, management were simultaneously improving their own structure and organization. The objectives of this effort were twofold. First, managers and supervisors at all levels were to accept full responsibility for managing their subordinates. This meant that many personnel matters, formerly left to the care of staff specialists, were to be handled directly by the managers and supervisors themselves. This also meant that managers and supervisors were to become deeply concerned with establishing relationships with their subordinates that would be characterized by mutual respect and trust.

The other objective of the program to improve management organization was that management should assume full responsibility for determining labor policy. Thus, the managers and supervisors were the ones to decide on the specific proposals for the changes in working practices, and on the methods for their accomplishment. The managers and supervisors were the ones to conduct the discussions of those changes with the men and with the union officials. Also, the managers were the ones to direct and conduct the negotiations with the unions.

The management organization was improved by several fundamental changes. The organization structure itself was simplified by a reduction in the number of levels in the hierarchy between the workers and the refinery manager, and also in the number of supervisors. The managers' and supervisors' salaries were increased, so that a proper incentive and reward could be introduced for the increased managerial competence and skills now required. Simplifying the organizational structure shortened and made more effective the lines of communication at all levels. There was a deliberate increase in the delegation of both responsibilities and the freedom to carry them out. This was particularly true of the management of people.

There was also a planned effort to involve supervisors and managers at all levels in discussing and solving the enormous number of problems presented by the impending changes. As a consequence of their involvement and participation, they developed a genuine team spirit. This, in turn, led to a unified understanding of and approach to solving these problems, as well as confidence that, no matter how difficult, these problems could be overcome.

Without this development and strengthening of the management and supervisory group, it is doubtful that the productivity proposals could have been introduced successfully. Certainly, neither the planning nor the communications phases of the changes could have been carried out with such telling effect. And even if the changes had been negotiated with the union officials, it is doubtful that they could have been negotiated with the union officials, without these improvements in the management organization.

Another factor in the success of these changes was the flexibility of the timetable. Senior management did not impose an arbitrary deadline for the start or completion of negotiations, or for the full implementation of the changes themselves. They realized from the outset that a great deal of time was necessary to plan for these changes, and to prepare the ground for their acceptance. Consequently, the timing of the negotiations was determined by the actual progress made during the communications phase of the changes. Sufficient time was taken during every phase for accommodation to the ideas of change to play a significant role. The climate of employee opinion toward the proposals was the primary determinant for establishing the start of the negotiations.

Another factor that contributed to the success of the changes is also worthy of mention. This was management's realism in their approach to the bargaining process. They understood that to gain something they had to be prepared to give something in return. The extent of the wage increases, the pledge of no redundancy, and the abandonment of at least one of their key proposals were all illustrations of management's attitude. Furthermore, a number of modifications and compromises were made to the original proposals during the process of negotiation. The final changes agreed by the unions differed in some respects from the original list of management's proposals.

Summary

Changes, even when the scope is substantial and the obstacles daunting, can be accomplished successfully provided that management take a planned approach that is comprehensive, systematic and thorough. Success is particularly dependent on the extent to which management make use of discussion with everyone concerned, and of participation. Success can often be assured when structural changes are made in the organization and an effective and unified management "team" is developed. Management must pay special attention to providing a high quality of supervision throughout the change, from its planning and communications phases through its transition period and concluding with its follow-up and consolidation.

11

Implications for Managerial Competence

> *A State which dwarfs its men, in order that they may be more docile instruments in its hands even for beneficial purposes .. will find that with small men no great things can really be accomplished.*
>
> John Stuart Mill

> *A State without the means of some change is without the means of its conservation.*
>
> Edmund Burke

Throughout this book, I have emphasized that managers, together with their subordinate supervisors, are together responsible and accountable for achieving successfully the full benefits from any change. But the routes to success contain many barriers and pitfalls. To overcome these obstacles is often difficult. To solve some of the problems can be at times almost impossible. Occasionally, management must settle for results that are less than what might have been potentially possible.

Enormous demands are made of managers and supervisors when they introduce and implement changes. Probably no other managerial task is more difficult. Yet, the ability to make changes effectively is, in my view, the principal value added to an organization by its managers. I believe this because no organization can maintain its vitality or even survive in the longer term by simply maintaining the status quo. The changing conditions of any organization's marketplace and external environment require continuous adaptation within that organization in order for it to remain viable. Such adaptation requires a never-ending series of specific changes. Instituting and implementing these changes are the core tasks for managers, and to a lesser extent, supervisors.

Required Attributes, Skills and Competencies

What competencies and attributes must managers and supervisors have to perform these tasks well? The list is a long one. At the outset of making a change, they must be able to understand the full implications of each impending change. They must be able to identify its objectives and supporting rationale, and grasp the nature of its probable effects. They must be able to imagine themselves in the positions of the people to be affected, and view the change through their eyes. Managers and supervisors must be able to visualize what employees might fear and regard as losses, as well as what they might hope to gain from the change. Managers and supervisors must be able to identify any prevailing cultural beliefs that might be in conflict with the change. They must be able to analyze probable attitudes and forecast likely reactions. They must be able to predict with some accuracy the nature and extent of any resistance, and then plan how such resistance could be minimized.

Any manager able to perform all these tasks effectively must have both intelligence and imagination above the norm. Furthermore, s/he must have a mind trained to approach problems analytically and logically, with a method that embodies systematic planning.

Furthermore, a manager who is to be effective in accomplishing changes must have a general attitude toward others (and toward subordinates in particular) that is characterized by confidence, consideration and understanding. Consider how Douglas McGregor defined this attitude:

> [Such a manager] has a relatively high opinion of the intelligence and capacity of the average human being. He may well be aware that he is endowed with substantial capacity, but he does not perceive himself as a member of a limited elite. He sees most human beings as having real capacity for growth and development, for the acceptance of responsibility, for creative accomplishment. He regards his subordinates as genuine assets in helping him fulfill his own responsibilities, and he is concerned with creating the conditions which enable him to realize these

Implications for Managerial Competence

assets. He does not feel that people in general are stupid, lazy, irresponsible, dishonest or antagonistic. He is aware that there are such individuals, but he expects to encounter them only rarely.

The climate of the relationship created by such a manager will be vastly different. Among other things, he will probably practice effective delegation, thus providing his subordinates with opportunities to develop their own capabilities under his leadership. He will also utilize them as resources in helping him solve departmental problems. His use of participation will demonstrate his confidence in them.[76]

Also, as they proceed with carrying out changes, managers must be skilled in communicating with people at all levels in the organization, whether they be workers, staff specialists, senior managers or even union officials. Managers must be good listeners, so that they can test out employees' reactions to the various elements of a change. Managers must be able to use skillfully the mechanisms of both individual and group discussions, so that those involved can develop understanding, and so that any potential problems can be identified and solutions found. Managers must also be able to make the best use of other, more formal means of communicating, and, in particular, those employing the written word.

In addition, managers must be persuasive in their approach to subordinates, superiors, staff specialists and union officials. In a logical and convincing manner, managers must be able to organize and marshal those arguments that support the need for the change, as well as for one particular approach to its accomplishment. They must be able to present and develop their arguments so as to persuade those involved to accept and support the change and a method for its realization. Similarly, managers must be able to convince their superiors when it is necessary to make certain modifications to the method of change, and possibly even to its objectives. A manager might also have to persuade senior management that it would be desirable to offer certain rewards so that some of the unavoidable losses from the change might be counterbalanced.

Moreover, managers must be systematic and thorough in their attention to the details of supervising the changing situation. They must follow closely the progress of the change. They must ensure that they receive a constant flow of accurate and timely information about what is happening "on the shop (and office) floor." They must maintain close contact with subordinate supervisors and ensure that all of the myriad and seemingly trivial difficulties that inevitably accompany any change get solved before they balloon into major problems. Finally, they must ensure that the necessary supporting functions, activities and systems (e.g. training, systems of wage and salary determination, engineering, quality assurance and control, economic evaluation, etc.) are provided in a useful form.

Still further, managers must themselves be personally flexible and adaptable to change. They must be able to view the developing situation objectively. They must be able to maintain their focus of attention on the objectives of the change and not on any single method of their accomplishment. Furthermore, in determining the particular method of change, a manager should not be preoccupied with any possible implications for personal status and career. Accomplishing the task and achieving the goal should be the manager's principal personal objectives. S/he should understand that the successful accomplishment of such objectives is a particularly effective means for furthering personal advancement and improving status within the organization. Managers with this understanding are often better able to maintain a dispassionate and objective view of the changing scene. They can remain uncommitted to any single approach to a change, and can be better able to modify or alter their approach when this seems to be justified by the developing circumstances.

Each manager should have a clear concept of her or his role in instituting and implementing a change. Earlier, I noted that the interdependence of managers and subordinates (and staff specialists) is particularly acute during periods of change. For this reason, the more conventional and authoritarian methods of managing such as delegating and following up, checking, and applying pressure when performance fails to meet expectations, are likely to be less productive than a more indirect approach. Thus, managers should regard their role less in terms of a "director of operations" and more in terms of a leader providing direction and inspiration. Managers should also see themselves as "facilitators of communications and developers of understanding" among people with different points of view. In effect, this latter role is more like that of a leader than a manager:[77]

> I do not mean that the executive should spend his time with the different people concerned discussing the human problems of change as such. He *should* discuss schedules, technical details, work assignments, and so forth. But he should also be watching closely for the messages that are passing back and forth as people discuss these topics. He will find that people – himself as well as others – are always implicitly asking and making answers to questions like: "How will he accept criticism?" "How much can I afford to tell him?" "Does he really get my point?" "Is he playing games?" The answers to such questions determine the

Implications for Managerial Competence

degree of candor and the amount of understanding between the people involved.

When the administrator concerns himself with these problems and acts to facilitate understanding, there will be less log-rolling and more sense of common purpose, fewer words and better understanding, less anxiety and more acceptance of criticism, less griping and more attention to specific problems – in short, better performance in putting new ideas for technological change into effect.[78]

Many managers may find it difficult to assume the roles described above. It is not uncommon for managers to feel that they must be in control of whatever goes on in their area of jurisdiction. The realities of their interdependence with superiors, subordinates and peer managers and staff specialists seldom lessen the fantasy that they are in a position of power and must therefore exert control. Managers afflicted with this outlook have difficulty in behaving rationally whenever they feel their "mastery" is threatened. This kind of management *machismo* can be a major obstacle to effectiveness in making changes. This is because during periods of change, managers are least able to control how people will react and behave. Their feelings, associated with their need to be in control, are most likely to be threatened by the unpredictability and disorder so characterstic of changing situations. Not until a manager recognizes and acknowledges that changes are inherently *uncontrollable* can s/he begin to approach the change more coolly and objectively. When a manager decides that her or his immeditate objective is to develop understanding, and when s/he takes action so as to catalyze this instead of behaving like a more traditional manager, s/he is enhancing the likelihood of achieving the change successfully.

A manager (or supervisor) who is effective in introducing and implementing changes should possess the following attributes, skills and competencies:

- Intelligence.
- Imagination.
- A mind that is analytical and logical.
- Sensitivity to and consideration for the needs of others.
- Ability to be a good listener.
- Skill in communications, particularly oral.
- Skill in persuasion.
- Personal objectivity and detachment with respect to the change.
- Personal flexibility and adaptability in approaching the change.
- Understanding the manager's special role requirements during periods of change.

The closer a manager comes to matching these characteristics, the greater will be the probability that any changes for which s/he is responsible will be successfully realized.

Development of Managerial Abilities

By the time one becomes adult, many of the above attributes have become well developed and established elements of one's personality. It would be difficult to bring about any substantial changes in such deeply rooted characteristics as intelligence, imagination, fundamental attitudes toward the self and toward other people, and the ability to be analytical, logical, systematic and thorough. Even the development of the skills of listening, communication and persuasion depend to a considerable extent on certain fundamental aspects of personality. On the one hand, it is improbable that any manager with modest abilities and fixed attitudes could even develop her or his capabilities to the extent required for truly effective management of changes.

On the other hand, however, there is no assurance that a manager with the requisite potential will necessarily be able to develop and apply his or her abilities effectively. The organizational climate or environment can be an important factor in controlling this development and application. These abilities can be either stimulated or inhibited by the structure, systems, procedures and cultural beliefs and norms of the organizational environment.

One of these organizational characteristics is the extent to which change is and is perceived as a continuing, normal, regular everyday activity in the organization as a whole. On the one hand, it is especially difficult to accomplish changes in an organization addicted to the status quo, and where any change is a rare event. In such a climate, managers would find it difficult to gain any experience with the problems of introducing and implementing changes. Furthermore, should a change be instituted in this environment, the shock effect would probably result in intense resistance, not only from employees, but also from the lower levels of supervision and staff specialists.

On the other hand, in an organization where changes are and are seen as a frequent and normal occurrence, it would be difficult for the status quo to become entrenched. People's expectation would be more geared to change. Hence, their resistance would tend to be less strong than in the prior instance. Also, managers and supervisors would have

Implications for Managerial Competence

ample opportunity to become skilled in bringing about changes and in coping with all of the attendant problems.

Another significant aspect of the organizational climate is the extent to which the responsibility for managing changes is considered a normal, regular part of the jobs of every manager and supervisor. In some organizations, the middle and lower levels of management do not regard it as their responsibility to introduce and implement changes. Instead, they believe this to be the responsibility of senior management and staff specialists (e.g. industrial engineers, organization and methods specialists, employee relations experts, organizational development specialists, etc.). In such organizations, middle- and lower-level managers and supervisors regard their jobs as being concerned primarily with administering and coordinating a set of existing and established conditions. They would consider it somebody else's job to change these conditions.

Where such views persist, it would be difficult to gain the involvement and commitment of lower-level supervisors to the realization of changes. These managers and supervisors would probably not identify with the objectives of senior management. When confronted with any resistance to a change by their subordinates, these managers and supervisors would be unlikely to find ways to lessen such resistance. Instead, they would tend to resist the change themselves. In such an organizational climate, the senior manager would have to assume the role of prime mover in accomplishing any change. Such a constrained concept of the managerial job can only inhibit the development and application of the requisite abilities and skills for managing changes.

How do lower-level managers and supervisors develop an attitude that the responsibility for making changes and improving conditions is not theirs but rather somebody else's? Probably the most important reason is that senior management have failed to make this responsibility an explicit part of the manager's and supervisor's job. For example, in evaluating and discussing the performance of these members of management, competence in the achievement of changes would normally not be one of the criteria considered or used as a basis for rewards.

Without such a stimulus, it is unlikely that most managers and supervisors would be willing to risk taking any initiative in managing changes. The chances for failure simply are too great. Accomplishing any change is far more difficult than maintaining operations on a smoothly functioning "even keel." When changes are initiated, there is much risk of "rocking the boat" by generating resentment, anxiety and insecurity. Also, when a manager or supervisor undertakes to bring about a change, the fact of her or his interdependence with subordinates is particularly highlighted. Because of this interdependence, most changes are difficult to accomplish through the traditional managerial methods that depend on the use of authority and control. Many a manager or supervisor would feel considerable discomfort in a situation where s/he could not rely on accustomed ways of managing. Thus, unless senior management deliberately establish the responsibility for managing changes as part of the jobs of lower-level managers and supervisors, these subordinate members of management would be unlikely to accept such responsibility on their own initiative.

The organizational structure and its systems and procedures all can influence how managers and supervisors regard their responsbility for making changes. For example, a "tall" structure with more than six or seven hierarchical levels tends to define managerial and supervisory responsibilities more narrowly (particularly at lower levels) and lessen willingness to take initiatives and risks. A "flatter" structure tends to force more delegation, and encourage local initiatives.

The control, reward and information systems all signal what the organization deems important. These indicators tend to shape people's priorities and behavior at every organizational level.[79] They inform managers and supervisors on a continuing basis what goals they should be striving to meet and what kinds of performance are rewarded. When these indicators signal managers and supervisors that making changes effectively is an important priority, and that their performance against this expectation will be assessed and rewarded accordingly, the overall climate in the organization will tend to be supportive to the kind of systematic approach to making changes that I am advocating.

If there is to be stimulation of the development and application of those managerial abilities needed to make changes, the organization's structure, systems and procedures should be designed accordingly. Further, there should be some protection of middle management from any arbitrary pressure imposed by senior management. The timing of management's actions in a changing situation is often a key variable in determining the outcome. The manager directly accountable for results should have the greatest latitude for making decisions and taking action relevant to the change. S/he should be able to time and relate his or her actions to the requirements of the developing situation, not to some arbitrarily imposed deadline. These changing events should be the primary factors that s/he considers before deciding what to do next. Any arbitrary external pressure imposed from higher levels in the

Implications for Managerial Competence

organization may circumscribe the manager's freedom to act in accordance with these events.

It is important, however, to distinguish between arbitrary, unjustified intervention and those senior management directives based on sound, considered judgments. This latter kind of decision should shape the entire strategy for accomplishing the change. When arbitrary deadlines or any other unjustified demands are imposed from on high, a manager's ability to achieve maximum benefits from a change may be seriously constrained.

Arbitrary and unjustified interventions are commonplace. For example, during the process of a change, senior management might issue a request, a "suggestion" or even an order which may be inconsistent with the plan as initially established. Or, senior management's expectations of the change may be unrealistic. Poor and irrational decisions are made in every organization.

When senior executives make decisions that may undermine the effectiveness of carrying out a change, it is essential that their effects be minimized. This can be achieved if the manager directly accountable for the change can tell these senior executives directly and truthfully what are likely to be the consequences of their directives on the success of that change. The organizational climate should be such that the manager's judgment and comments are given serious consideration before senior executives insist that their orders be implemented.[80] Where such a climate exists, managers and supervisors are encouraged to develop and apply those qualities necessary for realizing changes successfully.

There is yet another necessary characteristic of organizational climates that support managerial effectiveness in making changes. The organization's culture must place a high value on accomplishing tasks and achieving goals. In such a culture, when managers face problems requiring decisions and action, their first consideration will be, "What course of action will result in the most effective solution to the problem? What action would be likely to produce the best long-term results for the company as a whole?" Their first thought will *not* be, "What action will mostly likely further my own status and career within the company? How can I ensure that if all goes well I shall get the credit, and if problems arise, I shall not be left holding the bag?"

Several benefits result from an organizational value system that ranks successful task accomplishment uppermost, and that subordinates personal and political considerations. One benefit is that task-oriented managers are more likely to be open to criticism of their methods for approaching changes when such criticism is valid and directed toward improving the possibilities for success. They are also more likely to accept others' ideas and suggestions. Thus, such managers would be more likely to encourage the involvement and participation of others in formulating some of the decisions affecting the conduct and outcome of the change. Also, such managers would be more likely to share information about the change fully and honestly with everyone concerned. They would not be tempted to enhance their own power and status by withholding information, and would realize that they could often lessen resistance to changes by investing more effort and time in communications.

In addition, managers who value task accomplishment above personal status will probably be more willing to experiment with fresh ideas and to risk failure. Carefully controlled experiments that fail can often yield valuable insights about methods of solving problems. This fact is fully recognized by scientists and engineers. In the culture of the laboratory or development group, the failure of an experiment is not regarded as a personal failure. Yet in the culture of management, the reverse is often the case.

In most organizations, any kind of failure, whether or not it be of an experiment, is most typically seen as personal failure. Determining who is to blame is often the first executive response. When this is the case, managers are unwilling to expose themselves to the risks inherent in experimentation. They are reluctant to try out any ideas or suggestions that depart from well-trodden paths because such ventures often are vulnerable to failure.

When the consequences of experimental failure in a changing situation are perceived as a constructive contribution to organizational learning, leading ultimately to enhanced possibilities for success, managers will be more willing to try out approaches that depart from the norm. Such constructive perceptions of experimentation and failure are possible only when managers at all levels are concerned primarily with accomplishing the task and achieving the goal.

How can one develop such a constructive attitude toward sharing information, toward accepting criticism and ideas from other people, and toward experimentation and failure? How can the values in an organization's culture be restructured so that task accomplishment and results are ranked above personal and political considerations? Perhaps the most important factors influencing the development of any value system in an organization is the basis on which performance is measured and rewarded. Employees at every organizational level must be able to see a clear, consistent relationship between successful task and goal accomplishment and personal reward in terms of both

Implications for Managerial Competence

compensation and recognition (e.g. advancement, status). When this perception is widespread, goal and task accomplishment will assume primary importance in management's value structure.

In organizations where the people who are advanced or otherwise rewarded seem to be talented primarily in their political astuteness and ability to turn every situation to their own personal advantage, or where there is no apparent relationship between performance and reward, task accomplishment will often be regarded as secondary. In such organizations, before any decisions are taken, most managers' first and foremost concern will be for the consequences of their actions on their personal futures with the company. The values of an organization's culture can be altered, but change is difficult and typically requires several years to achieve. In my experience, there are three most powerful levers available to top management to change values:

1. What gets measured to track and assess the performance both of the organizational system as a whole, and of the individual employees within the system.[79]
2. How employees at every level are rewarded, in both monetary and nonmonetary terms; this includes how superior performance is defined, how personal performance is related to rewards, and how superior performers are differentiated from average and below-par performers in the rewards they receive.
3. How consistently top and senior-level executives behave as they model the desired values.

Senior management also control another organizational characteristic which can influence the development and application of those managerial attributes that are key to making changes effectively. This is the extent to which senior management understand and recognize that managers and supervisors can resist changes in the same way and for similar reasons as do any other group of employees.

When senior executives truly understand this point, they tend to encourage lower-level managers and supervisors to participate as fully as possible in making the decisions relevant to any change. The senior executives will take care to ensure that the individual fears, hopes and other personal needs of the other members of management will receive as much attention as will the fears, hopes and other personal needs of other employees. An uneasy and resentful manager or supervisor cannot be expected to cope effectively with the fears of an apprehensive worker. A deliberate policy of involving the lower levels of management in formulating those decisions relevant to accomplishing a change, will ensure that all members of management are united in a "common front" when they introduce and implement that change.[80] Such a unified approach is possible only when senior management have taken care to develop a common understanding and shared outlook and approach that encompasses all levels of management.

Another view of the characteristics necessary in an organization where changes can be introduced and implemented smoothly is proposed by R. Likert.[81] He suggests that the central problem is "not how to reduce or eliminate potential conflict, but how to deal constructively with conflict." He hypothesizes that an organization must have three characteristics for this to be possible:

> The organization must possess the machinery to deal constructively with conflict. This includes an organizational structure which facilitates constructive interaction between persons and between work groups. Furthermore, the organization's personnel must be skilled in the processes of effective interaction and mutual influence. These skills include those of leadership and membership roles, and of group building and maintenance functions. Finally, there must be a high level of confidence and trust among the members of the organization in each other, a high degree of loyalty to the work group, and a high degree of loyalty to the organization. Such confidence, trust and loyalty lead to earnest, sincere and determined efforts to find solutions to conflicts. These solutions can be highly creative and can represent better solutions than any stemming initially from the conflicting interests.
>
> An organization, therefore, must have an interaction and mutual influence process such that, consistent with their goals and needs, all persons who have an interest in the organization and its activities are able to exert at least some influence on the overall objectives and decisions of the organization, as well as to be influenced by them.
>
> In every organization, it is important to have an interaction and mutual influence mechanism which achieves and maintains the highest possible level of compatibility between the goals of the individuals who are in organization or affected by it, and the overall objectives of the organization... A maximum degree of compatibility should exist, but only between those goals and objectives which are important for the continued operation and effective functioning of the organization.
>
> In every healthy organization, there is, consequently, a continuous process of examining and modifying individual goals and organizational objectives, as well as the methods and rewards for achieving them. This continuous process is necessary for the objectives, methods and rewards to fit new developments and changing circumstances.
>
> In an organization in which there exists widespread acceptance of the objectives coupled with pride in these objectives, and in which the

objectives and goals of the sub-units are consistent with the overall objectives of the organization, the efforts of the members will be highly focused and polarized. This polarization will mean that the behavior of all members will be in the direction best suited to help the organization achieve its objectives.

Summary

The following characteristics are typical of an organizational climate where managers and supervisors are encouraged to develop and apply those attributes, skills and competencies necessary for the effective management of changes:

- Change is considered as a continuing, normal, everyday activity for everyone in the organization. Changes are a necessary frequent occurrence.
- Introducing and implementing changes are considered the responsibility of managers and supervisors.
- The organizational structure and its systems and procedures are designed to encourage everyone in management to regard making changes as the most important element of their jobs.
- The manager accountable for making a change is delegated sufficient responsibility and freedom of action to achieve the change. The influence of any arbitrary and unjustified pressures or interventions by senior management can be minimized if the manager's objections are considered seriously by his seniors.
- When making decisions, most managers and supervisors consider goal and task accomplishment as a more important immediate personal objective than they do the direct pursuit of political and personal aims.
- Senior executives understand and recognize the attitudes and needs of managers and supervisors with respect to the change and its consequences.

The last three of the above characteristics can occur in an organization only when there is mutual respect, trust and confidence between senior and middle management, and between middle management and supervisors. If an organization's objectives are to be achieved successfully, such a mutuality of trust must be based on a recognition of the fact that all levels of management are interdependent, one on another.

Implications for Managerial Competence

Similarly, it must be recognized that there is interdependence between management and the employees.

In any situation of mutual trust, there is an inherent risk that problems may be handled by the lower levels of management in quite a different manner from the way in which senior executives might have handled them. However, for the trust to exist, it must be accompanied by a measure of confidence that, although such problems may not be solved in precisely the expected way, the desired results will nevertheless be achieved. If, through experience, senior executives find their trust to be unjustified, then they should reassess the competence of that individual to whom they delegated the responsibility. It is not the concept of mutual trust that should be reconsidered.

When making change, true delegation of full accountability, responsibility and freedom to act must be accompanied by mutual feelings of respect, trust and confidence. Only in such a climate can the managers and supervisors be more concerned with task accomplishment that they are with the furtherance of their personal aims. Only in such a climate can senior executives develop a vertically integrated managerial and supervisory group that functions in a united way. And only in such a climate are management likely to achieve a high proportion of success in their realization of changes.

Conclusion

Introducing and implementing changes so that the anticipated benefits are fully realized are among the most challenging and demanding aspects of a manager's job. Making changes effectively is perhaps the most important value added by the manager's role. To solve the problems that arise from changes, and to minimize resistance, require that managers apply fully their intellect and imagination and their skills of perception, communication and conflict resolution. Coping successfully with changes is also a test of managers' sensitivity to and concern for the needs and goals of others. In short, the effective realization of a change is a stringent test of any manager's total abilities. And the success with which the anticipated benefits are achieved is dependent, in large measure, on the extent of that manager's abilities.

Thus, those periods when changes are being carried out in an organization can be the times when the most effective development of managerial talent and abilities is taking place. Thus, the process of introducing and implementing changes can be regarded as a crucible for both management development and organizational learning. True progress will occur only when managers and supervisors are helped by their immediate superiors to learn in a constructive way the most fruitful lessons from both their successes and their failures, and when learning is widely shared. Without such guidance, coaching and sharing, not only will the full benefits fail to be realized from these experiences, but also some wrong lessons might be learned as well.

Although accomplishing changes effectively presents formidable problems that are difficult of solution, the probabilities for success can nevertheless be increased significantly. Certainly, although there is no neat formula to guarantee this in every case, senior management can improve their chances for success by taking the following steps:

- Establish and maintain an organizational climate that stimulates the development and application of those managerial qualities necessary for the effective achievement of changes. The essential characteristics of such a climate are described in chapter 11.

Conclusion

- When a change must be accomplished, delegate the accountability, responsibility and freedom to act to a manager whose attributes and abilities most closely resemble those described in chapter 11.
- Ensure that the change is planned, discussed, introduced and followed up systematically, applying the concepts and approaches outlined in this book.
- Ensure that the manager receives support and assistance in whatever action is justified, to minimize any resistance to the change, and to increase the possibilities for its acceptance.

Thus, when management are unified in their understanding and attitudes, and when they approach any change objectively and systematically, they should be able to achieve, in most cases, their expected benefits.

Notes

INTRODUCTION

1 Frank B. Gilbreth, *Primer of Scientific Management*, Van Nostrand, New York, 1912; Frank B. Gilbreth and Lillian M. Gilbreth, *Applied Motion Study*, Sturgis and Walton, New York, 1914.
2 William J. J. Gordon, *Synectics*, Collier, London, 1968.
3 Charles H. Kepner and Benjamin B. Tregoe, *The Rational Manager*, McGraw-Hill, New York, 1965.
4 Arnold S. Judson, *A Manager's Guide to Making Changes*, Wiley, London, 1966.

CHAPTER 2 HOW PEOPLE ARE AFFECTED BY CHANGE

5 R. E. Coffey, A. G. Athos and P. A. Raynolds., *Behavior in Organizations: A Multidimensional View*, 2nd edn, chapters 1-6, Prentice-Hall, Englewood Cliffs, New Jersey, 1975.

CHAPTER 3 HOW PERSONAL ATTITUDE TO A CHANGE IS FORMED

6 A. Kardiner and R. Linton, *The Individual and his Society*, Columbia University Press, New York, 1939.
7 For example, see: C. Kluckholn and H. A. Murray, *Personality*, Knopf, New York, 1949; T. M. Newcomb, *Social Psychology*, Dryden Press, New York, 1950; K Lewin, *Resolving Social Conflicts*, Harper, New York, 1949; J. Gellin (ed.) *For a Science of Social Man*, Macmillan, New York, 1954; T. E. Deal and A. A. Kennedy, *Corporate Cultures*, Addison-Wesley, Reading, Massachusetts, 1982.
8 The process by which differences in needs and goals of individuals and the organization and the subgroups of which they are members become

rationalized has been termed by E. W. Bakke the "fusion process" (E. W. Bakke, *The Fusion Process*, Yale Labor and Management Center, New Haven, 1953). He theorizes that in this process all three elements (i.e. the individuals, the organization, the subgroup) are changed, and their behavior maintains the integrity of the organization in the face of divergent interests which each holder hopes to realize through contact with the others.

9 D. C. Pelz, "Influence, a key to effective leadership for the first line supervisor," *Personnel*, no. 29, November 1952.
10 A. H. Maslow, *Motivation and Personality*, Harper, New York, 1954.
11 C. Argyris, in "Understanding human behavior in organizations," *Modern Organization Theory* (ed. M. Haire), Wiley, New York, 1959, proposes as a definition of an organization that it is: (a) a plurality of parts; (b) each achieving specific objectives; (c) maintaining themselves through their interrelatedness; (d) simultaneously adapting to the external environment; and therefore (e) maintaining the interrelated state of the parts.
12 R. Likert, "A motivational approach to a modified theory of organization and management," *Modern Organization Theory* (ed. M. Haire), Wiley, New York, 1959, p. 187.
13 C. Argyris, *Personality and Organization*, Harper, New York, 1957; J. G. March and H. A. Simon, *Organizations*, Wiley, New York, 1958.

CHAPTER 4 HOW PEOPLE REACT TO CHANGE

14 J. Dollard, N. E. Miller, L. W. Doob, O. H. Mowrer and R. R. Seats, *Frustration and Aggression*, Yale University Press, New Haven, Connecticut, 1939.
15 W. F. Whyte, M. Dalton, D. Roy, L. Sayles, D. Collins, F. Miller, G. Strauss, F. Fverstenberg and A. Bavelas, *Money and Motivation*, Harper, New York, 1955.
16 G. Strauss and L. R. Sayles, *Personnel, The Human Problems of Management*, Prentice-Hall, Englewood Cliffs, New Jersey, 1960.
17 John P. Kotter, *Organizational Dynamics: Diagnosis and Intervention*, Addison-Wesley, Reading, Massachusetts, 1978.
18 E. H. Schein, *Organizational Psychology*, Prentice-Hall, Englewood Cliffs, New Jersey, 1965.
19 A useful summary treatment of the dynamics between individuals and groups can be found in A. R. Cohen, S. L. Fink, H. Gadon and R. D. Willits, *Effective Behavior in Organizations*, Irwin, Homewood, Illinois, 1976.
20 R. Dubin, "Stability of human organization," *Modern Organization Theory* (ed. M. Haire), Wiley, New York, 1959, p. 241.
21 R. Dubin, *The World of Work*, Prentice-Hall, Englewood Cliffs, New Jersey, 1958.

Notes

CHAPTER 5 PREDICTING THE EXTENT OF RESISTANCE

22 For example, see: Argyris, *Personality and Organization*; C. Argyris, *Executive Leadership*, Harper, New York, 1953; L. R. Sayles, *The Behavior of Industrial Work Groups*, Wiley, New York, 1958; work of the Technology Project at Yale University, New Haven, Connecticut.
23 Arnold S. Judson, *Making Strategy Happen*, Basil Blackwell, Oxford, 1990.
24 Sayles, *The Behavior of Industrial Work Groups*.
25 M. Haire, C. Argyris and E. W. Bakke, for example.
26 Argyris, "Understanding human behavior," p. 150.

CHAPTER 6 MINIMIZING RESISTANCE TO CHANGE: CONCEPTS

27 D. McGregor, *The Human Side of Enterprise*, McGraw-Hill, New York, 1960. See also R. E Walton, "From control to commitment in the workplace," *Harvard Business Review*, vol, 63, no. 2, March–April 1985.
28 Strauss and Sayles, *Personnel*, p. 272.
29 F. Cousins, "Industrial relations, a forward look," an address made to the British Institute of Personnel Management, October 1962.
30 A. H. Maslow, *Motivation and Personality*.
31 Allan Flanders, *The Fawley Productivity Agreements*, Faber and Faber, London 1964.
32 Likert, "A motivational approach," p. 209.
33 A. Bavelas, *Journal of Social Issues*, vol. 4, no. 3, summer 1948.
34 J. K. Liker, D. B. Roitman and E. Roskies, "Changing everything all at once," *Sloan Management Review*, vol. 28, no. 4, summer 1987.
35 Kelvin Cross and Richard Lynch, *Measure Up! Yardsticks for Continuous Improvement*, Basil Blackwell, Oxford, 1990.
36 Strauss and Sayles, *Personnel*, p. 166.
37 G. Strauss and A. Bavelas "Group dynamics and intergroup relation," Whyte *et al.*, *Money and Motivation*, chapter 10.
38 Strauss and Sayles, *Personnel*, p. 168.
39 N. R. F. Maier, *Psychology in Industry*, 2nd edn, Houghton Mifflin, Boston, 1955, p. 172.

CHAPTER 7 MINIMIZING RESISTANCE TO CHANGE: METHODS

40 "Eye on restrictive practice - 3," *The Times*, London, February 19, 1965, p. 7.
41 A. Zander, "Resistance to change - its analysis and prevention," *Advanced Management*, vol. XV, no. 1, January 1950, p. 9.
42 P. R Lawrence, "How to deal with resistance to change," *Harvard Business Review*, vol. 32, no. 3, May–June 1954.

Notes

43 Strauss and Sayles, *Personnel*, p. 150.
44 L. Coch and J. R. P French, "Overcoming resistance to change," *Human Relations*, vol 1, no. 4, 1948, p. 12.
45 Argyris, "Understanding human behavior," p.148.
46 An excellent and practical discussion of participation in decision-making in industry can be found in E. H. Schein, *Process Consultation*, Addison-Wesley, Reading, Massachusetts, 1969.
47 W. G. Ouchi, *Theory Z*, Addison-Wesley, Reading, Massachusetts, 1981.
48 Gary Katzenstein, *Funny Business: An Outsider's Year in Japan*, Soho Press, New York, 1989.
49 L. B. Moore, "Too much management, too little change," *Harvard Business Review*, vol. 34, no. 1, January–February 1956, p. 41.
50 Ibid.
51 Ibid.
52 Ibid.
53 A. J. Marrow and J. R. P. French, "Overcoming a stereotype," *Journal of Social Issues*, vol. 1, no. 3, 1945, p. 33.
54 Zander, "Resistance to change."
55 Condensed from W. F. Whyte. *Human Relations in the Restaurant Industry*, McGraw-Hill, New York, 1948, p. 319.
56 The Scanlon plan was the first of several similar strategies known collectively as gainsharing. The other two best known variations are the Rucker plan and Improshare. All three approaches share the same fundamental assumptions and concepts. The Scanlon plan is named for the man who devised it, Joseph Scanlon, who rose from a rank-and-file worker in a steel plant in the United States to become the research and engineering director of the steelworkers' union (United Steelworkers of America). Later, he became a lecturer at the Massachusetts Institute of Technology. For a more complete discussion of this plan, see: R. W. Davenport, "Enterprise for everyone," *Fortune*, vol. 41, no. 1, January 1950, p. 55; W. F. Whyte et al., "The Scanlon plan," in *Money and Motivation*, chapter 14; F. G. Lesieur (ed.), *The Scanlon Plan: A Frontier in Labor Management Cooperation*, Wiley, New York, and Technology Press, Cambridge, 1958; G, Strauss and L. R. Sayles, "The Scanlon plan: some organizational problems," *Human Organization*, vol. 16, no. 3, fall 1957, p. 15; J. F. Donnelly, "Participative management at work," *Harvard Business Review*, vol 55, no.1, January–February 1977; B. E. Moore and T. C. Ross, *The Scanlon Way to Improved Productivity*, Wiley, New York, 1978.
57 The Scanlon plan and other gainsharing plans have been achieving increasing acceptance. Although the exact number of such plans in operation is unknown, recent estimates by the General Accounting Office of the US government suggest that there are more than 1,000 companies in the United States with gainsharing plans. In the mid 1960s, this number was about 50.
58 Davenport, "Enterprise for everyone."

Notes

59 Condensed from G. P. Shultz, "Worker participation in production problems," *Personnel*, vol. 28, no. 3, November 1951.
60 A type of tool.
61 Lesieur, *The Scanlon Plan*.
62 Shultz, "Workers participation."
63 G. P. Shultz and R. P. Crisara, "The LaPointe Machine Tool Company and United Steelworkers of America," National Planning Association, November 1952.
64 J. Bourne, "The Linwood plan: a signpost for labour relations?" *Financial Times*, London, March 11, 1964.
65 Lesieur, *The Scanlon Plan*.

CHAPTER 8   PROCESS SKILLS

66 A more comprehensive discussion of process skills can be found in Schein, *Process Consultation*. See also M. Sinetar, "The informal discussion group – a powerful agent for change," *Sloan Management Review*, vol. 29, no. 3, spring 1988.

CHAPTER 9   DIFFERENCES IN THE PERCEPTION OF CHANGE

67 In the term "supervisor," I mean to include all those in first-level supervision, including foremen.
68 J. A. Klein, "Why supervisors resist employee involvement," *Harvard Business Review*, vol. 62, no. 5, September–October 1984.
69 Lawrence, "How to deal with resistance to change."

CHAPTER 10   A SYSTEMATIC APPROACH TO MAKING CHANGE

70 For a more complete discussion of these techniques, see A. Battersby, *Network Analysis for Planning and Scheduling*, Macmillan, Cleaver-Hume Press, London, 1964.
71 This approach to both developing action programs and using them for tracking implementation progress is discussed in greater detail in Judson, *Making Strategy Happen*.
72 Flanders, *The Fawley Productivity Agreements*. See also R. B. McKersie and L. C. Hunter, *Pay, Productivity and Collective Bargaining*, Macmillan, London, 1973.
73 Ibid., pp. 199 and 206.
74 Ibid., p. 210.
75 Ibid., p. 212.

Notes

CHAPTER 11 IMPLICATIONS FOR MANAGERIAL COMPETENCE

76 McGregor, *The Human Side of Enterprise*, p. 140.
77 For a discussion of the differences in role between leaders and managers, see John P. Kotter, "What leaders really do," *Havard Business Review*, vol. 68, no. 3, May-June 1990.
78 Lawrence, "How to deal with resistance to change."
79 For a more extended discussion of the relationship between control systems, measures and individual behavior, see Judson, *Making Strategy Happen*, chapters 3 and 12; and Cross and Lynch, *Measure Up!*
80 This might be considered in the same light as the "upward influence" discussed in chapter 3.
81 Likert, "A motivational approach," p. 204.

Index

abilities, managerial, 191–6, 203–4
absenteeism, 50
acceptance, reasons for, 66–75
acceptance of changes, 15, 21, 22, 23, 28, 33, 53, 102, 106, 114, 116, 129, 133, 135–6, 159, 167, 173, 183, 189, 206; *see also* gaining acceptance of the required changes in behavior
accommodation, 40, 91–2, 113–14, 159, 174, 189
accomplishment, 86
　personal, 94
　see also results
accountability *see* responsibility, managerial
accounting, 157
action, group, 51–2
　tendencies toward, 29
Adams, John, 15
adaptability, 28, 191–2
adaptive cells, 146
adjustment *see* accommodation
administration function, 197
advancement, personal, 37, 66, 79, 83, 194, 201; *see also* careers
adviser, role of, 152, 157, 163
aggression, 48–51, 59, 81, 111
　self-directed, 49–51
analogy, 112
analysis, accuracy of, 2, 73
　situational, 73–4, 151, 153, 155, 157, 167–73, 192
analysis and planning phase of change, 167–73, 175, 183, 186–7, 189
announcements, 110
anthropology, 29, 129
anxiety, 27, 92, 112, 197
apathy, 48, 50, 127
apprehensions, 26–7, 36–46, 48, 60, 77, 84, 93, 107, 156, 170–1

Argyris, C., 36, 41, 59, 61, 63, 121
assumptions, 34, 46, 84, 87, 91, 142–3; *see also* inferences
attitudes, intensity of, 24, 45
　management, 33, 136
　predisposed to changes, 25–7, 42–3
　resistant, 15–16, 24, 41–6, 48, 64–6
　stereotyped, 128
attitudes to change, 23–46, 48, 55, 57, 59–75, 87, 91, 140–3, 153, 161, 183, 185
audio-visual presentations, 109
authority, 68, 78–81, 94, 100, 136, 140, 144, 145–6, 153, 194–5, 198
　deference to, 79
autonomy, personal, 40

Bakke, E. W., 30, 61
balancing gains and losses, 71–4, 101, 170–1, 192
bargaining, collective, 100–5, 133, 136, 176–7, 184–9
bargaining position, 115
Battersby, A., 172
Bavelas, A., 92
behavior, changes in, 6, 16–17, 39, 45, 59
　group, 47–8
　individual, 47–54, 57, 59–60, 64–5, 78, 81
　managerial, 33–4, 126–7; *see also* resistance, by management
　resistant, 2, 15–16, 23, 48–54, 81, 85, 87, 90–1, 96–100, 112–13, 114, 132, 135, 137, 152–3, 155, 161, 196–7; *see also* resistance, extent of
behavioral norms, 28–32, 42, 46; *see also* beliefs, cultural
beliefs, cultural, 28–33, 42, 44, 46, 48, 60, 70, 77, 79, 87, 124, 127, 165, 171, 173, 175, 182, 186–7, 192, 196
benefits, fringe, 31, 101

213

Index

benefits from change *see* change, benefits of
bias, supervisor's, 156, 162–3
birth, 25
Blue Book, 88–90, 185
Bourne, J., 135
brainstorming, 3
bribery, 100
briefings, 117, 178, 180
bulletin boards *see* notice boards
Burke, Edmund, 23, 191
buy-in, 2

careers, 38–9, 68, 154, 194
catharsis, 111
ceremony, 129–32
change, after-effects, 32, 34, 180–2
  attitudes to *see* attitudes to change
  of behavior *see* behavior, changes in
  benefits of, 2, 4, 6, 43, 53, 86, 94, 100, 114, 141, 151, 153–6, 161, 163, 169, 173, 181–2, 191, 205
  certainty, 1
  coordination of, 114–16
  cultural, 186
  definition of, 5–14, 74, 86, 168–9, 186, 188
  design of, 186
  impact on people, 15–22, 40, 169, 187, 192
  implementation of, 45–6, 54, 141–2, 152–6, 165–89
  institutional, 186
  irrevocability of, 40–1
  of job, 50
  manner of, 34, 39–41, 52, 57, 60, 69–70, 77
  method of *see* method of change
  nature of, 16, 48, 74, 86, 168–9
  need for, 6, 86, 97, 150–2, 168, 173, 193
  objectives of *see* objectives, of change
  as part of organizational culture, 196–7, 203
  planning for *see* planning changes
  pressure to, 6, 86, 168
  reactions to, 49–54, 57, 66–75; *see also* acceptance of changes; behavior, resistant
  scope of, 6, 86, 93, 155–6, 168–9, 170, 172–3
  as a symbol, 54
changes, complex, 172, 175, 179
  early, 25–7
  environmental variables, 78
  failure of, 150, 155, 180, 200
  flexibility in approach, 7–8, 28, 86, 97–8, 132, 154, 157, 158, 172, 175–7, 178, 179, 180, 189, 194, 195
  perception of, 149–63
  poorly conceived, 72, 128
  rapid, 91–4
  slow, 91–4
  technology of, 158–60, 169
  types of, 12–13
checking up, 194
checklists, estimating resistance, 66–70
children, 25–7
coaching, 160, 205
coalition, dominant, 51–2
Coch, L., 120
coercion, 78–82
Coffey, R. E., Athos, A. G. and Raynolds, P. A., 19
Cohen, A. R., et al., 52
commitment, 96, 116, 126, 128, 132, 140–4, 156, 168, 177, 194, 197
committees, 105, 117, 133–4
communications, 40, 59, 91, 92, 109, 113, 129, 134, 136, 140, 145–7, 153, 159, 171, 173–9, 187–8, 195–6, 200, 203–5
  oral, 110, 174, 193, 195
  written, 109, 174, 193
communications phase of change, 173–6, 177, 183, 189
compensation *see* rewards
competitive position, 87, 136
complaints, 103–4, 106
compromise, 57, 104–6, 154, 156, 177, 185, 189; *see also* methods of change, changes in
compulsion, 78–81, 100, 135, 142
concessions, 104–6, 143; *see also* compromise
confidence, 192, 202–3; *see also* self-confidence
conflicts, 1, 24, 30–2, 36, 39, 42, 45, 48, 52, 55, 57–8, 77, 81, 82, 87, 92, 103–4, 145, 153–4, 177, 184–6, 192, 202, 205
conformity, 58
consensus of agreement, 117, 142, 146, 161, 167, 175, 176–7
consideration, 192
consolidation of new conditions, 180–2
consultation, 25, 117–19, 136, 143, 187
control, management, 8, 39, 41, 43, 52, 59, 63, 77, 79, 125, 169, 172, 195, 198
  over work environment, 94
  social, 52
cooperation, 2, 17, 37, 48, 53, 80–1, 146–7, 179
coordinating function, 179, 197
cost comparisons, 87, 104, 114, 116, 174; *see also* trade-offs

214

Index

countermeasures, 80, 100
courage, 27
Cousins, F., 84
craft, 17, 30, 88-9, 183, 185-6
craftsmen; *see* craft
creative thinking, 80, 150-1, 157, 160, 168, 202
Crisara, R. P., 137
critical path scheduling, 172
criticism, 3, 85, 129-32, 136, 151, 199-200
Cross, K. and Lynch, R., 94, 201
C.U.C., 184
cultural beliefs *see* beliefs, cultural
culture of organization, 13, 32, 36, 52, 169, 199-203; *see also* organization, context
customers, 38, 69
customs, 33

data, evaluation of, 166; *see also* cost comparisons
date of completion *see* deadlines
Davenport, R. W., 134
deadlines, 114, 169, 178, 189, 198-9
Deal, T. E. and Kennedy, A. A., 29
decisions, 81, 96, 116, 119, 128, 144, 145-6, 166, 176-7
decisions, irrational *see* irrationality making of, 3, 50, 81, 96, 116, 117, 119, 125, 136, 140, 143, 153, 166, 179, 198-9, 201
delegation of responsibility and authority, 13, 145, 188, 193-4, 203-4, 206
demarcation, 183, 185-6
dependency, 40, 79-81, 97; *see also* interdependence, mutual
desires, 48, 52, 58, 59-60, 64
development, human, 25-7
development of personal abilities, 102
diagnosis by participation, 128-9
differences, individual *see* individual differences
directives, management, 39-41, 141, 198-9, 203
dirt money, 183
discipline, 100
discrimination, 37
discussion, 72, 91-2, 101, 108-13, 115-29, 136, 141, 161, 173-89, 193, 195
distribution lists, 117
distrust, 26; *see also* trust
Dollard, J., 49
Doob, L. W., 49
Drucker, P., 23, 55, 99, 139, 165
Dubin, R., 53

earnings
 guaranteed, 101; *see also* income, maintenance of
 see also pay; salaries
economic evaluation, 194; *see also* cost comparisons
economic forces, 6
education, 158-60
effectiveness, individual, 36
management *see* management, effectiveness of
electronic mail, 109-11, 113, 117
Emerson, R. W., 149
Emerson Consultants, 88
emotions, 35, 81, 124
employee relations *see* personnel
employment, alternative, 34
 guaranteed, 106-8
empowerment, 80, 116
enforcement, authority, 79
engagement, 106
engineering, 157, 194, 200
 industrial, 20, 126, 197
engineering design, 12, 20
environment, external, 1, 6, 146, 191
 working, 13, 18-19, 78, 97, 196
equilibrium, homeostatic, 36, 52, 61, 63
equitability and fairness, 18, 106, 177
errors, 48, 51, 111
Esso Petroleum Company, Ltd., 88, 182
ethics, 78, 83, 88-9
events, external, 97, 114-15
 historical, 33-4, 42, 44, 46, 60, 72-3, 77
exceptions, personal, 177
expansion, business, 106
expectations, 24, 36-46, 48, 52, 60, 153-6, 161, 170, 199
expediency, 154, 156
experimentation, 200
expertise, 140, 150, 157-63
explanations, 159-60; *see also* discussion

factors, situational, 55
failure, personal, 150-1, 200-1, 205
 of change *see* changes, failure of
fairness *see* equitability and fairness
favoritism, 37
Fawley Productivity Agreements, 88-90, 182-9
Fawley Refinery, 182-9
FAX, 109-10, 113, 117
fears, 24, 26-7, 36-46, 48, 51, 81, 84-5, 92, 97, 110-11, 153, 170-1, 173, 178, 192, 201
 economic, 82-3
 job satisfactions, 67-8

215

Index

job security *see* security
personal inconvenience, 67
personal security, 67, 106–8
redundancy *see* redundancy
social, 68–9
unexpressed, 110
feelings, resistant, 35, 41–6, 60, 64–6, 117, 140–3, 145
films, 109
film-strips, 109
fixation, 50
Flanders, A., 88, 183, 184–5
flexibility, inter-craft, 183
  managerial, 7, 97–8, 140, 154, 182, 194, 195; *see also* changes, flexibility in approach; methods of change, changes in
flexibility in approach to changes *see* changes, flexibility in approach
flexible timing, 172, 175, 189
following up, 194
  of change, 180–2, 203
forecasting *see* predictions
foremen *see* supervisors
formulas, managerial, 46, 112, 165–6
Franklin, B., 1
freedom to act, 39, 80–1, 154, 156, 188, 198–9, 203–4, 206
French, J. R. P., 119, 127
frustration, 49–54, 57, 59, 81, 97, 111, 113, 159

gaining acceptance of the required changes in behavior, 176–8
gains, 66–75, 81–2, 101, 161, 169–70, 192
  economic, 66
gainsharing, 133–7
Gellin, J., 29
Gilbreth, E. B. and L. M., 3
Gordon, W. J. J., 3
government, influence on business, 34
gratifications, 25–7
grievances *see* complaints
group forces, 23, 30, 48, 51–3, 55, 59
groups, stability of, 53
  structure of, 61
groups and individuals, 37, 42, 46
guarantees, 33

Haire, M., 61
harmony, 36, 42
heat money, 183
historical events *see* events, historical
holiday benefits, 101
hopes, 171

job satisfactions, 68
personal convenience, 67
personal security, 67
social benefits, 68–9
hostility, 40, 48, 57, 81, 93, 111, 147
hours of work, 67, 183–4, 187
housekeeping, 13
human nature and change, 28
human resources *see* relationships, human

identification, personal, 150–2
imagery, 112
imagination, 170, 171, 192, 195–6, 205
impatience, 151
importance, self, 41–2
improvement, labor relations, 133
operating efficiency and effectiveness, 6, 11, 133, 136, 140–1
  see also labor, relations
inadequacy, 84, 108
incentives, 188
  group, 133, 135
income, maintenance of, 107; *see also* earnings, guaranteed
incompetence, supervisory, 155
inconvenience, 67
indifference, 48, 50, 53–4, 57, 163
individual differences, 28, 40, 58, 72, 160, 170
  and organization, 37
  and work, 36–7
  and work group, 37
industrial engineering *see* engineering, industrial
inferences, 46
influence, mutual, 203–4
  upwards, 33, 199
information, 3, 40, 109–13, 159, 173–6, 193, 200
  management, 157
  systems, 59, 198
  withholding, 51
ingenuity, 80, 97
initiative, 28, 57, 80, 97; *see also* management, initiative by
innovation, 1
insecurity, 27–8, 44–6, 84–5, 106–8, 156, 197; *see also* security
institutional requirements, 52, 174
institutions, 130
integrity, 1
intelligence, 192, 195–6, 205
interactions, 19–20, 32, 37, 68–9, 101, 153, 160, 202
interdependence, mutual, 80, 194, 198, 203–4

216

Index

interest, job, 37, 48, 53, 94
intervention, senior management, 198–9, 201
involvement, need for, 122, 124
    personal, 41, 94–6, 116–29, 136, 141–4, 151–3, 157, 174, 176–7, 196; *see also* participation
irrationality, 151, 158, 199
irrelevant asides, 54

jargon, 112, 159
Johnson, Dr S., 47
judgment, managerial, 154–5, 161
Judson, A. S., 3, 59, 71, 201
just-in-time, 122

Kardiner, A., 29
Katzenstein, G., 123
Kepner, C. H. and Tregoe, B. B., 3
Klein, J. A., 156
Kluckhohn, C., 29
knowledge, expansion of, 83, 86, 136, 159–60
Kotter, J. P., 52, 194

labor, agreement, 177
    mobility *see* mobility of labor
    policy, 188
    relations, 133, 183, 185–6
laboratory culture, 200
language, 111–12
LaPointe Machine Tool Co., 134
Lawrence, P. R., 112, 157, 195
layouts, work, 12
leaders, informal, 105
leadership, 144, 146, 193–4
learning, 18, 36, 48, 53, 109, 140, 159–60, 181, 202, 205; *see also* training
Lesieur, F. G., 135, 136, 138
leverage, 45, 55, 77, 81–5, 90–1, 94–8, 99–137
levers *see* leverage
Lewin, K., 29
Liker, J. K., Roitman, D. B. and Roskies, E., 92
Likert, R., 40, 90, 202
Linton, R., 29
Linwood plan, 134, 137
listening, 104, 144, 173, 193, 195–6
location of work, 12, 18–20, 67
logic, 151, 192, 195
losses, 66–75, 81–2, 170–1, 192
    counterbalancing, 71–4
    economic, 66, 104
    personal, 104
    social, 68–9, 104

loyalty, 30–1, 32, 52, 97, 130–1, 140, 202
Luddites, 85

McGregor, D., 79, 136–7, 192
machinery, 12
McKersie, R. B. and Hunter, L. C. 183
magazines, company, 109
Maier, N. R. F., 96
maintenance department, 184
management, 23, 31–3, 39, 44–6, 53, 54, 64, 74, 77, 85, 91, 92–4, 97–8, 102–6, 109, 113–16, 121, 124, 132, 136–7, 141, 144, 151, 159, 167–90, 191–206
    culture, 199–201
    development, 3, 128, 144, 196–205
    effectiveness of, 188, 191–204
    flexibility of *see* changes, flexibility in approach
    initiative by, 1, 6, 102, 165–84, 186, 198
    institution of change by, 1, 6, 52, 97, 152, 154, 165, 182–9
    Japanese, 123
    line, 152–5
    machismo, 8, 195
    objectivity of *see* objectivity, managerial
    prerogatives of, 125, 136
    resistance to change by *see* resistance, by management
    senior, 6, 40, 63, 134, 154, 163, 188–9, 193, 197–9, 202–5
    style, 145–7, 165
    structure of, 183, 188, 198
    training *see above* development
managers, 7, 8, 11, 20–1, 28, 31, 34, 46, 50, 64, 66, 71–3, 77, 80–1, 82, 85, 87, 99–100, 110–11, 116–29, 136, 141–4, 152–6, 160–3, 166–89, 191–206
manipulation, 4, 82, 123–5
manner of change *see* change, manner of
marketing, 86–7
Marrow, A. J., 128
Maslow, A. H., 34, 43, 85, 122
masterminding, 123–5
materials, 12
mates, craftsmen's, 30, 183, 186
measures, performance, 59, 94, 200–1
meetings, orientation, 110–11
    training, 110–11
memoranda, 109
memories of early changes, 27
metaphor, 112
method of change, 2, 7–10, 154, 168–9, 173, 179, 188
    changes in, 11, 87, 97–8, 125, 132, 151, 154, 156, 157, 162, 171, 175, 179, 182

217

Index

Mill, J. S., 77, 191
mistakes, 51; *see also* errors
misunderstanding, 87, 144, 181, 187; *see also* understanding
mobility of labor, 34
Moore, L. B., 123, 126-7
morale, 84, 87, 104, 115, 118, 153
morality, 78
motivation, human, 24, 133, 136, 140-1, 144, 151, 156, 160, 163, 169
Murray, H. A., 29
mutuality of interest (union and management), 136, 183
myths, 29

needs, analysis of, 82
  esteem, 35
  hierarchy of, 34-5, 73, 85, 122
  love, 35
  organizational and institutional, 1, 30, 36, 42, 44, 48, 102-3
  personal, 1, 19, 29-30, 36, 40-2, 44, 48, 52, 55, 58, 78, 82, 94, 98, 101-2, 106, 124, 130, 163, 177, 201, 205
  physiological, 34
  safety, 34
  self-actualization, 35
  social, 52
negotiation *see* bargaining
network analysis, 172
Newcomb, T. M., 29
news releases, 109
newsletters, 109
newspapers, company, 109
norms, behavioral, 28-32, 46, 58, 63, 87; *see also* beliefs, cultural
notice boards, 109

objectives, changes in, 1, 57, 65, 72, 153-4, 156, 193
  of change, 2, 7-14, 55, 151, 153, 155, 161, 168-9, 175, 186, 198
  identification of, 7-14, 86, 168, 192
  immediate, 1, 7-14, 86, 168
  long-term, 1, 7-14, 86, 168, 202
  managers', 65, 80, 128, 140, 150, 153, 154, 169, 198, 204
  vs. methods, 7-10, 126, 168-9, 175
  need for, 86, 154
objectivity, managerial, 7-8, 126, 153-5, 161-3, 181-2, 194-5, 206
  personal, 132, 157-61
operating system, 59, 61, 62, 63, 132, 201
operational effects of change, 16-17
orders, 39-40, 48; *see also* directives
organization, changes in, 13, 188

context, 15, 24, 42, 48, 57, 149, 161, 165, 196-205
definition of, 37-8
structure, 1, 13, 32, 59, 149, 165, 169, 188, 203
organization and methods, 157, 197
organization of work, 19, 32, 101, 157
organizational behavior, 3, 24, 30, 59-61
organizational development, 3, 197
organizational forces, 23, 55, 59-75
organizational theory, 24, 59-61
originator of change, 21, 149-54, 156, 157, 162-3, 168-9
Ouchi, W. G., 123
outplacement, 107
output, limitation of, 48, 51, 111
overtime, 30, 66, 88, 106, 183, 186
ownership, 141, 143

parents, 25-7
participation, 102, 116-29, 133-4, 136, 141-4, 176-7, 179, 193, 200-2
  benefits of, 127-9
  disinterest in, 124
  job rating and evaluation, 123
  location of plant, 123
  menu, 126, 144
  necessary conditions for, 124-7
  office problems, 124
  piecework rates, 120-1
  policy making, 118-19
  production methods and problems, 95-6, 118, 120-1, 134-5
  sales problems, 123
  supervisors and staff, 168, 187-8
pay, 19, 61, 66, 82, 100-1, 183-4, 187, 189; *see also* earnings, guaranteed; salaries
Pelz, D. C., 33
pension schemes, 101
perception of changes, 21, 93-4, 140-4, 149; *see also* apprehensions; attitudes; expectations; fears
performance, limitation of, 80; *see also* output, limitation of
performance, organizational, 1, 201
  business, 87
  managerial, 1
performance of work, 18, 84, 97, 108
perquisites, 31, 101
personality, 17, 18, 19, 23-4, 32, 41-5, 46, 48, 57-60, 78, 149, 160, 196
  changes to, 78, 196
personality and culture, 29
personnel, 1, 188, 197
perspectives, broadening, 160, 168

218

Index

persuasion, 73, 75, 79, 81-4, 100-2, 162, 176-7, 193, 195-6
PERT, 172
phases of managerial action, 166-7
piece-rates, 63
placement, job, 13
planning changes, 24, 54-5, 64-75, 87, 93, 99, 116, 136, 142, 165-73, 186, 189, 192
plant, 12
pleasures, 25
policies, 1, 13, 33, 59
political forces, 7, 153-4, 156, 163, 200, 203
posters, 109
practices, 33, 59, 87, 89, 183, 185
precedents, 34, 37, 69, 104
preconceptions *see* prejudice
predictions, 51, 55-75
  accuracy of, 24, 73
  attitudes, 28, 45-6, 72-5, 168-73, 192
  behavior, 24, 28, 45-6, 110, 168-73
prejudice, 42, 132
prerogatives *see* management, prerogatives of
Pressed Steel Company, Ltd., 134
pressures, external to organization, 6
  group *see* group forces
  job, 68, 81
  management, 48, 194, 198-9
prestige *see* status
priorities for action, 87, 104, 144, 162, 172, 198
probabilities, 36, 72-4, 167, 169, 205
problems, 156-7, 162-3, 167, 178-9, 188, 191
  analysis, 2
  avoidance of, 53
  identification of, 2, 151, 153, 156-7, 168-71, 193
  individual, 177
procedures, operating, 1, 12, 59, 183
process skills, 62, 124, 139-48, 202
  clues, 142
  defined, 139-40
  development of, 147-8
  importance, 140-2
  supportive atmosphere, 144-7
processes for gaining support, 2
productivity, 62-3
  bargaining, 88, 184, 189
  improvement in, 115, 133-6, 140, 141, 182, 184, 186, 189
products, improvement of, 11-12
professional help, 79
profitability, 10
profits, sharing of, 133

programmed instruction 109
progress, measurement and evaluation, 172, 180-2, 189, 193
protests, 48
psychological concepts, 48
psychological effects of changes, 17-18, 20-2, 157-8, 162
psychosomatic illness, 50
public image, organizational, 11
public relations, 104
punishment, 79-80, 81

quality, assurance, 157, 194
  defects, 67
  product, 104
  standards, 13
questions, predictable, 16-20, 36-9, 43-4, 66-75, 168-71
questions about changes, 86, 98, 110-13, 173, 180-1
quits, 106

rapport, 19, 38
rationalization, 30, 45, 58, 59, 92, 113-14, 124, 150
reactions, preparation for, 71-5, 170-3
reactions, testing, 132
reassurance, 171
recognition, 127, 130, 144
  personal, 37, 127, 201
  union, 52, 174
redundancy 37, 39, 67, 69, 84-5, 106-8, 115, 136, 184, 187, 189
regression, 48, 50
relations, management and union *see* labor, relations
relationship, attitude and behavior, 24, 45, 47, 55-65
  information and resistance, 96
relationships, human, 18-22, 37-9, 80, 83, 103, 130, 131, 157
reports, 181-2
research, industrial, 20
resignation, 48, 50
resistance
  extent of, 55-75, 159
  group, 60-1; *see also below* organized
  by management, 7-8, 162-3, 172, 182, 197-9, 201
  minimization of, 15, 53-5, 64-5, 73-5, 77-98, 99-137, 165, 171-89, 192
  of organizational system, 59-63
  organized, 51-2, 59-63, 93
  by originator, 151
  passive, 48, 50
prediction of *see* predictions

Index

reasons for, 66-75, 187
 as a symptom, 78
 see also attitudes, resistant; behavior, resistant
resonance, 61
resourcefulness, 28
respect, mutual, 203-4
responsibility, acceptance of, 80, 96
 for making changes, 152-6, 197
 managerial, 152-6, 162-3, 167-70, 186, 191-204, 206
 personal, 37, 39-40, 68-9, 178
 social, 1
 staff specialist, 156-63, 167
 supervisory, 156, 162-3, 167, 191-204
restrictive practices, 48-9, 51, 107, 111, 183, 186; *see also* output, limitation of
restructuring, organizational, 122
results, evaluation of, 93, 172, 181-2
retirement, 106
reward systems, 13; *see also* pay; rewards; wage systems
rewards, 37, 79, 82-4, 100-2, 135, 161, 172, 176, 186-8, 193, 197, 198, 200-1
 economic, 82-3, 201
 non-economic, 83-4, 201
 see also pay; wage systems
risks, evaluation of, 87, 153, 174, 197, 198, 200
rituals, 29, 123, 129-32
rivalry, sibling, 25
roles, organizational, 149-50, 157, 194-5
rules, shop, 184; *see also* practices; procedures, operating

sabotage, 48-9, 51, 100, 111
sacking, 79, 100, 106
safety, 12, 67, 157
salaries, 188
satisfactions, work, 37, 39, 52, 68, 94, 102, 113, 116, 160
Sayles, L., 59, 61
Scanlon, J., 133
Scanlon plan, 133-7
schedules, 86, 114, 172
Schein, E. H., 52, 122, 139
school, 25
scientists, 200
scope of change *see* change, scope of
secondary effects of change *see* change, after-effects
secrecy *see* security, information
security, financial, 27
 information, 86-7
 personal, 1, 27-8, 32, 38-9, 41-2, 44-6, 51, 67, 78, 81, 84-5, 106-8, 125, 127, 136, 143, 198
self-actualization *see* self-realization
self-confidence, 26-8, 127
self-protection, 51
self-realization, 94, 122
self-sufficiency, 40
selling ideas, 82
sensitivity to others, 195, 205
service, length of, 30-1, 53
Shakespeare, W., 47
Shultz, G. P., 134-5
sickness protection schemes, 101
signs, 109
Simon, H. A., 41
Sinetar, M., 139
skills, 18, 19, 20, 30, 54, 66-7, 83, 108, 136, 139-48, 159-60, 178, 202
slowdowns, 48-9; *see also* output, limitation of; restrictive practices
social arrangements, 87, 101, 159
social effects of change, 18-22, 68-9, 157-8
societies, 28
 primitive, 29
solicitation, 117-19
specifications, 12
spoilage, 48-9; *see also* errors
staff specialists, 40, 80, 87, 112, 124, 128, 150-2, 157-63, 167-8, 174, 179-81, 193-4, 197
standard management approaches *see* formulas, managerial
standards, 12-13, 36, 51, 84
status, personal, 20, 31, 38-9, 46, 48, 68, 83, 101, 125, 127, 143, 145-6, 153, 156, 163, 194, 199, 201
 union, 52
stewards, shop, 184
Strategic Business Units (SBUs), 59
strategic plans, 1, 2, 3, 167-73, 186, 199
strategy *see* strategic plans
Strauss, G. and Bavelas, A., 95
Strauss, G. and Sayles, L., 51, 83, 95, 96, 118
structure, organizational *see* organization, structure
subcontractors, 106, 115, 184
subculture, 52
sublimation, 51
subordinates, 8, 41, 66, 74, 80, 97, 100, 124, 127, 133, 143, 145, 153, 155, 188, 191, 193, 198
suggestions, 7-8, 54, 57, 68-9, 80, 92, 96, 102-6, 116-29, 134-6, 141, 143, 144, 151, 157-9, 162, 173, 179, 200

Index

supervision, levels of, 13
  relations with, 37-8, 69; *see also* subordinates
supervisors, 15, 32-3, 39, 63, 80, 85, 97, 112, 124, 131, 136, 141-4, 150, 152, 155-6, 158-63, 173, 179-82, 184, 188, 191, 196-7, 201, 203, 205
suppliers, 38, 69
surplus labor, 106-8, 136
survival, organizational, 52, 174
suspicions, 26, 28, 40, 43, 48, 111; *see also* apprehensions; fears
Swift, J., 5
symbols, 129
synectics, 3
synergy, 144
systematic approach, 3, 73-4, 165-89, 192, 198, 206

tactics, 2, 140
task, accomplishment of, 194, 199-200, 203-4
task forces, 117, 145
tasks, undifferentiated, 61
tea breaks, 183
teamwork, 11, 80, 133, 163, 168, 188-9, 202, 204-6
technology of work, 16-19, 32, 59-61, 67, 157
technology project, Yale U., 60-1
tenure, 30-1; *see also* service, length of
termination, 50, 79
Thoreau, H. D., 149
threats, 27, 34-5, 52, 60, 73, 80, 82, 100, 132, 135
time, 41, 91-4, 111, 113-16, 132, 140, 144, 159, 169, 175, 178-80, 187, 189
time and motion study, 20, 157
The Times (London), 107
timetable for action, 167, 172, 173, 175, 189
timing of change, 40-1, 113-16, 136, 159, 162, 169, 189, 198
titles, job, 101
tools, 12
total quality management, 122
trade-offs, 87, 104, 107, 113, 116
tradition, importance of, 130-2, 183, 187
training, industrial, 20, 101, 106, 108, 136, 160, 178-80, 194
training, toilet, 25
traits, inherited, 26
transition to new conditions, 178-82
Transport and General Workers Union, 84, 183

travel, 67
trial and error, 3
trials, 33, 135, 169, 178, 180
trust, 32-3, 42, 44-6, 60, 72-3, 78, 106, 111, 125, 128, 140, 147, 188, 202-4

uncertainty, 17; *see also* apprehensions; fears
understanding, 25, 53, 70, 85-91, 94, 102, 108-13, 116-19, 127, 133, 135-6, 140, 141, 159-61, 167-8, 172-6, 183, 188, 192-5, 206
unemployment, 34
unemployment benefits, 107
unified approach *see* teamwork
uniformity, 177; *see also* equitability and fairness
unions, 15, 18, 19, 21, 32, 42, 45-6, 51-3, 60-3, 69, 72, 80, 84, 86, 88-9, 102-6, 133, 169, 173, 174, 177, 179, 183-9
  leadership, 124, 134, 174, 179, 186-9, 193
  membership, 52, 177, 179
  representatives, 102, 180-1; *see also* stewards, shop
unlearning, 108
upgrading, 106

values, constancy of fundamental, 130
  cultural, 29-30, 89, 94, 183
vendors, 38
visual displays, 109

wage systems, 82, 101, 194; *see also* pay
walking time, 183
Walton, R. E., 79
washing time, 183
weaning, 25
welfare, personal, 32
Whyte, W. F., 49, 131
withdrawal, 48, 50
work, individual, 36-7
  methods, 12, 16-17
  simplification, 20; *see also* engineering, industrial; time and motion study
  study, 20, 157; *see also* engineering, industrial; time and motion study
working conditions, 13, 61, 67
working environment *see* environment, working
working-to-rule, 48-9
workmates, 68-9, 84

Zander, A., 109, 129